Sons of the Machine

MIT Press Series on Organization Studies
John Van Maanen, general editor

Sons of the Machine

Case Studies of Social Change in the Workplace

Charles H. Savage, Jr., and George F. F. Lombard

The MIT Press
Cambridge, Massachusetts
London, England

This book was set in Melior by The MIT Press Computergraphics Department and printed and bound by Halliday Lithograph in the United States of America.

Library of Congress Cataloging in Publication Data

Savage, Charles H.
  Sons of the machine.

  (MIT Press series on organization studies ; 7)
  Bibliography: p.
  Includes index.
  1. Organizational change—Colombia—Case studies.
2. Industrial relations—Colombia—Case studies.
3. Industrial sociology—Colombia—Case studies.
I. Lombard, George F. F. (George Francis Fabyan),
1911-   . II. Title. III. Series.
HD58.8.S29 1986   / 306′.36′09861   85–15133
ISBN 0–262–19243–8

Charles H. Savage, Jr., dedicated this book to his wife Mary Elene and to the potters at La Nueva, the plate makers at La Blanca, the tailors at El Dandy and their associates, supervisors, managers, factory owners, families, and friends; their wholehearted cooperation and hospitality, generously given, made possible the data for this book.

Contents

Foreword

The stories told in this book are small gems. They tell of the raw forms and forces of labor and production as they clash in several Latin American settings. They tell also of distinct work cultures at the margin where change is both a curse and a promise for worker and manager alike. The little dramas of *Sons of the Machine* transcend time and place, however, for the industrial ironies so carefully evoked in the tightly drawn case examples of this book reach to the very core of work relations everywhere.

What Charles Savage and George Lombard have to say comes not from comparative surveys of the workplace, rigorously controlled experiments on shop floors, or general precepts culled from a prescriptive literature designed to hasten organizational change. There is no golden path to industrial progress to be found here for, as the authors suggest, progress is very much in the eyes of the beholder. This is primarily a descriptive work based on Charles Savage's lengthy, highly focused fieldwork on the shifting and always contextual character of everyday social relations at work. It is ethnography to be sure, but it is of a committed and caring sort, written to detail and potentially ease the pains of economic and social change.

We are fortunate to be able to publish this book as part of the Organization Studies Series. Charles Savage died of cancer in 1973 and, with him, the manuscript might also have perished. George Lombard, however, acting on the request Savage made when realizing he would not live to finish the work, pulled together this manuscript from Savage's papers. This is an uncommon scholarly project, undertaken with affection and, most critically, respect. It was not an easy project because the unfinished character of Savage's analysis left much of the explanatory framework open. The results of intertwining two voices separated by time and field experience are obvious in the book: Savage provides the empirical narrative marked by personal reflection and style, Lombard contributes a sort of general voice-over for Savage's observations in a fashion consistent with the intellectual currents of Savage's time. That these currents still run deep gives the book its lively and relevant tone.

I first saw the manuscript in 1982 after George, driving up from his home on Cape Cod, left it in my office wrapped in a brown paper bag. Suspicious of unsolicited manuscripts and preoccupied, *par normal*, with my own work, I reluctantly began glancing through the contents of this curious grocery bag, prepared for a quick, perhaps dismal, read. What I discovered was a manuscript of considerable force that swiftly gained a hold on me and wouldn't let go. Telling others of my excitement with *Sons of the Machine*, I also discovered selected pieces of the substantial reputation Charles Savage left behind in Cambridge. He was, in his time, regarded as something of an intellectual presence on the business school scene, although something of an outsider and deviant as well. In particular, he was seen as unusually frank with colleagues and sharply critical of the prevailing management wisdom found at both M.I.T. and Harvard. His distrust of conventional case studies and, more vehemently, survey and laboratory work was apparently overshadowed only by his impatience with those who conducted such studies, who, Savage felt, were intent on increasing the distance between the researcher and researched.

In many ways, Charles Savage was a man well ahead of his time, for he anticipated much of the current critique of the arid, ritualistic, and impersonalized research methods used in organizational and management studies. He was also well ahead of his time in topical and analytic circles where now so many organizational observers are jumping aboard the proverbial cultural bandwagon. Indeed, much of the descriptive ground covered in *Sons of the Machine* represents a model for what careful ethnographic work can obtain in studies of the workplace. Intensive work of this kind is today regarded as critical if we are to gain more than remote and cold versions of organizational life. Savage was already well aware of this 25 years ago while traveling those dusty roads in Colombia trying to learn first-hand of the changing industrial scene. I suspect he would be both amused and yet a little angry at our recent rediscovery of both culture at work and naturalism in research.

Many of the stock villains identified in this book are alive, well, and still kicking in the industrial worlds of developed and developing countries. Standardization, automation, routinization, autocratic management, and, more generally, "Taylorism" have hardly disappeared. Savage would not be surprised to learn of the reactions of workers in what are regarded as advanced industrial plants, to robotics, computer-aided machines, attempts to speed up production, or any other social and technical promise to improve efficiency. The managerial assumptions guiding organization change seem remarkably the same whether we are reading Savage's account of the *doctores*' scheme to increase production in Colombia or of the latest management plan to automate the office in Chicago. Technology per se is not at issue in either case but, as this book so clearly announces, at issue is the meaning of technology for those who must put it into practice. In this regard, technology means nothing without context, for it cannot be considered apart from the meanings people at work attach to it. From this perspective, new technologies are, most assuredly, not neutral.

Sons of the Machine is both a tale of penetration and a tale of traces left after new ways are introduced to do old things. It speaks of disruption, misunderstanding, altered social relations, and costly social change. The message that emerges is not necessarily a grim one for those who seek change at work. But it is a message that conveys with quiet strength that attempts to impose meaning on new techniques for those who must artfully employ them are likely to be quite troubled ones. This is an ancient message to be sure, but it is one that requires frequent retelling for it seems so easily dismissed. Readers of Savage and Lombard will have fewer excuses at hand to allow such dismissals.

John Van Maanen
Cambridge, Massachusetts

Acknowledgments

For Charles H. Savage, Jr., and for myself I wish to express deep gratitude to the many people who contributed to this volume.

My first thanks—and Savage's—go to the persons who allowed Savage to study them both at work and away from work. To protect their privacy, their names and the names of the towns and factories where they lived and worked have—with the exception of Medellín—been disguised. No disguise, however, can shield their identities from persons who participated in or were close to the events Savage reports. Hence their willingness to let Savage study them and tell their stories is dependent to a significant extent on their trust in how he recounted these events. Both his and my deepest and sincerest thanks go to them, the members of their families, and the managers and owners of the factories where they worked.

I would like to thank the President and Fellows of Harvard College for permission to use copyrighted material from the teaching cases listed below.

I would like to thank George P. Baker, Lawrence E. Fouraker, and John H. McArthur, successively Deans of the Graduate School of Business Administration, Harvard University, under whom Savage began this work and I completed it, for their long-continued support and encouragement. I would also like to thank Associate Deans Richard S. Rosenbloom and E. Raymond Corey, Directors of the Division of Research, for their substantial help and other assistance.

Savage's first written report of his studies was his thesis *Factory in the Andes: Social Organization in a Developing Economy*, submitted in partial fulfillment of the requirements for the degree of Doctor of Business Administration at the Harvard Business School in 1962. As his studies continued, his material became available in the form of teaching cases through the Intercollegiate Case Clearing House, now HBS Case Services. In the classification system of that organization these cases—most of them copyrighted by the President and Fellows of Harvard College—are identified by the following numbers: 370-119A and B; 371-569, 570, 571, 582, 583, and 584; 372-012, 028, 042, 043, 044, 332, and 333; and 373-102, 105, and 106.

In addition to these teaching cases, Savage wrote a monograph and several articles and working papers based on his research; they are listed in the references. In writing them he drew heavily on the material in the teaching cases and added additional material when it was relevant. For use of material in the monograph I wish to thank the Society for Applied Anthropology, the copyright holders. I also wish to acknowledge the Working Papers of The Alfred P. Sloan School of Management, Massachusetts Institute of Technology, including the Work Group Structure Series sponsored by the Inter-American Program in Civil Engineering. Alfonso Rojas, a member of the Economic Research Center of the University of Antioquia, collected much of the data at one of Savage's research sites and co-authored a working paper with him. David C. Korten prepared revisions of and additions to some of Savage's cases with support from the Instituto Centroamericano de Administracion de Empresas (INCAE), Managua, Nicaragua. I thank both of them.

In his publications Savage acknowledged support from the Agency for International Development (AID) of the United States Department of State, the Carnegie Corporation, Coca-Cola Export Corporation, Dow Chemical Company, Esso Inter-America, Organization of American States (OAS), and the Latin American Divison of Xerox Corporation. Savage also received important assistance from the Economic Research Center of the University of Antioquia and the Escuela de Administracion y Finanzas (EAFIT), both of Medellín, the College of Business Administration at Boston College, and INCAE.

Everett E. Hagen of the Center for International Studies, Massachusetts Institute of Technology, arranged Savage's original introduction in Colombia; and as Savage recounts in chapter 1, he used Hagen's insightful studies of that country as a starting point for his own work.

Savage also thanked the Directors of The Associación Nacional de Industriales, the Programa de Becas of the Pan-American Union, and Dr. Rodrigo Uribé. All these persons graciously welcomed Savage into their countries, opened their traditions and customs to him, extended their warm hospitality to him, and embraced and helped him in other ways.

In addition, Savage expressed appreciation to Anne Orlov of the Harvard University Press and to Frederick McGarry, Thomas J. Allen, Jr., Warren G. Bennis, the late Douglas McGregor, and Edgar H. Schein of the Massachusetts Institute of Technology; John Platt of the University of Michigan; Jack Rosin of Boston College; Lamar Carter of the International Center for Integrative Studies in New York; and Robert W. Ackerman, Kenneth R. Andrews, the late Raymond A. Bauer, James P. Baughman, Alfred D. Chandler, Jr., Charles J. Christenson, Stanley M. Davis, Cyrus F. Gibson, David F. Hawkins, Albert O. Hirschman, the late Robert W. Merry, and Allen P. Sheldon of Harvard University "for other services contributed."

Savage would also want me to express his thanks to his students at the Harvard Business School, MIT, and INCAE and in his management training seminars in Latin America, many of whom discussed these cases with him and gave him the benefit of their comments and insights.

To my regret, many others people who helped Savage are unknown to me. They know who they are, and I hope that they will both accept my apologies for leaving them nameless and be assured of his and my thanks for their contributions to this book.

Mauricio Obregon gave me much-needed help at an important time in the progress of the manuscript. Hernan Echavarria O. read the whole manuscript, made several concrete and specific suggestions, and gave me other helpful advice. I am grateful to both.

Paul R. Lawrence gave me many helpful suggestions in connection with my drafts of the manuscript, as did John J. Gabarro, George C. Lodge, the late Fritz J. Roethlisberger, C. Wickham Skinner, Harold S. Spear, Arthur R. Turner, Richard E. Walton, Louis T. Wells, Deirdre Strachan, and Davis Dyer. While F. J. Roethlisberger lived, his experience and insights were readily available to me. Abraham Zaleznik's work called James MacGregor Burns's writings on leadership to my attention. Ernesto R. Cruz, formerly Rector of INCAE, read the manuscript and encouraged me to complete it. Harry Strachan went way beyond the courtesies he originally offered in commenting on the manuscript and in renewing some of Savage's contacts in Colombia.

Jinny Rosenthal devotedly helped Savage with the preparation of his early drafts of the manuscript. Cheryl Talbott, Rachael Daitch, Hedwig E. Pocius, and Robin Quinn typed and retyped many pages of corrections that were especially difficult because of my handwriting. Pauline B. Henault added new momentum to the project at a time when my interest in it was low. Rose M. Giacobbe, Manager of the Word Processing Center, and the staff of the center, especially Aimee B. Hamel, typed and proofread the later drafts of the manuscript with accuracy and care and *mirabile dictu*, on schedule.

Joanne F. Segal, Audrey Barrett, and Judith Uhl of the Division of Research at the Harvard Business School gave me substantial help. Carol B. Allen, Helen G. Cauchon, Elinor Goodale, Janice L. Fleischner, Nancy Hansen, Rita McAleavey, Dolores Mullin, Nancy Freitag, and Barbara Shank cheerfully and promptly helped me with various responsibilities along the line.

Charlie Bond of Graphic Design Associates and Jay's Publishers Services, Inc., drafted the original diagrams.

Max R. Hall gave me clear, concise, and helpful editorial suggestions on an early draft of the manuscript. John Junkerman spent many hours adding clarity and structure to the final draft, which no doubt would have further benefited had I accepted even more of his suggestions. I am most grateful for his assistance. John Van Maanen was of invaluable assistance.

Mary Savage and the members of the Savage family—Mark, Charles, Hugo, Mary C., Andrew, and Matthew—cooperated with my every request and supported me with understanding, patience, and encouragement despite disappointing delays in my work. I am most grateful for this help and for that of Mary Esther Lombard and the members of my family.

Sons of the Machine

1

Introducing Savage's Studies

In 1972, when Savage learned that he would not be able to finish his book about his research on three factories in Colombia, he asked F. J. Roethlisberger, Paul R. Lawrence, and me if we would see it to completion. The three of us, as members of his thesis committee while he was a student in the Doctoral Program at the Harvard Business School, had been in close touch with his studies from their beginnings. Circumstances among us led to my taking on the task. Shortly after his tragically early death in January 1973, I started revising his manuscript, together with his teaching cases, working papers, journal articles, and other memoranda. Thus, rather than being joint authors in the usual sense, Savage's work and mine have been done in sequence with the result that, although I have reviewed and edited his, he has not done so with mine.

These circumstances constitute an infringement of the meaning of joint authorship as it is customarily practiced. Even though some readers will recognize the authors' separate contributions because of the differences in our styles, it is desirable to clarify them further. One of my principal motives in undertaking the completion of Savage's work was to bring the products of his clinical research skills, his data, and his ideas to the attention of general readers. In these circumstances a reader could easily be misled into believing that I, as the senior author, was seeking credit for myself on the basis of a junior's work when the true situation is the opposite. Thus in this chapter, which is an introduction to Savage's work as well as to this book, I will identify each contribution.

Savage's Initial Studies

Savage began his studies in a remote mountain village in Colombia in 1960. In one of his early memoranda he wrote that his "initial curiosity about the behavior of workers in industry grew from anger. This was my reaction to the views that veteran managers passed along to us, when I worked with management trainees in the oil fields of South America during the late 1950s. The veterans enjoined us newcomers to be tough, realistic, and hard-headed and to accept the principle that money constitutes the only effective means for disciplining workers. We were told that managers should view workers as self-centered and irresponsible, motivated only by fear of not receiving the pay they required for squandering on wine, women, and song. These strictures were an affront to the views about the dignity of work and workers with which I had been reared.

"Some of us understood that the workers played a game with us that confirmed the old-timer's views. At other times, glimpses of true humanity broke through in our encounters, brief flashes of something different and authentic that disappeared as quickly as they came.

"I became curious about what was happening in these encounters and about how managers had come to adopt their views of their roles and the roles of workers. I wondered how we expatriate managers had gotten ourselves into the fix we were in. Why was alienation all around us? Where had things gone wrong?"

At the time, in the late 1950s, Savage was working for a large international oil company, primarily in the Andean region of northern South America. "I traveled widely throughout the region, wherever there was oil, the prospects of it, or a market for it, from the jungles of the Orinoco and the islands of the Caribbean to the heat-soaked basin of Lake Maracaibo and the snow-capped peaks of the Andes. The visitor who concentrates on these sights easily misses the most interesting feature of the scene, the Andinos themselves, who live in the backwash of a violent history that has seen the successive impact of the Incas, the *conquistadores*, the Spanish friars, the liberators and, most recently, the modern techologists." In learning about this world, its history, and the people who inhabited it, Savage wrote, "I had trouble escaping from the breakfast trays of airliners, the gin and tonics of cocktail lounges, and the swimming pools of management training centers. I felt separated from the world outside, as though I was behind a picture window. I could see the world beyond the window, but I was cut off from understanding it. I heard a great deal about the 'Juan Bimba' of the region, but he remained as faceless as John Doe, his North American counterpart. I took the opportunities that came my way to escape outside the compound gates of the training centers to sit with the *campesino* at his door, quietly smoking, while the children ran to a neighboring *tienda* for ice and Coca-Cola to lighten the rum of our drinks."

In Savage's longest assignment in one of South America's largest oil fields, he found that the dominant managerial ideas being applied were those of Frederick W. Taylor.[1] Taylor, from studies of industrial efficiency in the United States at the turn of the century, concluded that workers could not be depended on to carry out their tasks in the most efficient manner. As is well known, he proposed a corps of independent observers to study job design and motion economy and to discipline workers according to management standards. The indicated tactic was to break the work into units that could be measured and then to pay each person only for the work that he or she actually produced.

Taylor recognized that the introduction of his new corps of work specialists would create resistance both from workers and from their non-Taylorist management leaders. To counter this resistance, Taylor and his followers developed an ideology based on the premise that workers were motivated only by money. In this ideology, managers were viewed as the activating subjects, who paid workers to the degree they would or could act as compliant objects of the managers' initiatives.[2]

During this assignment, Savage found that in Latin America Taylorism was being applied in the context of the older, indigenous approaches that it was replacing. Taylorism concentrated power in the hands of technological specialists, whereas traditional Latin American management centered on the leadership of the *patrones*. Despite this difference, both doctrines assume that motivation proceeds from outside the workers. The patrones imposed it by the force of their long-standing personal presence, something the oilfield Taylorists were denied, for their tours of duty were limited. They had neither the taste nor the talent to replicate the patronal manner. They depersonalized their presence and substituted cold output-reward formulas. The workers appeared to conform to their managers' views of them.

Savage recalled that most of the novelists, philosophers, and historians that he had studied in college also presented industrial workers as faceless automatons who surrendered themselves for eight hours of tedium each day in return for the benefits enjoyed after hours. Transparent in their alienation, they were considered unworthy of artistic treatment. In academic fields primitive peoples received more attention. The intellectual community locked workers into rigid categories and forgot them. In doing so its members withdrew from them the touch of illusion that helps to dignify the human condition, the essential service that poets, songsters, and shamans offer a society. Stripped of romance, industrial workers were left to their bosses as objects to be manipulated and motivated.

Octavio Paz, Mexico's Nobel laureate in literature, stated this tendency as follows: "The peasant . . . has always had a certain fascination for the urban man. In every country he represents the most ancient and secret element of society. . . . It is noteworthy that our images of the working class are not colored with similar feelings, even though the worker also lives apart from the center of society. [W]hen a contemporary novelist introduces a character who symbolizes health or destruction, fertility or death, he rarely chooses a worker, despite the fact that the worker represents the death of an old society and the birth of a new. D. H. Lawrence, one of the profoundest and most violent critics of the modern world, repeatedly describes the virtues that would transform the fragmentary man of our time into a true man with a total version of the world. In order to embody these virtues he creates characters who belong to ancient or non-European races, or he invents the figure of Mellors, the gamekeeper, a son of the earth. It is possible that Lawrence's childhood among the coal mines of England explains this deliberate omission: we know that he detested workers much as he did the bourgeoisie. But how can we explain the fact that in the great revolutionary novels the proletariat . . . does not provide the heroes, merely the background? In all of them, the hero is an adventurer, an intellectual, or a professional revolutionary; an isolated individual who has renounced his class, its origins or his homeland. It is, no doubt, a legacy from Romanticism that makes the hero an antisocial being. Also, the worker is too recent, and he resembles his boss, because they are both *sons of the machine.*"[3] (Emphasis added.)

Savage and the fellow members of his company's management training center debated these matters during the long tropical nights. True, there was a need for a core structure of task discipline that could be ignored only at an organization's peril. But beyond that, what did Taylorist bosses really know about workers and their leaders? For that matter, what did intellectuals working from second-hand sources know? Were intellectuals imposing on workers their own criteria for work, that it be creative and thus reflect something of the workers in the product? Were intellectuals making themselves feel guilty because they derived something from their efforts that workers were denied? Could this be why they judged workers harshly and withdrew their attention from them? Could it be that, unknown to Taylorists, patrones, and intellectuals alike, industrial men and women had created their own myths and ceremonies and erected their own romantic shields?

It is possible to make such a case. There is a certain redundancy to many of the routines to which workers submit and that intellectuals find abhorrent. But there is also deeper evidence of encounters that workers appear to cherish. Do modern people gather at the factory each day in the same spirit that their predecessors had when gathering at the marketplace? Is industry our age's part in the course of history? People in other ages farmed or fished; ours operate machines and conveyor belts. Is a machine more alienating than a plough, a conveyor more divisive than an outrigger canoe? Both can be said to create community as well as to displace it. Will novelists one day turn to men and women of the factory to illuminate the age-old complexities as they did in the past with workers of the soil or men of the sea; will scholars one day find themselves as much at home in the factory as in the primitive village?

Savage's Doctoral Studies

Savage came to realize that he had pushed his quest as far as he could within the confines of industrial employment. He resigned his post in South America and returned to New England and its universities. He hoped to acquire a fresh lead in the work being done at the academic centers of management science. During the ten years that followed, his search to understand workers and their managers became a full-time pursuit. He became a doctoral student in organizational behavior at Harvard University's Graduate School of Business Administration. During his work in the program, he became acquainted with a wide range of the ideas then current in academic and professional circles about work groups and their management.

At this time, during the late 1950s, Taylorist ideology was still pervasive in industry, but alternate views of work and workers were being developed in academic circles. The principles of work engineering and efficiency, on which Taylorist ideology was based, were valid, but their psychological and sociological implications were different from what Taylor assumed. Not every worker in industry, for example, was motivated solely by money. Douglas McGregor at the Massachusetts Institute of Technology stated one alternative in *The Human Side of Enterprise*.[4] He contrasted the Taylorist view, a closed, suspicious interpretation of industrial encounters that he called Theory X, with what he called Theory Y, an open, trusting interpretation. Theory Y assumed that motivation was in the worker. Thus the job of the boss was not to motivate workers but to remove blockages so that workers' natural motivations could be expressed. The first blockage that had to be overcome, frequently enough, was the Taylorist perception of a factory, a perception to which the bosses themselves often subscribed.

McGregor's views are associated with what has been called the human relations school, one of the origins of which was in the Hawthorne studies at the Western Electric Company. F. J. Roethlisberger and W. J. Dickson, who wrote up these studies in *Management and the Worker*, suggested that a factory work group, like any group that engages in sustained activity, could be conceived as a human community attempting to come to terms with its environment.[5] Although the Hawthorne studies of workplace behavior did, in fact, record evidence of the patterns that Taylor assigned to workers and their bosses, these patterns were only a small proportion of the ones that Roethlisberger and Dickson described.

In his doctoral studies, Savage became acquainted with the writings of other researchers who dealt with the relationships between economic and social phenomena. Max Weber, for example, viewed economic behavior as an extension of the social.[6] He coined the term "Protestant ethic" to describe a socially based attitude toward hard and dedicated work. He went on to point out that there is nothing incompatible about the holding of religious or mystical beliefs and the pursuit of practical ends. Religious beliefs eliminate for their holders, he wrote, "all those questions about the meaning of the world and of life, which tortured others"[7] and allowed them, as it did, for example, the Puritans, to take up their industrial pursuits with assurance of the spiritual salvation of their souls as well as the material success of their industrial efforts.[8]

Savage also became acquainted with the work of Bronislaw Malinowski, an anthropologist who was stranded on a Pacific island during World War I.[9] There, Malinowski studied the culture of the Trobriand islanders, with whom he lived. When the islanders turned from ceremony to work, Malinowski did not lay aside his notebook. He could not, because the islanders used ceremony to sanctify the instruments and products of their work, just as work defined the content and direction of their ceremonies.

For example, the islanders, who were deep-sea fishermen, ceremonially sprinkled powder on their fragile outrigger canoes, for they could not face both the force of Pacific storms and their own fears and insecurities. The ceremony quieted their fears and left them free to give their full attention to the work of seamanship, even under conditions of stress, when their concentration was especially needed to ensure their personal safety and the well-being of their tribe. Similarly, the islanders stored the yams that they cultivated in open bins in front of their huts, but they had more than storage in mind. The quality and size of the displays projected individual differences in productivity and helped to express each individual's position in the tribe's structure, which assured the continuity of its culture.

The fact that Roethlisberger and Dickson's book retained a lively sale 20 years after its publication and that McGregor's became a best-seller in business literature soon after its publication suggested to Savage that the Taylorist views of industry were ready for further breaching. Yet he also believed that the ideas he was studying were ahead of the times, for the idea of a factory as a social unit with significance for society beyond its output had still to come into its own. In industry, management's ultimate standard for judging workers' behavior remained work for work's sake without explicit consideration of its contribution to the growth and development of individuals. And in the academic world, with few exceptions, students of modern factories either restricted themselves to the surface or productive aspects of factory life or contented themselves with superficial reports acquired from secondhand sources.

Savage's Plans for Fieldwork for His Dissertation

In particular, the limitations of two studies, of which Savage thought highly, influenced the design of his own fieldwork. The first was a study of industrial life in a Guatemalan village, in which the author, Manning Nash, entered the village factory only briefly.[10] He picked up the factory's impact obliquely, as it were, as it expressed itself at other centers of assembly in the community.[11] The other study was James C. Abegglen's *The Japanese Factory*, in which the author, having visited several dozen Japanese factories, interpreted how the organizational arrangements that he found in them differed from those in comparable factories in the United States.[12]

Savage thought that he could go beyond the limitations of these studies by designing one in which he, as observer, spent generous amounts of time in the factory itself and in which he attempted to interpret what he found there in terms of its own internal consistency rather than in terms of his own country's practices. Where might the study of factory workers lead, Savage wondered, if they were treated as a tribe and if the chieftainship of the Taylorist tactic was given only the weight that observation supported? If from this perspective Taylorist premises about workers and supervisors loomed large, he would report it, but he would make an effort to suspend judgment until after he had taken testimony and marshaled evidence.

The option of undertaking his fieldwork in the United States was unsatisfactory to Savage. He was concerned that the assumptions of his own culture would restrict his observations to familiar patterns. He wanted to go beyond those to where subtle shifts in social contexts would by their novelty stand out and lend themselves to precise documentation. He thus decided to conduct his fieldwork outside the United States and to follow the research methods of Malinowski.

Although choosing Malinowski's methods, Savage was aware of the need to avoid adopting the condescending attitudes toward non-industrialized peoples held in Malinowski's time in many Western societies. If he did not, he realized that he would fall back into the attitudes toward workers that the old-timers in the oil fields held and thus, by adopting the attitudes from which he sought an escape, defeat his search before it started. Savage thought, though, that he could separate Malinowski's research methods from the political attitudes of his times.

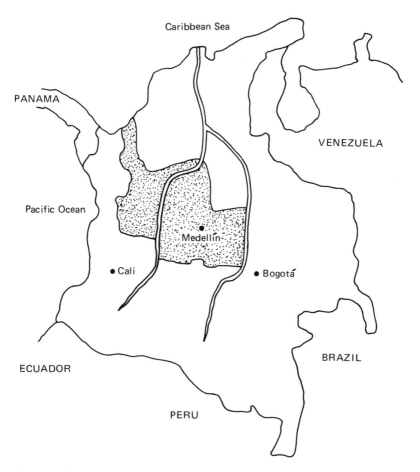

Figure 1.1
Map of Colombia showing the Antioquia region (shaded).

Antioquia as the Study Site

Latin America, neither completely familiar nor completely strange, appeared ideal to Savage as a site for his work. Everett E. Hagen, a colleague at the Massachusetts Institute of Technology where Savage had held a part-time appointment during his doctoral work, had just completed a survey that documented the entrepreneurial values of Antioquia,[13] a mountainous region of central Colombia that Savage thought held great promise for his study (figure 1.1). From Hagen's description, Antioquia appeared to be an example of indigenous industrialization powered by a Catholic version of Weber's Protestant ethic. Because the area was isolated by geographical accident from adjacent historical and cultural experience, a unique ethic about work had taken root there.

Until well into the twentieth century, Antioquia had been a two-months' journey by foot or mule from the nearest river port.[14] People made the trip only if they planned to stay. The region was avoided by most military adventurers, Spanish grandees, missionaries, and traders. The scant population was made up of a small number of Europeans and Indians who had survived the Conquest. They were later joined by a smaller number of Africans brought up from the coast to supplement the labor force. The three groups mixed to create the region's ethnic stock. The population settled in narrow canyons and valleys to engage in subsistence farming and placer mining of gold and silver, endeavors that never lived up to their original prospects.

Coffee played an early role in opening the region and helped finance the industrialization that followed. Coffee was cultivated easily on the region's shaded hillsides by independent families and was shipped leisurely by mule over the hills to the river. At the turn of the century, gangs of men and mules hauled textile machinery over the mist-shrouded trails; later, cotton cloth was shipped back by mule train to the river steamers. Antioquian merchants proved to be adroit entrepreneurs and the Antioquian people capable of the discipline of purposive activity. With few resources, distant markets, and little outside assistance, the people found within themselves the genius to industrialize on an important scale.

Hagen based many of his views on Rostow, who proposed a theory about how economic growth occurs in stages.[15] Although Rostow's ideas have been challenged by further research and are largely outmoded,[16] interest in the takeoff,[17] the initial stage of growth, and how and when growth occurs are still questions with important theoretical and practical implications.[18]

Hagen believed that the takeoff could not be explained by economic factors alone, for example, by the availability of natural resources. He thought that cultural and social forces underlay the economic ones.[19] He defined economic growth as "the process by which the affluence of a society increases,"[20] and he spoke of takeoff as the period when change becomes the normal state of a society that is becoming modern. Though less specific than Rostow about the duration of the takeoff, Hagen believed that it lasted for perhaps a decade. To present his views, he used Antioquian society, particularly changes in relations between fathers and sons, as an especially interesting illustration.

Antioquians have a long history of harboring odd and unusual elements, a trait that may have been a function of the stability of their institutions and the confidence with which they looked to the future. "We should be proud of our odd ones," Julio Arroyave wrote.[21] "They introduce into our life a note of color, ingenuity, originality, and eccentricity. The fact that our society produces them gives testimony to the vital energy that dominates us."

A further distinctive characteristic of Antioquian society was its capacity to maintain cohesiveness at the same time that it encouraged entrepreneurial activity. Its people practiced conservatism, but they also encouraged innovation. Established ways of doing things did not smother new ways, and new ways were not walled off in separate sectors of the society. Rather, they spread through it and thus preserved the society's integrity.

Antioquian families tended to work as units, sometimes with other families. When one family gained economic ascendancy, it was careful not to make this too obvious. The founder of the region's largest textile complex maintained his small home like those of his neighbors, and the heads of the workers' families that joined him in his enterprises continued to visit him at their pleasure.

By the middle of the twentieth century, the region's isolation was ruptured, and its distinctive ethic was exposed to outside scrutiny. An airplane in the 1920s was the first mechanical vehicle to arrive under its own power. Next came overland communication by a combination of train and truck. At the time of Savage's study, it was possible to travel by automobile, but it was still an overnight journey from Bogotá or Cali. The traveler followed dirt roads that sometimes led through crag-hugging mountain hamlets. At the end of his journey, a visitor found industry employing some 27,000 individuals in textiles alone and moving confidently into chemicals, electronics, and machine tools.

By the 1960s, Antioquians dominated the industrial and religious life of their nation. They were also prominent in export and in the establishment of Colombian subsidiaries abroad, which they tended to manage themselves with employees from other countries only at subordinate levels of their organizations. At the time of Savage's studies, there were only two manufacturing establishments in Antioquia with important foreign ownership, and both were experiencing administrative problems. Thus Antioquia featured the same linkage of strong, broadly dispersed religious beliefs and industrial capacity—social stability plus innovative entrepreneurship—that has been noted in Calvinist England[22] and in Japan.[23]

Savage wanted to find a concrete instance of Hagen's thesis about social and economic change—namely, that social and cultural factors underlay the economic ones—and to see what light a description of its events cast on the idea. To choose a site, Savage visited a dozen work communities in two countries. A broom factory in a sleepy tropical village seemed too small and somnolent; a giant textile firm was too large. Appendix A gives a description of the criteria that Savage used in selecting his site and an account of how he made the selection.

La Blanca: The First Site

The work community that Savage chose was engaged in the manufacture of chinaware in the village of La Blanca.[24] Its single factory was populated with strong examples of Hagen's entrepreneur. Before Savage arrived, the patrones, the owners, had withdrawn from the factory and moved to the city. They had recently introduced a corps of Taylorist-oriented managers to run the factory. La Blanca also possessed a work force that Hagen, the entrepreneurs, and the Taylorist managers assumed to be a passive or at least a neutral factor in the developments that were occurring. In 1960 Savage settled in for what turned out to be a three-month visit, the first of a series that extended over eight years; his objective was to establish just how neutral a factor the work force actually was.

At the time of Savage's arrival, the work force was experiencing the early trauma of separation from its patronal leaders. Like the managers in the oil fields, the young engineers that the owners had hired to replace themselves had neither the inclination nor the resources to assume the substantial responsibilities of patrones. For the patronal presence they substituted Taylorist-oriented systems of work measurement and individual compensation that they had learned at the university.

This substitution provided Savage with an opportunity to examine workers and their bosses at that critical juncture at which they attempt the difficult passage from a patronal culture to early Taylorism. Did they convert to the intellectual's faceless automaton?

Did their traditional sense of community give way to a Taylorist emphasis on increased personal income? Or, hidden from both intellectual and Taylorist, did some spirit of community survive, nurtured by its own imagists? Within La Blanca's factory, Savage hoped it would be possible to trace the initial impact of Taylorism on industrial workers; to raise questions as to whether technological considerations, including the organization of work (even when screened by the patrones' concern for the dignity of individuals), constituted sufficient explanation of workplace behavior; and to relate this behavior to the total human adventure.

In due course Savage completed his intensive visits to La Blanca, wrote his dissertation, entitled *Factory in the Andes: Social Organization in a Developing Economy*, and received the degree of Doctor of Business Administration in 1962. His own interests and the urgings of others led him to continue his research as time and funding permitted, even while he held faculty positions at the Massachusetts Institute of Technology and at Boston College and while he was concurrently visiting professor at Harvard and academic advisor to Instituto Centroamericano de Adminstracion de Empresas (INCAE) in Managua, Nicaragua.

Savage found in La Blanca, that the passing of the patrones left behind such conflicting views of the earlier period that it was difficult to understand what the period had really been like. For the older workers the time had been a golden age of factory employment, to which they wished they could return. The new managers referred to the time as a "cult of the patrones" and believed that the workers preferred it to the more equitable arrangements that they were carefully introducing. The younger workers believed that a return to traditional relationships with the patrones would threaten the new structures that were emerging. To understand more clearly what work at La Blanca had really been like during the village's long patronal prelude, Savage moved from La Blanca to Santuario, a nearby village that had not yet made the change.

Santuario: The Second Site

Santuario is an hour's drive from La Blanca along a poorly maintained gravel road that leads nowhere else. At first impression, the village appears to be a brooding, silent place. A visitor arrives in Santuario with the sensation of having entered a museum after hours, followed immediately by the sensation that someone else is watching.

Santuario provided the patronal context that Savage sought, for resident owners native to the village managed all productive activity. Like La Blanca, the village industry was the manufacture of chinaware, but with a difference. La Blanca's single factory employed almost 1000 workers. Santuario's 14 small factories each employed from 20 to 100 workers, with a combined total of 400 employees.

At the time of Savage's first visit, moreover, the village was not hooked into the regional power grid. For power the small plants depended on waterwheels, some of which were as old as the industry in the village. Here Savage could study what the economic history texts refer to as cottage industry, chat with classical entrepreneurs, and sit with workers at night while their wives—in a contemporary version of the putting-out system—molded cup handles by candlelight.

During his first two years of visits to Santuario—two hours, two days, two weeks, then two months—Savage's early impressions of Santuario were approximately sustained. The village was, indeed, a silent, brooding place. It had protocols and routines in which everyone had an assigned place. There was no way for either patrón or worker to contest the rigid destiny he or she had been assigned.

By the time Savage had almost completed documenting the nature of the social encounters on the floor of one of Santuario's factories, a combination of psychological, sociological, and technological forces broke down the established order. The flash point was reached at the factory where he was making his study, but the explosion engulfed the whole village. During the next two years, Santuario was catapulted from medieval calm into a situation approaching La Blanca's. Since Savage had the setting under scrutiny before, during, and after the explosion, he had a ringside seat from which to view the effects of a cycle of change on industrial workers and their managers.

During the six years that Savage visited Santuario, he spent a total of four months there and formally interviewed on at least one occasion each member of the work group that he selected for study. He observed them repeatedly at work. Though Savage did his fieldwork in Santuario after he had visited La Blanca, he begins his account of his research with Santuario's story.

El Dandy: The Third Site

When Savage had completed the major part of his studies at La Blanca and Santuario, he decided that to round out his research, he needed to find out what work and workers were like in a setting where industrialization had arrived earlier, lasted longer, and was more advanced. He turned back from Santuario, past La Blanca, to Medellín, the region's capital in the valley beyond, a thriving industrial center, home to almost a million Colombians.

El Dandy, the factory that Savage studied, was one of the city's principal textile and garment-making establishments. The forces that worked among El Dandy's employees mirrored its environment. Family heads worried that their children were being exposed to street vice. There were new arrivals from the mountain villages, militant unionists attempting to achieve a sense of fraternal support, and post-patronal industrialists and later-generation Taylorists seeking some measure of worker loyalty and task organization. Only representatives of the lowest stratum in the social structure of Medellín's society—the vagabonds, waifs, prostitutes, and drug addicts, who constituted a large part of the population of the center of the city—were missing at El Dandy.

During Savage's stay, however, El Dandy was not a success story. Its failure added depth to his understanding of industrial life. An impasse developed between the owner and his managers on the one hand and the workers and their unions on the other, and a subtle balance was upset. There followed a long strike that no one wanted. Managerial misassessment eliminated conditions essential to workplace collaboration, and the workers lost the shelter they required to sustain their efforts. Unintended consequences of actions taken for the best of reasons but without understanding of the actual situation lies behind the last story in Savage's trilogy.

Writing Up Savage's Data

When the time came for Savage to return to the United States, he bundled up his field notes and headed north once more. He began to publish summaries of his data soon afterward.[25] He also wrote teaching cases, which he and other faculty members at the institutions where he taught used in their classes. He found, though, that strange things began to happen in his data.[26] The first patterns that he had seen in them did not hold. Like aging wine, these first descriptions continued to mellow. There were a number of reasons.

A first refinement came about because the surveys that Savage undertook at subsequent sites cast new light on interpretations of events at the locations he had studied earlier. In his first report of La Blanca, for example, he did not mention that the factory had a team that played football (the game called soccer in the United States), even though he had traveled with its members for Sunday competition away from home. It was only when similar teams loomed large in the workplace configurations at both Santuario and El Dandy that he went back and plugged the game into the La Blanca study. The results proved surprising. If there was a single pivot on which events turned during that location's critical trials of passage, it was the activities off the playing field of the members of the factory team.

A second refinement came about because the extended time horizons built into Savage's studies permitted return visits to sites where his intensive studies had already been completed. Five times a year he was able to spend two or three days talking with the workers and managers who were the principal actors at his research sites. They read his first accounts. Both their reactions and the passage of time helped clarify his reports. The new data they introduced over the years gave Savage a chance to test his early conclusions. Between 1960 and 1972 he made both long, intensive and, later, short, follow-up visits to each of the sites (La Blanca, 2 intensive visits, 8 follow-up visits; Santuario, 2 and 6; El Dandy, 2 and 4).

The individuals who were principal to the events that Savage reported reacted to his initial accounts, as did his students at Harvard, the Massachusetts Institute of Technology, Boston College, and INCAE. In addition, Savage took the three stories "on the road" and used them in management training seminars that he conducted from Mexico to Argentina, including three in Antioquia. More than 500 Latin American managers spent an average of ten hours each studying and discussing the cases in programs that companies and industrial and trade union associations sponsored. The comments of the participants in these programs added further depth and dimension to the versions presented in the chapters that follow.

A final processing of the data occurred during my preparation of Savage's manuscripts for publication. The draft of this book on which Savage was working at the time of his death consisted of eight chapters, of which the first seven and a part of the eighth were in first-draft form. Some of what he intended to say in the second half of the concluding chapter existed as rough notes. In his manuscript alternate chapters presented the data from each of his three field sites, followed by a chapter that interpreted this data.

As is apparent from the table of contents, the book follows this general structure. Within each case report, the first chapter (in the case of Santuario, the first two chapters) presents data about the environment and the work of the group that Savage studied. The next chapter presents data about the individual workers and their behavior, and the final one describes the long-term outcomes of interactions between the workers and their environments.

In these chapters, a first-person pronoun always refers to Savage, except, as in a direct quotation, where the context clearly indicates otherwise. I added the notes and references to materials published since Savage's death. Translations of conversations conducted in Spanish and of quotations from newspapers and other published sources are Savage's except as otherwise noted in the references. He also chose the title of the book[27] and took the photographs.

Savage's manuscript drew heavily on the teaching cases he prepared. Since these cases were intended to be taught as separate units rather than in a series, my main task with respect to them was to eliminate repetition and to clean up the order of presentation to fit more appropriately than in Savage's first drafts into Homans' conceptual scheme. I also completed the statistical analysis of the potters' output, pay, and productivity in chapters 4 and 5.

During the decade that I worked on the manuscript, my main efforts went toward clarifying a theme to integrate the case studies. As the length of time that the task took me clearly indicates, I did not find it easy to do so, though once made, as so often happens, the choice seems obvious. Yet I found the problem compelling, for from my first reading of the chapters I sensed a unity in Savage's data. In addition, I knew, especially from my work on Roethlisberger's *The Elusive Phenomena*,[28] which took much of my time between 1974 and 1977, that the problem of moving from clinical levels of knowledge toward analytical levels was a significant problem of the social sciences. The opportunity to work on a concrete instance absorbed my attention.

In selecting the notion that change in the structure of the social organization of a work group happens rapidly and in bursts, I drew on ideas that Savage stressed in the context of his individual cases without having raised them to the level of a unifying theme. I was also influenced by recent debates about the pace of change in biology, where, as elsewhere, the conventional wisdom since Darwin's time has been that change occurs gradually and continuously at a uniform rate rather than rapidly and at an uneven rate.

To assist in making these themes explicit, I extensively rewrote the interpretive and explanatory chapters that follow each case in Savage's manuscript. In the data chapters in this book, the interpretations of events and the discussions of theory are at the minimum needed to tell the story and to clarify the continuity in a conceptual sense of the events that Savage witnessed.

I added the ideas about leadership from Burns[29] to chapters 6, 8, and 11 and the material from Brinton[30] and from Homans[31] on social mold and social contract theories to chapter 8. I also reconceptualized Savage's account of events at El Dandy to describe the group in workshop A as a frozen group. To do so, I added material in chapter 10 from Maslow,[32] McGregor,[33] and Zaleznik et al.[34] The material from Erikson[35] in chapter 12 and the discussion of how managers might behave to support changes in the structures of the social organizations of workers in chapter 13 draw heavily on Savage's manuscript.

Other modern themes of importance in Savage's research, including the introduction of women into industry and the relative productivity of workers from urban and rural backgrounds, are commented on in the conclusions to the appropriate case studies.

As is apparent, Savage and I are not conceptual innovators. Thus readers who approach the book with the expectation that conceptual innovations are the justification for a publication in the behavioral sciences will be disappointed. Others may be disappointed that Savage did not collect his data more systematically. Why did he not quantify some of the interaction patterns he described? If only he had been able to overcome the difficulties he encountered in the field and collect data on the ethnicity, class, and other status characteristics of the members of the groups that he studied! Why did he not tell us more about the market conditions that the products of each of the three factories faced and about the financial and investment problems of their owners?

Lack of information about some of these matters is particularly troublesome in Savage's account of events at El Dandy. It would be desirable to have even a little more information about the role of the supervisors in workshop A and about the role of women. How about the strike and its outcomes from the perspective of the unions? And what about data with respect to the social organization of workshop A after the strike? Savage was aware of these questions, but at El Dandy the situation from the point of view of field research was the most complex of the three sites that he visited, and the time that was available to him for study was the most restricted. Such limits affect all research. In Savage's case, he was working without assistance in a foreign culture and, for much of the time, with pressing responsibilities from other duties.

The value of *Sons of the Machine* is to be found primarily in the richness of Savage's data, in the style of his writing, and in the syntheses he made between his data and the theories to which he refers. Though 20 years have passed, his data and the questions they raise are as fresh and original today as when he gathered them. His style is lively and vivid. As a result the people and events about which he writes come alive to us, even though they are from a culture that is different from ours. He thus joins the group of social scientists who have earned their way into the respect and friendship of the members of work communities in foreign lands. On all these counts his data and his ideas speak for him; my aim has been to order them in ways that assist them in doing so.

I

Santuario: A Time of Change

Santuario and Its Traditions

Santuario has a long history. It was settled in one of the later Spanish migrations during the seventeenth and eighteenth centuries. The settlers crossed the Atlantic Ocean and made the tropical journey up the Magdalena River. They left the river and traveled by mule train over the wild mountains and through empty canyons. Their destination was the high, narrow mountain valley, two months' journey from the river, where Medellín was located. The founders of Santuario discovered on their arrival that all the land in the valley was taken, so they had to move back toward the river. At the lip of the valley the trail crossed a broad, cool plateau with deep woods and many streams. At the far side of this plateau on the mule trail between the capital and the river port, where the mountains began and continued on toward the river, the settlers established their village. A small Indian settlement nearby was absorbed into the new community. The land that the immigrants occupied was full of pines, flowers, and pleasing mountain vistas but was of marginal value agriculturally.

At the turn of the twentieth century, Santuario was just another small village on the Antioquian plateau. Although it was not a primitive village, neither was it in any sense a modern one. The world had left it to its own rhythms and purposes. Farmers came there on Sunday mornings to hear mass and to exchange their sacks of corn or beans for bars of sugar or cocoa or perhaps a few candies; their spiritual and economic needs could be filled at opposite ends of the village's plaza. The picture of the church and market-day activities at La Blanca is similar to the scene at Santuario. Though the merchants made occasional trips to Medellín, a day's journey away, most villagers never went there. They made their life by the far mountain wall.

At the time of my visits, Santuario was still isolated, difficult to enter and difficult to leave. Though there were perhaps 20,000 inhabitants in its environs, only a single dirt road in poor repair wound up from the river and across the hilly plateau to the village. Except for a truck that carried passengers and produce daily to Medellín, transport in and out was sporadic. The round-trip fare amounted to almost a day's wages, and the villagers did not have the time, the money, or the appetite for such excursions. Occasionally a private car accepted a passenger for the trip. There was no travel after dark. The arrival of a visitor was a rare event, for the village did nothing to encourage immigration or tourism.

Nevertheless, my acceptance in the village came naturally and almost without incident. Once I had chosen the site for my studies, I rode out each day to the factory on the truck that carried the workers from the plaza. I spent the day on the factory floor, where there was ample opportunity for conversation, even while the men were working. In the evening I talked with them at the plaza or sometimes in their homes. As we will see, the church is important in Santuario; my own religious beliefs permitted me to enter easily into its activities. I found it a pleasure to work with Santuarians in all walks of life.

The Founding of Santuario's Potting Industry

Shortly after the turn of the century a stranger named Jésus Alvarez breached Santuario's isolation. He had climbed up from Medellín looking for clay for a pottery where he was employed. He found a good deposit and made the acquaintance of Don Enrique over bowls of hot chocolate at the latter's establishment in the plaza. Don Enrique, one of Santuario's principal citizens, traded sugar, kerosene, and chocolate for the farmers' corn, beans, and potatoes. He and Jésus Alvarez soon decided to go into the chinaware business together. Jésus Alvarez provided the technical know-how, and Don Enrique made the local arrangements; the partners also became workers in the new enterprise. Don Enrique invited his son Don Bernardino and his brother Don Tómas to join in the undertaking (figure 2.1). Four neighbors completed the original work force.

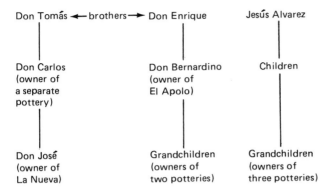

Figure 2.1
Three generations of the potting industry's founding
families at Santuario. The founders are Don Tomás,
Don Enrique, Jesús Alvarez, and Don Bernardino.

It took this team of eight men the better part of a year to get their factory going. The men mounted a huge waterwheel by the stream at the edge of the village. With the help of the village blacksmith, carpenter, and mason, they created a series of gears, axles, belts, mixing vats, kilns, and potting wheels, many of which were still in service at the time of my visits.

A low, open-walled, tile-roofed factory soon became part of the Santuarian landscape. At first the work force remained the original eight. On Saturdays Don Enrique packed the finished ware over the mule trails to Medellín to be peddled in Sunday's open market. Gradually more neighbors left their corn and their beans to join in the work. When the work force reached 40, a significant event happened. Don Bernardino set up a second factory, known as El Apolo, 100 yards upstream. There was no animosity behind the decision. It simply seemed appropriate for each of the two patrones to preside over a part of the expanded work force. El Apolo was still there 60 years later.

At the time of my studies there were 14 potteries in Santuario. One made porcelain cups and saucers, a thin ware preferred by many of the local cantinas and restaurants. Another produced special industrial products. A third sold its entire output to a large dry-goods store in Bogotá. The others manufactured standard lines of low-priced household chinaware, similar to what can be found on sale in most parts of the world. These products served the lower-priced half of the Colombian market; the higher-priced half was served from the large, more modern plant at La Blanca. A small portion of Santuario's pottery found its way over the borders to Colombia's neighbors, Venezuela and Ecuador.

The owners of all the potteries still traced their lineage to the original group of relatives and neighbors. Members of Don Enrique's family owned three, as did Jésus Alvarez's grandchildren. The owners of the others were descended from neighbors who associated themselves early with the founding families. Only once had another outsider come up from the valley to try his hand at running a factory; he soon failed and returned to Medellín.

Most of the factories had fewer than 40 employees. This number seemed to set a ceiling on the size of a work force, which most of the owners respected. One had as few as 20, but Don José's employed over 100, a special case that invited investigation.

Don José's family had been a pillar of village society for as long as anyone could remember. He was unique among the patrones in having had important exposure to the outside world. When he complete the five years of schooling that Santuario provided, his father sent him to Medellín to a religious high school that doubled as a junior seminary. His schooling completed, Don José tried his hand at managing a retail establishment before returning, as he always knew he would, to serve an apprenticeship at his father's pottery. When his presence and expanding sense of command started to tax the limits of the family factory, Don José, then nearly 30 years old, separated from his father, as custom dictated. He acquired his own pottery three miles from the village against the mountain wall. Its formal name was Ceramica Nueva, S.A., but it was usually known as La Nueva—The New One. Don José liked to think that the organizational arrangements he contrived there were somehow distinctive: "We have a different *ambiente* here," he told me. "Workers who leave us are never satisfied anywhere else, and those who come here from other factories need time to adjust." Whatever the distinctiveness of these arrangements, they permitted him to pass the ceiling on the size of a factory's work force that the other patrones considered fixed. In ten years he quadrupled the size of his work force, production, and sales, which were now at the level of $200,000 a year. His pottery was the largest and most progressive in the village.

At the same time, Don José continued to carry undisputed credentials as *patrón*. Together with his father (Don Carlos) and Don Bernardino, he served on the village's eight-man village council and was a leading participant in church affairs, notably in the Saint Vincent de Paul Society, a charitable organization that served the community. He received villagers warmly in his home, attended to their petitions during his nightly round of the plaza, and fully carried out his patronal role during religious and civic assemblies.

The Arrival of Electricity

Don José did not intend to bring tradition in his village tumbling down, but his decision to electrify his factory started this process. Until that time village industry had been without electricity. Recently, the regional power authority had extended its cables across the plateau to Santuario as part of a national plan to develop the country's industrial infrastructure.[1] For months the cables had ended there at the plaza, unconnected—the terminus, at least temporarily, of a "trickle-down" process of development begun, no doubt, by economists in far-off Bogotá, perhaps supported by international commercial and government agencies in New York or Washington, D.C.

The development posed for the village fathers the issue of converting the town's modest lighting system, which used a local generator, to the new source of power. The matter was raised at a meeting of the village council. The village priest told me, "Our people are so pleased with things the way they are that they won't even discuss change. Even with the power lines in place, they refused to believe that a new source of illumination was available. They saw the lines and the poles, but they just refused to admit that they could in any way be connected with the reality they knew. The matter of appropriating a few thousand dollars for a transformer that would convert the new system to our needs came up before the town council. The members could not visualize such use of town funds. I had to go to the meeting and fight with them."

Only Don José, the youngest of the current factory owners, thought of connecting the cables with the village's archaic chinaware industry. His first undertaking was to draw up a plan for a cooperative program designed to cover all the factories. His vision was that power-driven mixing machinery would prepare a better clay at one location. Power-driven kilns would reduce the baking time at a second. The plan provided for a marketing cooperative that would maintain prices and control production in times of short demand. Costs of the program would be allocated among the factories on the basis of output. Don José offered to give up the management of his factory and to administer the program from Medellín. The proposal was designed to update the local industry, provide for its gradual mechanization through electrification, and improve its competitive position in a way that would offer the national market more than just the economies of hard work and low wages. The village would meet outside competition on its own terms, and manufacturing in the village would enter a new era.

Don José submitted his proposal for consideration by the other owners. According to Santuarian protocol, he first discussed it with the village priest. The priest arranged for his bishop to nominate a leading industrialist from Medellín to preside over the meetings of Santuario's patrones. The plan was considered and in most part rejected. It may have been a sense of the pervasiveness of the required changes that unsettled the patrones. Or perhaps the quasi-monopolistic flavor of the proposal offended the patrones' entrepreneurial instincts, embedded as they were in the cultural traditions of the Antioquian region. In any case, Don José underestimated the patrones' resistance. Only the priest supported him. Even his father and Don Bernardino remained silent; the other patrones were against his proposal. A modest effort at price maintenance did result from the meetings, but even this broke down the next time that prices were cut, when some of the owners were suspected of smuggling goods out of the village at night to sell at prices below the agreed-to minimums. "Our people are great egoists," the priest told me. "They don't know how to cooperate. Each one wants to go his own way."

Don José was hurt by the rejection of his proposal. "I plan no more approaches to the others," he told me. "Now I compete with them. I prefer to stay out of their affairs and to deal with them from a distance. It is impossible to do business with them. We must wait for another generation to take over." Yet Don José did not give up. He decided to go it alone, a decision that was as much an emotional as an economic one. It started him on a lonely voyage.

Don José built walls around his factory, which made it the first in the village to be so enclosed, and posted a gatekeeper at the entrance. He brought electricity into his plant, so that the molding apparatus could be operated either electrically or by waterpower. The electricity also made it possible for him to convert his ovens from coal to oil burners and thus to double their capacity by cutting the firing time in half. He purchased an electric oven for finish firing. Later he put up a new building that nearly doubled his floor space.

From the beginning the new equipment required individuals with technical skills that the local educational system did not provide. Don José went to the city and hired two young mechanics. One stayed only briefly, but the other was to have a role in the change processes that went far beyond his technical responsibilities.

Inside his factory's new walls, Don José found himself condoning social and organizational experiments that unsettled centuries-old village values about how people should relate to one another. Don José was the only patrón who employed a substantial number of women among his workers; most of the potteries had none. He received scant support for his efforts from any of the other patrones. One of them told me, "This time José has bitten off more than he can chew." His father and Don Bernardino supported him privately, but more as an act of faith in a close relative than out of belief in the changes he was introducing. "José is one for reaching up and ahead," his father said.

Don José's factory became a seedbed of new social arrangements that spread rapidly to the plaza, bringing down the conventions that had provided the village with its social rationale. To appreciate the significance of these developments, we need to understand the historical context in which they took place. To do so, I describe the previously existing social arrangement in Santuario. These arrangements were deeply embedded in the Antioquian culture. Thus their description provides the background for events that are described in later chapters.

The Concept of Fixed Destinies

Every society develops values that make social intercourse possible, and every society disciplines its members to observe these values. Primary among these values in Santuario was a sense of fixed destiny. Only at great peril did a Santuarian disregard the destiny to which he or she was born. I came to recognize this fact in the following way. Late at night during the months I was in the village, I made notes of what people told me during the day. Within a few weeks certain words began to stand out because of their frequent use. For instance, workers told me over and over that they were "poor" and "cold" and "bored." But the word that was used most of all was "destiny." I began to use it in my conversations with the villagers in order to find out what it meant to them.

A destiny specified the appropriate behavior for a family's status, its social and economic heritage, and even the temperamental and psychological characteristics into which a person was born. Children in Santuario, I found, did not do household chores; they did *destinitos*, little destinies, a usage of the term that I did not encounter elsewhere in Antioquia. Destiny determined job classification, group membership, and level of productivity. The workers said, "Nuestro destino es ser pobre" (Our destiny is to be poor). Others were born to be patrones or owners of property, a role that included responsibilities for sponsoring and protecting those who worked for them. If a patrón provided a service to someone who depended on him, he merited no special thanks, for he was simply doing what his destiny required. Since destiny was externally imposed, there was also no point in struggling against it.

The concept of destiny specified for all parties with whom the initiative for action resided and absolved from responsibility those not so charged. Both parties accepted the changelessness of the assigned categories and the rigid prescriptions of behavior that accompanied them.

One day I had lunch by the river and talked at length with an articulate young man who had recently returned to Santuario after working in the city. He came back full of Marxist dogma about human misery and those who fed on it, but he indentured himself to a patrón because it was the only way he could get the $100 he needed to buy exemption from military service. I asked why he did not take over and manage El Triunfo, one of the small potteries that had not been in use for some time and that could be run with ten or twelve employees. At first he did not understand my question, but when I pressed, he exclaimed in disbelief, "You don't understand! My destiny is not to be a patrón. My destiny is that of the poor. No one would lend money to me to buy a pottery, and if they did, no one would work for me. You take over El Triunfo, and I'll come work for you."

Little Pablo Mejia was 16 years old when I first came to Santuario, though he looked more like 12 to me. He worked around the plaza and was the first friend I made in the village. Pablo dearly wanted to be a potter, and sometimes Don Bernardino gave him odd jobs at El Apolo. But Pablo's father was the village bootblack, and everybody expected that the youngster would succeed him in that occupation. Everything congealed along this bias, including the hovel where Pablo lived with his parents and their brood of sickly children. It was the kind of living arrangement and family situation that would be supported by and in time produce bootblacks. Furthermore, a factory patrón took on a whole family when he employed one of its members, and Don Bernardino would have thought twice before undertaking so heavy a burden. The destiny concept made his reluctance to employ Pablo legitimate.

On return trips I watched Pablo's physical and psychological transformation into what fate held in store for him. As he grew older, he lost his teeth and his shoulders bent forward. Instead of the searching upward glance with which he had greeted me on earlier visits, his eyes went to my shoes to see if he had another customer. As Pablo grew toward manhood, Don Bernardino turned to him less frequently, and he finally stopped seeking factory work. When I asked him when he was going to apply for it, he answered, "When they send for me."

Pablo came to look, talk, and think like a bootblack. If his neighbors had any qualms about the process, the destiny concept made it palatable. His destiny was, after all, that of village bootblack. His transformation, although personally distressing, served larger community purposes in which all parties had a stake.

For Colombians—and, I suppose for Latin Americans generally—the concept of fixed destiny undergirds a fondness for tradition and the old ways. If there was anything unique about its expression in Santuario, it was its extensive application. Elsewhere it assigned an individual's occupation; in Santuario it prescribed his temperament and character as well. Don José told me that he had all his factory families categorized. The Garcias, for instance, were moody people but hard workers. Woe to the Garcia who tried to be anything else! Public expectation would inexorably bend him to his assigned character.

Young Marco Antonio Sanchez provided a particularly poignant example of this process. When I first met him, Marco Antonio was 15 years old, wide-eyed, and open. He went to mass early and attended the evening recitation of the rosary as well. After mass on Sundays, he used his few remaining coins in the open market to buy holy pictures to bring home to his younger sisters. Marco Antonio's principal pleasure in life consisted of playing chess with a crippled neighbor. Don José used him to do odd jobs at the factory, where he occasionally filled in as a potter's assistant. Like Pablo Mejia, Marco Antonio also wanted to be a potter. Working as a potter's assistant was a first step, but the conventional wisdom was not to be denied.

When Marco was transferred off the job, I found him crying; I talked to Don Ignacio, the *mayordomo*. "Yes, Marco Antonio is doing well," he told me, "but he will have to wait. After all, Marco is a Sanchez." And the Sanchezes were the village drunkards. One patrón told me, "I wouldn't have a Sanchez in the factory." Although Don José kept the boy's father busy around the plant, it was Marco Antonio's destiny to be a drunkard. I remembered how proud the boy had been when he had brought his father, a gentle man whose affliction had reduced the family to the most abject poverty, to my room to meet me. When I returned the visit, I found that the household contained no furnishings beyond a double bed, a corn grinder, and a table. The children slept on mats that were rolled up against the wall.

Toward the end of the six years during which I visited Santuario, I found the expectations others held about Marco Antonio's future beginning to be fulfilled. As with the bootblack, Pablo Mejia, Marco Antonio was permitted some early leeway in adjusting to his destined role. The interests of the community did not yet reside in exerting its power, but as the boy approached manhood, this leeway was withdrawn. In Marco Antonio's case, the expectations that surrounded him and thwarted his efforts to escape his destiny, plus the poverty to which his father's weakness had reduced the family, led him to increase his drinking and thus combined to verify the general expectation in his behavior. His associates found themselves faced with the problem of getting him home after a Saturday night of drinking. Happily for Marco Antonio, he soon left the village for military service.

Some fought the concept of destiny, but their struggles only served to underscore its general applicability. A few of the boys took off for the city. Some returned penitent. The villagers circulated horror stories about those who did not return. Alcibiades, the village carpenter, was one who returned without the proper penitence. The toll of his long, losing battle showed in his face. His father had been a carpenter, an important man with a house and shop on the plaza. While still a boy, Alcibiades ran away to work on the railroads and exposed himself to the variety of lifestyles that he encountered wherever the tracks took him.

When his father passed away, Alcibiades came back to take charge of the family property, especially the house on the plaza, but the damage had already been done. He refused to discard some of the ideas, strange to village ways, that he had picked up on his travels. The neighbors' children sought work when they finished primary school; he sent his to the city for further schooling during the few years that he could afford it. They always wore their suits, their one set of clothing, threadbare though they were and at odds with what their companions wore. Although the neighbors' children went barefoot, his went shod even when there was no food in the house. In Santuario it was cool enough in the mornings and evenings for the men to wear woolen ponchos or *ruanas* over their suit jackets on the way to mass. Patrones wore them for comfort at home but did not wear them in public. Alcibiades wore neither ruana nor suit jacket. He had purchased instead a short military-style jacket that in all likelihood cost him more than the other garments without being as warm. Men in the village who had attained Alcibiades' years—at least those who did not have strong Indian features—were referred to as *don*, a traditional Spanish title that once meant *de origen noble*. Alcibiades resisted this designation. "Let them keep their titles," he said. "I'll take the money instead."

Alcibiades had looked beyond the community's conventional wisdom, and the resulting vision cost him his tranquility. The years that followed were an unending struggle to realize that vision or at least to gain the privilege of pursuing it in private. The struggle served to underscore the rift that separated him from his neighbors. His carpentry business had remained static, though the village had grown and others who owned property had prospered with the growth. By the time of my arrival, Alcibiades' house had become a symbol of his situation. Inside, around the interior patio, was a litter of bricks, a sagging staircase, and walls propped against imminent collapse, 20 years of disintegration that Alcibiades had neither the time nor the interest to repair. But all this was hidden from the community. The plaza saw only a typical facade, and on fiesta days its occupant surveyed the crowded square from a second-story balcony. At night we sat by candlelight in the single cavelike room where the family lived on the far side of the patio, and we reflected on the erosion of the family's fortunes.

A rumor circulated that Alcibiades practiced black magic, which he had picked up on his travels. The story was that he had been a *duende* (male witch) and that he had brought back from his travels the implements of witchcraft to use in healing the sick. One day his young son became seriously ill, but his magic was of no avail. He went to the priest, who said to him, "Kneel before the Virgin and repeat three Hail Marys with the same fervor that you apply to your black arts." Alcibiades did this, and when he returned home, he found his son cured. According to the story, he never again practiced sorcery.

The Plaza Phenomenon

Up to now I have been dealing with primarily the unusual cases, the young who were being conditioned and the marginal who were being disciplined to an abiding social reality. There was nothing personal, perhaps nothing unkind, in the treatment accorded Pablo, Marco Antonio, and Alcibiades. It was simply that there was too great a social stake in maintaining the only operational principles that this small society had at its disposal, the ones that had brought it intact through a difficult past deep into the twentieth century. But just as the conventional wisdom punished deviation, it also supported those who made the commitment to its cultural values.[2] It rewarded compliance by means of social mechanisms that were small miracles of invention.

I had long sensed that the plaza played a symbolic role in Colombian life. It was not until I studied Santuario that I understood that this role was instrumental as well. The plaza was the size of a large city block and paved in cement. In the center was a small plot of grass surrounding a modest-sized statue of Simón Bolívar. Directly across from Alcibiades's house was the church, topped with two towers, a clock, and a large cupola. The largest building in town, the church, dominated the plaza. Flanking the church was a rectory for the village priest, a maternity clinic operated by the church, and meeting rooms for the savings and loan association and other church societies. Thus church buildings occupied the entire north side of the plaza.

The government building on the west side was less imposing. It housed the mayor's office, the police rooms, a clinic, and a small library. The mayor and policemen were from outside the village and served more as agents of the state government than of the local establishment. They were appointed by regional authorities for short terms. The roles they played as well as the building that housed them proved to be less dominant in village affairs than those of the church.

The plaza also featured a movie theater that operated twice weekly, a pharmacy, a soft goods store, and a number of cantinas, coffeehouses, and taverns, some with sidewalk tables. Rum, beer, and *aguardiente* sold for ten cents, Coca-Cola and other soft drinks for four cents, and coffee for one cent. The schools and other commercial establishments were located in the blocks that bordered the plaza.

Many of the patrones had their homes above the shops. I noticed when I visited that without interrupting our conversation, a patrón would stand from time to time, hold aside the full-length drapes that covered his window, and look out over the busy scene in the plaza.

The plaza was the stage for the village's annual fiesta, its great feast days, political rallies, and important funerals. It also featured rhythms that marked the hour of the day and the day of the week. It was largely empty when the men were at work, the women in their homes, the priests in their quarters, and the mayor and the policemen in their offices. The only visible activity during these daytime hours was the play of a group of boys whose games helped them fill the months between school and work. Their meeting place was the grassy spot at the center of the plaza. Pablo Mejia, the shoeshine boy, sat near them.

At night and on Sundays the plaza filled. Trucks brought the workers in from the factories some time after 6:00. At 6:30 there was a public recitation of the rosary. Many of the men came back after going home to change, clean up, and have their evening meal. Only men came to the plaza at night, although women, who were seldom seen on the streets, occasionally passed through on errands or on the way to mass. On Saturday nights activity became more intense as the midnight closing hour approached. Policemen circulated more pointedly, and the senior patrones discreetly absented themselves.

Sunday was the day for mass and the open market. Activity started at 4:30 A.M., when the schoolchildren paraded in the streets and chanted hymns and their responses to the rosary in their high sing-song voices before disappearing into the cavernous church. The plaza was then restored to silence. I remember standing there one morning in the predawn. A flood of candlelight from the church provided the only relief to the darkness and the cold. Promptly at 5:00 A.M. the bells started pealing, and the rapid patter of hurrying feet gradually built up from all directions. Scores of villagers converged on the plaza and the church. There was no other sound. The patter subsided as rapidly as it had begun, leaving the plaza empty again except for the lighted windows on its north side. Most of the early churchgoers were women who hurried home as soon as mass was over. Men attended the later masses, typically accompanied by their unmarried sons. Santuarians attended mass regularly and all eight Sunday masses were crowded, jovial, bustling, and full of song and loud prayers.

Since the men did the shopping, stalls and tents were set up later in the morning in order to catch them as they came out of mass. The market occupied the southern half of the plaza, opposite the church. Here one could purchase beans, corn, potatoes, and other local products, together with a limited number of items produced outside the town. By midafternoon, market activity subsided and the vendors started taking down their stalls. The villagers rested at sidewalk tables or conversed in groups on the pavement beyond. The hour for a symbolic ritual arrived then. The two senior industrial patrones, Don Bernardino and Don Carlos, left their homes and crossed the plaza to the rectory to await the priest in his parlor. Then the three men made a leisurely circuit around the plaza. The gentry nodded as the three men passed, reminded once again that the old marriage of the economic and the spiritual, the work place and the church, the linkage to which the villagers attached their well-being, still prevailed.

When a Santuarian was not eating, sleeping, or working, he went to the plaza. There was no other place to go, no secondary plaza or cantina away from the center. Social recreation and sports were unknown, even among the young men. In Medellín major sporting events electrified the population from time to time, but the few newspapers that found their way to Santuario were not read for their sports pages. There was little discussion of sports of any kind.

It was not customary for men to visit each other in their homes. When Javier, a popular young worker, was away from the factory for ten days with an illness, none of the other young men visited him. When I went to greet the families I knew after a trip away from the village, any young men who accompanied me hung back at the door of each house that I approached. They knew that the housewife was not prepared for such visits. Since the front room was used for sleeping, it would be necessary to sit among the beds, which would be a source of embarrassment, and coffee would have to be sent for, an extra expense when there was little to spare. Custom thus precluded meetings at homes except on such ceremonial occasions as funerals and weddings, when the hosts were prepared and the ceremonies were supervised by the appropriate persons. Social dancing was forbidden by the pastor. Courtship took place at the entrance to a girl's home. Rio Alto, a nearby town, had a *barrio* where those who were so inclined could consort with prostitutes; Santuario had none.

If a Santuarian sought contact with another villager, he did so at the plaza. Until 10:00 P.M., when activities in the plaza ceased, the patrones circulated there and drank coffee with the principal men of their factory families. This was the time and place to air a grievance, to petition for a son's employment, or to get counseling on a domestic matter.

The village custom of treating interactions in the plaza as public encounters imposed a special burden on me as a visiting social investigator. I gave up trying to talk with individual workers at a canteen table in the plaza and retreated to my rented room, also on the plaza. Even there personal conversation became impossible. The room was constantly full of people arriving and leaving, each of whom had to be greeted. The mayor rented a room in the same house. He sent word to me through the landlord that, unless this commotion abated, he would issue a public denunciation.

Toward the end of my stay, this absence of privacy unsettled my personal habits. I was crossing the plaza to visit a family in which recently there had been a death. As usual, a dozen or so small boys were trailing me. I spoke to them harshly and asked them to leave me alone, whereupon a worker who overheard gently reprimanded me, "They are only showing interest." He was defending the Santuarian custom of public encounter in the plaza, which was at odds with the privacy to which I was accustomed.

The archaic routines of the plaza might have appeared amusing to the village's neighbors and especially to Sunday drivers from the city. Outsiders did not come to Santuario to buy or to sell. The market did not have a reputation with itinerant peddlers or visiting tourists.

Both the location and the dynamics of the plaza protected Santuario's routines from exposure. Consider the prospect that confronted a family from Medellín planning a Sunday outing to Rio Alto, as contrasted with the possibility of continuing on to Santuario itself. A good asphalt road took the family to Rio Alto, where they found at its plaza music, food, and commercial hospitality catered to their tastes. If they desired, they could patronize a second recreational center at the edge of town, where dancing was possible. The sun would be bright, the flowers ablaze against green pines and mountain vistas, making a Sunday vist to Rio Alto a happy experience.

By contrast, the prospect of a visit to Santuario was unnerving. Santuario enjoyed the same natural beauty, but once Rio Alto was passed, the visitor traveled a poorly maintained, winding gravel road that led only to Santuario. There was no other place to go. Only feeder roads, white with crushed ceramic shard, led out past the potteries to end by a mountain stream or some impassable country lane. At the plaza the arriving visitor felt ill at ease and unsure of the appropriate behavior. Its commercial establishments were not geared to family requirements. Most of them served only men. Women were served at only one cantina, operated by the church, where a single Ping-Pong table was also available. Dancing was not permitted, music was reserved for special occasions, and in a setting in which codes of dress and comportment were carefully observed, the reaction to different apparel or behavior was sharp, brusque, and discomforting. Girls from the city in toreador pants and boys in open shirts, tight trousers, and jewelry—all welcomed in Rio Alto—faced a web of hostility, resentment, and derision at Santuario. So the visitors stayed away.

I first became fully aware of a visitor's malaise when I innocently tried to introduce the village to friends. A group of young workers from neighboring La Blanca came over to visit me one Sunday afternoon. I expected them to mix readily with their Santuarian counterparts, but the latter fell completely silent and watchful. In turn, the visitors became unsettled. They never returned. Another time, when two young professors came up from Medellín at my invitation, I discovered that the pervasive Santuarian insularity that had driven off the young workers now conditioned my responses as well. I desperately wanted my colleagues to understand the village's unique qualities. But when they aggressively questioned the villagers whose table we had invaded, I found myself unexpectedly reacting against behavior that I myself had exhibited a few months earlier. A short stay on the plaza had made me a part of the insulating response that functioned to protect and perpetuate routines and customs that appeared ridiculous to a visitor.

The plaza—the policing instrument for the community—had the automatic control features of an electric circuit. The tripping device was the group of urchins playing at the little park in the center. These youngsters were alert to any elements of potential drama that passed their way. Every arriving vehicle attracted their attention. A stranger's dress or initial hesitation was enough to cause them to coalesce around him in a moment's time. I could never light a pipe without creating an audience before the match was shaken out. Such attention served to disconcert the uninitiated, thus adding to his dramatic appeal. If the gathering held for a few moments, a second level of attention became activated. Those strolling around the plaza or sitting at sidewalk tables came over to see what was happening. The invading element was now a prisoner of Santuarian values. He could not flee, for there was no place to hide. By this time the final level of attention had come into play. A priest or patrón overseeing the plaza from his second-story balcony or the mayor or policeman standing by the government building came over to investigate. By these processes, behavior not consistent with what the village considered appropriate was rapidly spotlighted and delivered over to authority figures for disposition.

Most Santuarians were not the kind of travelers who found respite from behavioral surveillance away from their village. They felt uncomfortable and uneasy in the city. Occasionally I invited some of the younger workers to visit Medellín with me on a Sunday. I thought they might enjoy going to the airport, where jets would be landing. Their reaction was why go to all that trouble when the real Sunday action was here at the plaza. Their younger brothers were more candid. They told me of the fate that befell townspeople who went to the city and recounted stories that hinted at masked supermen and human vampires who wandered the streets. Only the younger workers said, "Medellín is expensive, dangerous, and noisy, but very nice!" The others were unsettled by its noise and by the prospects of being cheated and robbed. These prospects also served to restrict the migration of Santuarians out of the village, as returnees were forced to submit to a strict inspection of their behavior, as in the case of Alcibiades. The chances were that when a Santuarian sought social contact, he did so in the plaza and with other Santuarians subject to the same codes of behavior. "Here you are safe," they told me, "but Medellín, whuffff!"

Thus, as Santuario entered the final third of the present century, it had a clear identity and effective measures by which this identity could be maintained. The identity specified the destinies of each individual—the hierarchical, psychological, and economic role that each was expected to play. Some individuals suffered because of the destinies that they had been assigned, but the general welfare outweighed the suffering of individuals. The community policed adherence to one's destiny at the plaza, its one site of legitimate assembly, at which dependable monitoring apparatus was available. The activation of this apparatus not only applied sanctions to the deviant but also served to remind the spectator of the consequences he could expect should he depart from his assigned role, thus reinforcing his allegiance to all aspects of his destiny. Since this allegiance was at odds with the values of neighboring communities and might have been seen as somewhat amusing to visitors from outside, some kind of protection was required against external reproof. Again, the social phenomenon of the plaza served as this agency. Outsiders shunned the village, as they were shunned when they happened into it. Don José commented on observing these processes: "It's like maintaining the purity of a herd on a *hacienda*. If a stray wanders in, you drive him out. It's not just a biological matter. It has to do with moral and spiritual integrity as well."

Central to these arrangements was the concept of destiny that attached to authority relationships. The entire community was geared to perpetuating a hierarchical emphasis in relations between people. This emphasis had brought the community to its present condition of relative health and stability. Historically this achievement was a function of the integrity of authority relationships in all their manifestations, including father-son, patrón-worker, and priest-patrón. Everything about the village—its productive activities, its traditional technology and style of management, its locale and conditions of assembly, its values and the ceremonies by which they were reinforced—constituted a pervasive system with a consistent rationale of authority relationships tested and proven in the plaza.

Custom required, for example, that patrones who had their homes in the plaza—except when the family was dining—always had their doors open, so that villagers could call. One Sunday I visited a recently bereaved family. While I was there, a farmer arrived to ask his patrón's advice about his inability to dispose of his chickens in the Sunday market. The patrón's response, in keeping with his role, demonstrated interest in and attention to the farmer and his complaint. They acted in terms of a well-understood social compact, which stated how both parties manifested their destinies, the one seeking help and the other giving it.

In other parts of Latin America, the patronal arrangement blended with ancient Indian systems of social organization to provide the social basis for large agricultural complexes. In the region surrounding Santuario, the terrain was not suitable for the establishment of large haciendas or *encomiendas*. Patronal units remained small, and families moved into and out of them at will. But even though the arrangement might be temporary, the participating families undertook the reciprocal obligations of the relationship seriously. This seriousness in observing fading protocols was what others referred to when they spoke about Santuario as "more traditional." They meant that the bond between fathers and sons and between patrones and working families remained strong in comparison with neighboring villages, where it had already yielded to modernizing influences.

Community Traditions and the Potteries

Earlier in the century, new values had taken root in Medellín, welled up over the rim of the valley, and spread across the plateau to Santuario. These values affected everything in their path. The other villages offered little resistance. Tradition and the devices by which tradition had been perpetuated had run their course, and the new values promised better solutions. But when the new values reached Santuario, they encountered stout resistance. Long before the outside world became aware of the fate of rural villages, Santuarians had adapted its traditional ways to industry, and the adaptation worked. Village products, if not its people, entered into the national life. Santuarians used the fruit of these activities to shore up the old values. Industry gave traditional values a new lease on life, for the manufacturing families applied tradition—the concept of fixed destinies, the patronal system, and the plaza phenomenon—to industrial purposes. Modernization did not follow industrialization, at least until electricity arrived.

Although Don José was not born to social disruption, it was he who let down the bars. This came about because the village came to possess a second site of general assembly when its manufacturing methods were modernized. If change was to occur, the only places where it could begin were the plaza and the work place. Although I knew of studies that documented how changes in the environment of factories affected the work groups within them, I was unaware of studies in which the lines of influence flowed in the opposite direction.[3]

When I thought about it, though, I realized that there were ample reasons why they might, for even a traditionally oriented industrialist is committed to the success of the business venture he fosters. If new social models promise to reinforce the venture by opening previously untapped reservoirs of talent and productive capacity, he may close his eyes to the weakening of tradition that results. Were he to do otherwise, he would forego the opportunities that the new arrangements make possible and yield advantage to more venturesome competitors. The workplace could become a unique site of continuous congregation, where influences originating elsewhere converged and where the forces of reform intersected the forces of tradition under technological and economic conditions that favored reform. It provided the specific conditions that allowed structural reform to be carried to completion.

I came to understand these circumstances more clearly when I moved out of the village itself and went up the river that provided the power for Santuario's potteries. There I observed how behavioral conformity was monitored and maintained among the different categories of people—the patrones, workers, fathers and sons, and women—who gathered for work nine hours a day, six days a week. I could assess how adequate the concept of destiny, the paternal system, and the plaza phenomenon were as the basis for dealing with manufacturing activities.

The patronal system predated industry in Santuario. Farming and shopkeeping had always been carried on by sons working with their fathers. When a farmer or shopkeeper was successful enough to require additional help, he entered into a contract with a second family. The arrangement was made with the entire family through its head, the *padre de familia*. The padre de familia held himself responsible for the behavior and output of the entire family, particularly his adult sons. In this sense he stood between his sons and their employer, who in turn became a super-father or patrón to one or more neighboring families.

The employment relationship was thus a contract between families rather than between individuals. When an owner wanted to expand his work force, he himself did not recruit new workers. Rather he turned to his padres de familias to do so for him. In sponsoring brothers, sons, cousins, or in-laws for employment in this way, a padre de familia obligated himself to the owner or patrón for his relatives' comportment, including their productive behavior and output.

In support of these arrangements, in earlier times, the patrón paid the padre de familia for his own work as well as for the work of the members of his team. Thus a patrón paid a potter, the position usually held by a padre de familia, for each 100 pieces of good pottery that he and his team turned out. Out of what the padre de familia received, he paid one or two assistants who prepared the clay for him, and, before waterpower was available, a boy who provided handpower to turn his machine. A subsidiary employee came to realize that his behavior reflected not only on himself as an individual worker but also on the whole family as an employment-securing, benefit-obtaining entity. An employee's actions were thus directed at sustaining his patrón's concept of his family as a "good factory family." An old-timer recalled, "We potted during the early part of the week and then polished the potted pieces. If a truck arrived, we all pitched in to load it. On a warm afternoon we might take off to go swimming; but when there was work to be done, we would stay until two in the morning."

Older workers still occasionally spoke of the factory as their home, of the company as their family, and of the patrón as their father. The patrón was obliged to behave in ways that reinforced the basic reciprocities. He was also intent on perpetuating the image of his patronal family as a "good family to work for."

Strict protocol was also carefully followed within the patronal families. Even when an adult son who had established his own family called on his father, he sat respectfully silent. The primacy of the father, thus confirmed in the social spheres, freed the son, at least initially, to learn the technical management of the business. Furthermore, it was not difficult for the son to subordinate himself to the father, for doing so validated the importance of the father's role to which the son aspired. This social contract eased the son's entry into factory employment by reducing the areas of new knowledge that he needed to learn. He had still to acquire new technical knowledge, but under this arrangement he could do so in the context of familiar social responses. In short, when a son entered industrial work, relying on the concept of destiny benefited both him and his father.

In applying the old ways to industrial practice, Santuarians gave tradition its broadest test. This test required that both the patrón and the working families be meticulous in fulfilling their assigned destinies. Once the work association was made, the patrón was careful to see that his padres de familias received his most affectionate greetings and closest attention as well as the most rapid disposition of their petitions.

The old ways passed the industrial test in Santuario, but with an important limitation. In the factory and in the village, application of the concept of destiny required a policing mechanism. In the village this mechanism was the social phenomenon of the plaza, where visual connection and instant feedback combined to ensure that an individual followed the destiny he was assigned. If the factory was to depend on the same concept for its organizational rationale and motivational source, equivalent capabilities for feedback were required. Physical arrangements at the factory, therefore, were limited to those that would permit a miniature version of the plaza phenomenon to operate.

At first this limitation created no problem. A typical Santuarian pottery, 30 yards square, permitted ready scrutiny. The workers could look out over the cornfields to the village and its church. Children came and went with their fathers' lunch pails and sold cheese wrapped in banana leaves. Women came to search for good pieces among the shards. The priest came to chat with the patrón. What the visitor from the village found in the factory, despite its strange wheels and belts and gears, was a familiar setting. The villager understood that his arrival was monitored by all present.

Rather than being laid out in the arrangement of a long, narrow assembly line, the four production operations—clay preparation, potting, baking, and decoration—typically occupied a building's four quadrants. There were no walls and no places to hide, conspire, or experiment with new behavior. Sons worked by their fathers' sides. All parties knew that any action not congruent with their destinies would trip a delicate mechanism in each of their work associates, regardless of the patrón's presence. Adherence to the familiar social mechanism brought Santuario a smooth conversion to industrial practice. The cost was a limitation on the size of its factories.

This cost was real, for it included what would be considered wasted effort in other industrial settings. The plate makers and polishers, for instance, congregated around a worktable in a way that required extra manual transport for the work in process. The pieces of clay first had to be carried to the table for the potters to work on. After shaping, they were placed on a plank and carried outside to dry in the sun. Then they were brought back for the polishers, and then carried to the ovens for baking.

When the sons were 12 or 13 years old—the age at which boys in Santuario sought employment—fathers brought them to the factory to do much of this transporting. They also shoveled ashes and did other work for their fathers around the ovens. "There is a lot of restlessness in youth today," one of the men told me. "It is better to have them where you can watch over them. In that way a father can teach his son about life and see that his lessons are followed." Work activities shared between generations thus served to perpetuate and reinforce the unchanging values of village life and work.

The factory families had still other stakes in the established system. Some of them availed themselves of a special "putting out" system to take cup handles and other small pieces home with them for wives and sisters to mold during breaks in their household routines or for the whole family to work on by candlelight in the evening.

I asked the patrones why they did not build larger factories that would employ more than 40 workers. Their answers were technical and related to the baking process. A factory with two or three kilns could keep 40 workers busy preparing the greenware that would be fed into them and processing the work that came out. But the technical answers the patrones gave me were fictions. They could just as well have built six kilns or a dozen. What they correctly predicted, although their answers were couched in technical considerations, were the social consequences of increased size. Such expansion would have required extension of the patronal services to a larger number of families, a frightening prospect considering the role that the patrón was expected to play in fulfilling the destinies of his workers. For example, the factory truck, usually with the patrón as driver, could transport a group of nearly 20 men and boys to work in the morning. A second trip could bring the women and girls who did the decorating. Transporting additional workers would have required a third trip and thus small changes in the existing routines of many people.

Such expansion would also have strained the operation of the plaza mechanisms in the factory, creating secondary work centers, out of range of general scrutiny and reaction. Policing mechanisms would lose their effectiveness, and the patrón would somehow have to step in to replace them.

These were the reasons that the sons of patrones left their fathers to establish second factories when the work force approached the ceiling of 40 employees. This also explained why there were 14 small factories in the village rather than a few large ones. It was not technical but organizational capability that kept Santuario's industrial units small.

Outside events conspired to confront the village with the cost of this limitation. The small factory became uneconomic, and the usefulness of ths old system was called into question. Yet the village lacked the social architecture to support new organization.

Nearby La Blanca, Santuario's principal competitor in the national chinaware market, had abandoned the patronal system five years before my visits began. The events surrounding its demise constitute a dramatic story, which I describe in the next case study, and gave La Blanca an economic edge. The patrones' successors there were graduate engineers who converted their factory's operations to more efficient machines and standardized work practices, advances that the small Santuarian factories could not afford. I knew from my conversations with La Blanca's industrial engineers that they cast covetous glances at Santuario's "simple but sound" labor force and speculated about how it might be combined with the economies of scale for productive purposes. Village tradition in Santuario was ripe for change. The question was whether the change would come from within or from without.

In the short run, traditions that function are not subject to external subversion. Surrounded by contrary values and fragile as they were, Santuarian traditions still had momentum going for them. The industrial application of these traditions validated the old ways and disciplined Santuarians to their perpetuation. Don José's father referred to this view when he spoke about Rio Alto: "As a village with its own integrity, Rio Alto is finished. Its best people no longer take part in its civic affairs. The town council is composed of taxi drivers."

Any outside agent of change who visited Santuario found cohesive arrangements that, although not to his tastes, were still functioning and enjoying broad support. Two Peace Corps workers from the United States made many friends in the village during a two-year stay. Probably their best friends were Alcibiades's sons and other marginal types. The Corps men organized these people into work teams to build culverts and do other jobs, but they made no impact on the community's traditions and way of life. Thus if tradition was to be subverted in Santuario in the short term, it was likely that Santuarians would do it themselves. We turn now to Don José's factory, where the transitional action occurred.

3

La Nueva: Don José's Factory

At 7:00 each morning I rode in the factory truck to La Nueva. Four people sat in the cab: Don José, who did the driving; Don Ignacio, who served as Don José's assistant or mayordomo; Rodolfo, who kept the books; and I. The workers were in the back. The fathers with woolen ponchos worn against the morning cold stood with their backs against the rear of the cab; the sons sat on the floor with their bare feet hanging over the tailgate. Later, Don José made a return trip to pick up the women and girls, who arrived late and left early. The road led through rolling country planted with corn. The other potteries hugged a depression by the river, so that sometimes the only evidence of their location was the smoke rising from their kilns.

Don José, now in his late thirties, spoke little as he drove, for the rough road demanded his attention. En route, we went through two small residential areas and passed several farms. There was a small school, which farm children attended for the first two grades. After a gradual climb and just short of the mountainside itself, the road turned sharply left, climbed over a flank of the mountain, and dropped rapidly into a final extension of the valley floor before the river narrowed into a gorge. Here sat La Nueva, together with the modest farm buildings to which Don José and his family came during school vacations (figure 3.1). He took a special pleasure in showing visitors his stables and fields as he explained his plans for increasing their productivity. Before he drove his workers back to the plaza at night, he pulled up the truck to the buildings to allow the mayordomo there to load milk and vegetables for his family's table.

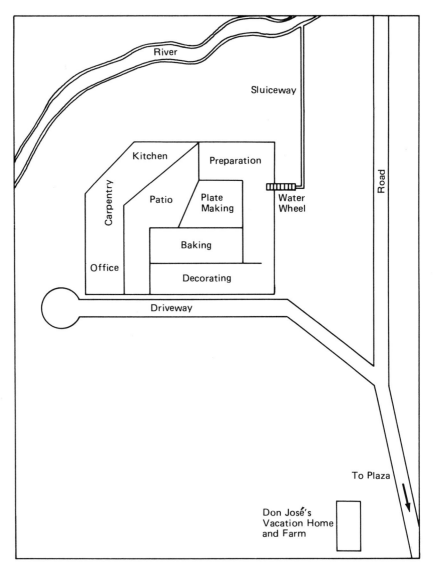

Figure 3.1
Layout of La Nueva before expansion.

When the truck arrived in the morning, its riders complained about the cold. Other workers who made the trip by foot waited by the entrance. A group of farm boys sat beside the road, waiting to fill their sacks with coal ashes from the kilns to take home for their families' kitchen hearths. At midday the youngsters came back across the fields with hot food for their fathers and brothers, and some of the family groups lunched by the river.

The Work Groups at La Nueva

Before Don José's decision to electrify his factory, La Nueva's production process was the same as that used at other locations. All its sturdy machinery was constructed locally. The clay was mixed in casks rotated by belts connected to the slowly turning waterwheel and then dried over a coal fire. Great masses of clay were then pounded manually before being cut into plate-, bowl-, and cup-sized slices. These were turned on a potter's wheel, on which a lever operated by the potter lowered a form against them to give them their final shape. Next, a polisher smoothed the rough edges with a wet sponge. After drying in the sun, the pieces were baked in batches in crude brick ovens, which were sealed and fired by coal heat for 36 hours. The ware was then decorated and given a second gentler baking for glazing. It was then packed with wood shavings in rough board crates and trucked to selling agents in the city.

The preparation or mixing room was at the far end of the building, and the members of the work group there were somewhat isolated both physically and socially. These men operated the stone crushers, vats, presses, and drying pans used to mix quartz and other additives with the clay. They then battered the masses of prepared clay or *pasta* into shape for slicing. Most of them wanted to work elsewhere. Young Marco Antonio, heir apparent to the destiny of village drunkard, wept when he was temporarily transferred to this area from the plate-making room. I had the impression that these individuals were not senior enough to qualify for duty at the kilns and had not yet met the social tests necessary for acceptance by the higher-status potters, who formed a more cohesive group. In any event, these men seemed lonely souls with whom it was easy to establish rapport, for they received visitors eagerly.

The plate-making or potting room was located between the preparation area and the baking area. Its most prominent feature was the large table at which men and boys formed and polished the pieces of pottery.

The baking section was dominated by three kilns, each 20 yards in circumference, that reached up through the roof. The bakers stacked the partially dried greenware from the potting room in these ovens until they were full. Then the ovens were sealed and the firing commenced. Most of the dishes were baked several times and glazed before the final baking. The bakers as a group, though reserved, were receptive to visitors. Senior fathers liked to work in the area, because the ovens warmed them during the morning chill. They also valued the work arrangements that provided them with more of an opportunity than other areas in the factory to work at their own pace and to avoid comparisons with the quantity of work that others were turning out. Moreover, they could have their sons at their sides to help shovel out the ashes and load the kilns. During the morning break, fathers and sons squatted by the ovens to consume a breakfast of the local corn bread, called *arepa*, and hot chocolate that had been warming there. The kiln workers responded with an easy hospitality to Don José when he stopped to visit them. They sometimes used the affectionate diminutive Josito in addressing him. There was a warmth in the baking room that was social as well as physical.

After the electrical cable had been extended from the village to La Nueva, Don José installed oil burners in place of coal furnaces to fire his kilns. This innovation cut baking time from 36 to 18 hours. Twice as many dishes could now be baked in the same ovens, which meant that production and employment in the preparation, potting, and decorating areas could be doubled. To achieve this increase, Don José constructed a second building, equal in size to the first and facing it immediately across the driveway. The new construction gave La Nueva a modern look that was less congruent with its setting.

When the new building was finished, less than six months before I began my intensive visit, the women and girls who worked in decorating and packing moved into it to provide space in the older building for the other operations to expand (figure 3.2). In decorating, a girl placed a piece of baked ware on a disk, which she rotated by means of a foot pedal while she held a paint brush against the edge of the piece. Occasionally she added a hand-painted floral design. The pieces then went into an electric oven to be baked.

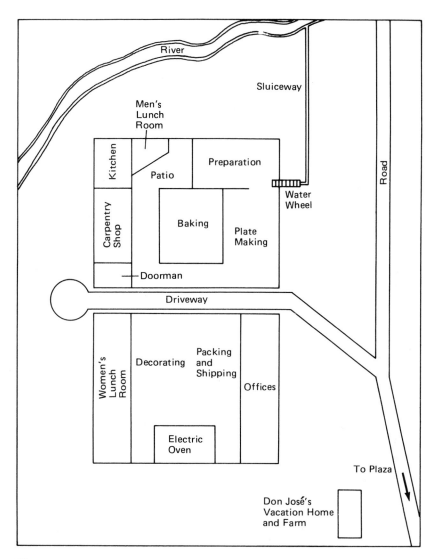

Figure 3.2
Layout of La Nueva after expansion.

Afterward they were tested by a group of girls who worked near crates set on the floor in the packing department. They struck each plate with a small metal rod to make it ring; if it did, the plate was sound and it was packed for shipment.

The decorating area was a happy, responsive place. The girls enjoyed visitors. They carried on protracted conversations without slackening the pace of their work. Don José paid long visits to them on his morning tours of the plant. The girls sometimes passed through the baking department, but none of them ever went through the plate-making room. "The potters wouldn't let us; they would yell at us," the women explained, and the younger potters told me, "They are afraid they would lose their virginity if they came here."

On my last day at the plant I gave the potters, with whom I had spent most of my time, a simulated oil painting of John F. Kennedy as a memento of my visits with them. I suggested inviting the girls in for the presentation ceremony. The plate makers, however, would have none of it. If one of the women wished to speak to me while I was at the plant, she sent a boy to summon me from the plate-making room.

There was a hunger in the mixing, baking, and decorating areas for the old unity of the plant and an uneasiness with the new separations; not so in the plate-making room, where the new arrangements reinforced a sense of separation from the rest of the factory that the plate makers seemed to favor. The large worktable was fitted with potter's wheels and polishing disks. Below the table were a number of crude belts that communicated power by means of gears and axles from an electric motor or, when the new source of power was interrupted, from the giant waterwheel at the rear of the plant. The belt that linked the table's machines to the plant's power system passed through an opening on one of its sides. Racks of dishes in process separated the potters from the rest of the plant on all four sides and provided them with some privacy. The older men from other parts of the plant rarely came to the room.

One entered the area from the mixing room through an aisle between the drying racks. The first sensation was of grayness and, especially in the morning, cold. The polishing operation raised dust that settled over the machines, the table, the men, and their clothing. Even the floor had taken on the gray of the broken ware trampled into it over the years. The grayness accentuated the cold, and the men complained constantly of the chill. The brilliant glow of an opened oven door, the touch of brightness in a dress pattern, paint, or white enamel, and the splash of tropical sun that one encountered elsewhere in the factory did not occur in the potting area.

The men looked up from their table when a visitor arrived, responding more as a group than as separate individuals. It was as though some time-consuming group process had to work its way to consensus before individuals could open their hearts to visitors and their purposes.

The cohesiveness of the men in the room was evident in other ways. Don Ignacio had hung a pipe from a beam at the edge of the patio. When he sounded it to signal a work break, the plate makers, eager to gather for lively conversation among themselves, were the first in the factory to leave their machines. Some of the boys ran to eat with their fathers by the ovens but hurried back with a haste that was almost disrespectful. A mixer told me that he longed to be transferred, but "plate making is not my art or my destiny," he said.

Don José must have noted the special climate. On his morning rounds, after lengthy visits with the women in the decorating area and the senior men at the kilns, he hurried through the potting area without stopping to talk. When I questioned him about his haste, he explained that potting required close supervision, and that for this reason he had delegated the task to his mayordomo; but I found Don Ignacio responding in the same way on his tours through the plant. For a while Don Ignacio had a foreman under him in the room, but the foreman never rose above the status of an expediter or production clerk and did not remain. When circumstances forced Don José to deal with the plate makers, his behavior seemed to become gingerly and stylized. In any event, I concluded that the social dynamics of the plant that interested me were centered in the potting area, and I decided to give it priority during my visits.

Changes at the Work Level

In doubling the size of his plant, Don José dealt a mortal blow to previously existing social mechanisms which, like the plaza phenomenon, required direct scrutiny and the opportunity for instant reaction to deviant behavior.

The expansion of the plant increased the separation of the production departments from each other. In some cases the physical distance between them became greater; in all cases the intervening spaces filled with work in process, which further separated the departments. Moreover, Don José and the other authorities in the plant were kept busy making the new apparatus work and had less time to devote to individual departments. These changes provided the opportunity for the workers in the several departments to develop new behavior patterns without workers in neighboring departments having an opportunity to monitor them.

The first and fairly rapid response to the new circumstances was a sorting out of workers, which had both social and technical characteristics. The men who operated the kilns no longer needed assistants to shovel ashes. Their sons were transferred to the potting area, where increased production was required to satisfy the kilns' new capacity. This transfer disturbed a subtle age balance around the potting table. The potters whose sons already worked there became uneasy. The malaise was increased by the excitement with which their sons and the sons of the bakers welcomed the new arrangements. The bakers' sons still returned to breakfast with their fathers by the ovens, but they gulped their food and hurried back to the less somber atmosphere of the potting room.

The changes proved to be too much for the father-son potting teams. The teams drew some of their strength from the reinforcement of their traditional behavior patterns that they received from those who worked near them. Thus the breakup of the father-son teams in the baking department weakened the teams in the potting room. Moreover, the old format suffered in comparison with the new relationships that were developing between the younger and more gregarious potters and their assistants, who were now released from their fathers' immediate supervision. Several of the older potters requested transfer to the kilns. The last of the father-son potting teams collapsed when the sons who remained left the factory's employment.

The countervailing pressures tended to push the younger element out of the baking department and the older element out of the potting room. The migrations that the introduction of the oil-burning equipment sparked made the kiln area the gathering place of fathers and converted the potting area into Santuario's first youth center. The wall between the two had physical, social, and psychological aspects.

At the time of the plant expansion, Don José arranged for a lunch-room to be set up with tables and chairs and a place where the workers could heat their food. No other pottery provided such arrangements. But the family groups that went there to eat dispersed as soon as the boys received their food; the boys ran off to eat or play with their peers or a sympathetic potter for whom they served as assistant.

The unitary plantwide control system was thus destroyed. Where there had been one plaza, there were now several.

Changes at the Supervisory Level

The management organization of the firm was also undergoing revision. When I first visited La Nueva, its management organization was not noticeably different from those of its neighbors, at each of which the patrón directly supervised the workers with a mayordomo to assist him in matters of maintenance and materials supply.

At La Nueva this form of organization was beginning to change. Partway through my stay there, I drew a diagram (figure 3.3) to represent the supervisory relationships as I understood them. As I saw it, Don José, without in any way losing status as La Nueva's owner, had limited his supervision to the baking department, where the older men and the padres de familias worked, and to the decorating department, where the women and girls worked. These were the departments where he had introduced mechanization. At the same time, he was giving Federico, one of the young mechanics he had recently hired, broad supervisory responsibilities in the decorating department. Day-to-day supervision of the mixing and potting departments was in the hands of Don Ignacio, who had one foreman, a former potter, working under him. In contrast to Don José, Don Ignacio restricted his foreman's activities to matters connected with maintenance and materials supply.

I showed the chart to each of the individuals concerned and found that none of them agreed with me entirely about the way I had drawn it. Their comments, however, contradicted each other. So far as I could tell, the ambiguities in these relationships did not adversely affect the way the organization operated in any serious way. For one thing, La Nueva, though growing rapidly, was still small enough that the people who worked there could keep in touch with one another easily. In addition, everyone, even Don Ignacio, understood that Don José had the final say. My conclusion was that

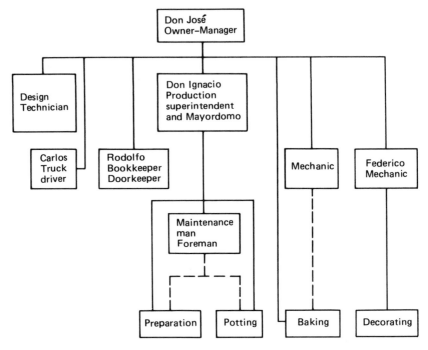

Figure 3.3
Inferred organizational relationships at La Nueva after electrification.
Solid line indicates a supervisory relationship, dashed line a technical
one.

the participants were sensitive to making explicit the changes in La Nueva's supervisory organization while it was in transition.

Don José's behavior was much the same in the plant as outside of it. His early morning tours of the departments had many of the symbolic undertones of his tours of the village plaza. Although he usually completed the trip from the village in silence and without greeting anyone, in the plant he discussed production problems and passed the time of day with groups of workers. He appeared alert and attentive and obviously enjoyed conversation with everyone, especially the older heads of factory families. Talking with people and listening to them was what he did best. By midmorning he was at his desk with a bowl of hot chocolate in his private office above the decorating department. There he studied his financial records, answered correspondence, and held searching conversations with his assistants, Don Ignacio and Rodolfo. He also welcomed whatever visitors made their way to the plant. They might include his part-time accountant, a cousin who came from the city, the parish priest, or a government official. Sometimes he read slowly through one of the English-language trade periodicals to which he subscribed. He received numerous requests to help in charitable and civic undertakings.

Don Ignacio had served Don José as production superintendent and mayordomo in the traditional style for a number of years. He was about Don José's age and was related to the patrón of another factory. Many of the workers addressed him as though he was a patrón, but he preferred the role of mayordomo. He upheld Santuarian traditions wholeheartedly. He believed that a patrón who became too familiar with his workers lost their respect. He conceived of himself as an expert in personnel matters. He expressed his views to me as follows: "You have to be firm with the workers but have respect for their differences. You have to take into account the genio [temperamental destiny] with which each is born. Some people you shout at; others you coax. The people we have here are good, but sometimes they have trouble with their wives or girl friends or they just get bored [aburrido]. Then they may speak disrespectfully to their supervisors. Usually they come back in a few minutes and apologize. 'I was bored,' they will tell me. I forgive them. If they don't apologize, I send them home. They must show respect. When they do, I make allowance for their genio.

"Don José is in command, both here and in the plaza. When any of the others have a problem, they come to me. If I can't solve it, I go to him. He is the supreme court."

The third member of the supervisory staff, Rodolfo, who was 25, was bookkeeper and payroll clerk. He was the son of an older worker, whom he introduced to me with obvious affection. He had left the village for three months for training in bookkeeping. Don José and Don Ignacio were active in the socially central Saint Vincent de Paul Society; Rodolfo worked with the church savings and loan association. Rodolfo checked in the workers in the morning when they arrived at the plant. Another of his duties was to greet visitors.

During my early visits, he ate breakfast alone, except when I joined him, and rarely left his cubbyhole by the entrance. I never saw him in the production areas of the plant. His attitude to authority was respectful but with a touch of humor uncommon in Santuario. He told me, "We call Don José 'Papa.' Oh, not to his face, of course; but if I see him coming, I say, 'Here comes Papa.' It started one day when Don José told us, 'The plant is our mother, and we must always strive to protect her.' To this someone replied, 'If the plant is our mother, you must be our father.' Since then we have called him 'Papa.' "

Expansion at La Nueva meant that Don José needed to add to his supervisory staff. For one thing, he needed more transportation to get his increased complement of workers to the plant in the morning and the larger stock of finished goods to market. He purchased a second truck and engaged as its operator a young nephew, Carlos, age 23, who had traveled the country for several years as an assistant to an older driver before returning to the village. He delivered finished goods to outlets in the city and brought clay back to La Nueva. Like Alcibiades with his house on the plaza, Carlos had looked beyond Santuario's limited horizon; however, he was spared the carpenter's fate.

Don José also hired two mechanics from the city to tend his new furnaces. Santuarians had impressive ability to invent and service traditional, waterpowered machinery, but villagers had little competence in servicing equipment manufactured elsewhere. Don José had little choice but to look outside the village for such talent. The first mechanic he hired, who was put in charge of the oil burners in the baking department, was unable to adapt to the village's peculiar requirements. He returned each weekend to the city, where his wife and family lived, and failed to report back to the factory after one of these trips. His absence on Sundays, the principal day at the plaza in Santuario, precluded him from establishing any important relationships in the village. Before he disappeared, he commented to me, "Changes always hurt someone. For instance, the workers like to take home sacks of coal ash to use in their kitchens. With the new oil burners this is no longer possible for them. Previously we needed 36 hours to heat the kilns. Now we do it in 18. Time is the key to the production process, and we gain time. But someone else loses."

Federico (age 22), the second mechanic Don José hired, fared differently. Don José placed him in charge of the electric oven in the decorating department. When he demonstrated his ability to proceed moderately in installing the new techniques and to deal effectively with the problems that they generated, Don José began to give him supervisory responsibilities in the department. He was a bachelor, and the girls called him *muy querido* (very cute). He began courting a village girl, an affair that led to a good deal of lighthearted joking. He eventually married the girl, and the workers took him to their hearts. Don José invited him to his house for dinner and sponsored him for membership in the Saint Vincent de Paul Society.

Rodolfo, Carlos, and Federico became a separate social force in the plant on the basis of age and exposure to the outside world. They gathered in Rodolfo's cubbyhole and in the cab of the second factory truck.

For the social investigator, a work break is a prime time for learning about the attitudes of workers. For this reason, I sought to vary the groups with which I shared my midmorning bowl of chocolate. But Don Ignacio would have none of this. He made strong efforts to see that I breakfasted with him in his office across the plant from Rodolfo's cubbyhole.

When Don Ignacio's gong sounded the breakfast break, a steaming bowl of chocolate, made up the way I liked it, always awaited me there; he had his wife bake fresh bread for me and send along soft cheese wrapped in wet banana leaves. "This is your home, this is your hearth," he told me. If my arrival was delayed, he went looking for me. He was equally intent in preserving the travel arrangements that the new social separation required. The younger threesome drove back to the village together in the cab of the second truck.

Whenever I tried to join them, Don Ignacio saw to it that I traveled with Don José and him. Thus I learned from second-hand accounts rather than from direct observation how a proposal to establish a football team started in Rodolfo's cubbyhole. Looking back, it seems almost preposterous that the formation of a football team was one of the elements that allowed changes to occur in the behavior of the workers in the factory and to be transmitted to the wider community.

In the little-understood kingdoms of men at work, historic junctures that lead to social change are more often marked by events than by words. So it is to an account of events, the persons participating in them, and the tasks assigned to them, that I now turn.

4

The Social Organization of the Potting Room

The potting community at la Nueva had little to work with in designating its leaders. Moreover, the potters were biased against promotion and differentiation. Nevertheless, they used what they had—primarily, their job assignments and job locations—to mark those in their ranks whom they considered influential and worth listening to. To understand how these designations were made and which individuals they identified, I first describe the group's tasks and note their dispositions.

The principal tasks in the potting room were plate making and plate polishing. The nine potters worked at adjacent stations on both sides of the table at the end near the area where the raw material was prepared (figure 4.1). The eight polishers filled in at the remaining work stations. Each worker, whether a potter or a polisher, had a boy to help him. Each boy worked behind and slightly to one side of the man he helped.

A potter's assistant cut the chunks of clay that came from the mixing department into slices with a wire knife, as one would cut a brick of cheese. Next, the assistant put a slice of clay onto a plaster mold. The clay and its mold were then placed on the potter's wheel, which rotated while the potter held a tool of the proper size and form against the clay to shape the piece. The piece was then placed on a rack to dry.

The work of a polisher was to smooth the rough edges of pieces that were half dry. A polisher's assistant placed the pieces on a rotating wheel, and the polisher trimmed and smoothed the edges with a hand tool. The assistant sponged and rubbed the pieces to

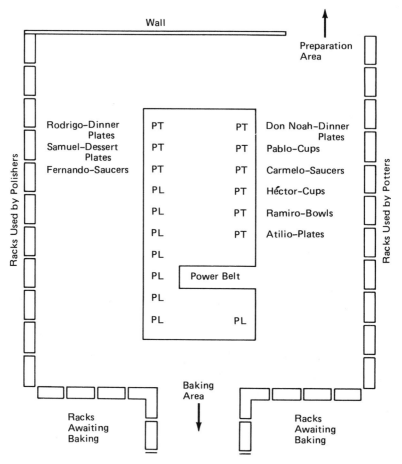

Figure 4.1
Layout of the potting room at La Nueva showing the work locations
of the potters and the products on which they worked. PT stands for
potter and PL for polisher.

remove any remaining blemishes. The greenware was then inspected, stacked, and taken to the baking room.

Potting was relatively skilled work and took longer to learn than polishing. One of the difficult aspects was learning to work with variations in the consistency of the clay. These variations made a difference in the amount of pressure that a potter applied to the piece to shape it and in the length of time that he rotated it in order to get finished pieces that were uniform in size, shape, weight, and thickness.

Differentiation among the Potters

The men in the potting room made little visible effort at differentiation.[1] Some of the shorter men and smaller boys equipped themselves with low platforms to bring themselves up to a comfortable level in relation to the table. One had fashioned a crude cross of twigs that he placed in front of his station. Several had made up sheets on which to tally their output. All wore aprons made of fabric or leather to cover their cotton shirts and trousers. On a typical day, I noticed that three potters, three polishers, and nine boys were not wearing shoes. Headgear was the sole exception to this lack of personal differentiation. The potters favored baseball caps; the polishers, modern straw hats with narrow brims and colored ribbons; and the boys wore berets. A few men wore military caps or the old-style felt hats that the local farmers used. Several wore no hats at all. The kind of headgear a man wore said something about his place in the social fabric of the plant.

The potters were clearly the most influential men in the room. Seven of them were married. Six of the nine were in the highest of the three pay categories in use throughout the plant. Their average age was nearly 37 years. None of them directly took part in the football venture, although some of them supported the idea. The sharpest differences of opinion about the football team and other issues occurred within their ranks.

The boys who served as assistants classified the potters as simpático or bravo. A potter who was simpático was easygoing. An assistant would lunch with him, joke with him, and ask to run his machine. The boys addressed him with the honorary title don. A potter who was bravo was stern and strict and even gruff. A boy lunched with him only if he was his father and showed him respect by not taking initiative in setting up or operating his machine.

The polishers represented an emerging influence in the department that had yet to come into its own. Two were in the highest pay category, five in the middle, and one in the lowest. Their average age was 26 years, and four of the eight were single. Three of the married polishers, men whom the boys designated simpático, supported the football proposal, although they did not become players. One of the polishers, the only one old enough to have a son in the plant, requested a transfer to the kilns after Don José's new machines upset the old balance. He reported, "I would rather be a potter than a polisher, but it's not my destiny. One must observe one's destiny." The boys respected this individual but rated him bravo.

The boys who served as assistants constituted an appealing group that the men enjoyed having around, but they had little influence at the potting table. Their average age was 16 years. All were single, and all were in the lowest pay category. As workers they were entitled to enter the taverns at the plaza and drink with the men, but their views of the world were innocent and full of fantasies about masked supermen to be found in both Rio Alto and Medellín—characters derived perhaps from comic strips or stories about the professional wrestlers found in the city.

When Don José announced that he was going to change the potters' pay from day rates to piece rates, only the assistants voiced objection. They were unhappy at the prospect of losing their recreation periods, which they lost whenever the potters decided to cut short their breakfast or lunch breaks. One of the assistants told me, "There was a time when some of the men beat us with their hands or sticks. They don't do that any more, but when we are on piece rates, there is no time to rest or relax with friends."

The boys' eagerness to please was a solace to the men they served and to me. Once I expressed an interest in the arepa or corn bread that one of the boys brought to the plant. The next day as I was concluding my visit and preparing to leave the village, he arrived at the plaza breathless after a race from his mother's kitchen. He wanted the arepa that he was sending with me to the United States to be warm when it arrived.

The Potters as Individuals

The potters' attitudes toward change in the factory and the village can be described along a spectrum with Don Noah at one end and

Atilio at the other, the same positions that they occupied at the worktable. The attitudes of the other potters fell between them.

Don Noah, at 44, was the oldest. He was also the only one who owned his own home; he and his sons were constructing it in their spare time. The son of a farm laborer, Don Noah started factory work at the age of 14. During the nine years he had been at Don José's factory, he had acquired a work position at a corner of the table, and he refused to leave it even for short assignments elsewhere. He also refused to make anything but plates, although making cups and bowls required more dexterity. Atilio and some of his associates criticized Don Noah for his inflexibility in this regard, but most saw it as Don Noah's right. Don Noah himself shrugged, "Making plates is my destiny."

Don José and Don Ignacio both considered Don Noah to be the most influential of the potters. The younger men respected him but considered him bravo. He breakfasted alone at his work station and never moved from his location to initiate conversations. People came to speak with him. Everyone used the honorary prefix *don* in addressing him. "It wouldn't sound right not to use it," one of the boys reported, "and Don Noah would wonder why I stopped."

Don Noah was the last of the potters to lose the sons who served him as assistants, one for three years, the other for four. He remained a bastion of the old order in the midst of social ferment, and he was not about to surrender his post. He could not, because, as uncrowned king of the potters, he had too much at stake. but in the post-electrification shake-up, both his sons, now approaching 20 years of age, left the factory to work in another pottery.

In the potting room Don Noah made the final intervention on all issues. He thus performed the decision making and closure function that human communities require. He maintained this role because, more than any of the others, he personified the traditional values, including their industrial applications, that held the community in place.

To underscore the centrality of the values that he symbolized, the other potters accorded Don Noah clear differentiation. They permitted him a distinctive work location at the corner of the table, and he emphasized the distinctiveness of the position by his effective resistance to efforts to transfer him out of it. He was also permitted to establish for himself and effectively defend a distinctive work assignment, the manufacture of plates alone. He wore a beret rather than the baseball cap favored by most of the potters. He was one of two men in the room who were not members of a small company union, which one of the priests in the village had recently been instrumental in establishing.

Don Pablo, 40, was a large, light-complexioned man. He wore old-fashioned, bell-bottom trousers and went about barefoot. One of his brothers was a key figure among the older polishers; another brother, also a polisher, had recently left La Nueva. When they were young, they had worked with their father on the family's farm. Don Pablo had come to La Nueva 14 years previously from another pottery. He considered making cups to be his destiny and, like Don Noah, his neighbor at the table, resisted efforts to transfer him, even temporarily, to any other activity or location.

Don Pablo was always busy with his work, but not too busy to carry on a running conversation with anyone who stopped by. When talking, he would not look up from his work. Only one theme interested him—poverty and its consequences. One morning I asked him, in the local idiom, how he had awakened. He answered, "Always bad, Don Carlos, always bad. In our poverty one always wakes up poorly. We are terribly poor. We are lost. Here I am working all these years, and what do I have to show for it? Mine is the destiny of the poor. I am dead but not yet buried. I should leave now and start planting corn, but I don't have the money to get started. It's warmer working in the fields. Here it's always cold. We don't eat enough to keep warm. We don't have the money to buy proper clothing."

Some of the men did not think it proper when Don Pablo spoke in this way to a relative of Don José on the day of his child's funeral. Usually, though, they smiled when Don Pablo started talking, and they did not interrupt him. It was as if he was their spokesman on a theme that concerned all of them but that they found difficult to talk about. The other workers called him "Pablito," "Little Old Pablo," but not to his face. He went to the baking department to eat. He was considered bravo on work-related matters but friendly enough, if somewhat eccentric, on other issues. He was a member of the union and wore a baseball cap.

Carmelo, 26, was the youngest of the potters. He was Don Pablo's protégé, a shy, friendly young man, well liked by his associates. The youngest boys called him Don Carmelo; the others sometimes referred to him as Lover Boy. He was brought up on his family's farm above the pottery, the youngest of 12 children. As a young boy, he traveled an hour by foot to attend school near the plaza. After three years he dropped out and found work at the factory as Don Pablo's assistant. Don Pablo taught him to pot; usually he made saucers, but sometimes he shifted to bowls or cups. He ate his breakfast with a friend from the baking department at a little table they set up off to one side, hidden by the racks of goods in process.

Samuel, 37, was the most experienced potter. Although he had worked at potting for 16 years, he had the lowest production. He was single and still lived with his parents. He kept to himself and seldom initiated conversations. He was the only plate maker who did not work at a corner of the table. One got the impression that his interests outside the factory limited his activities at work. His father owned cattle and was also a roofer. Samuel helped him whenever time permitted. The boys considered him bravo, a man who started work before any of the others and without preliminary conversation. They noted that he cut his breakfast short in order to get back to work. He also tried to set up the next day's work before leaving in the evening. Not a union member, he was addressed using his last name only. Atilio said of him, "Samuel has money and should speak up more, but he's afraid of losing his job."

Fernando, 34 years old and the son of a farmer, said that he would go back to farming if he had the money. He was a small man with the reputation of being simpático and easy to get along with. Through his wife he was related to Don Ignacio. The boys were fond of him and referred to him as "Little Fernando." Marco Antonio Sanchez was his assistant; there was a special bond between the two. When the group shifted to incentive pay, the potters increased their output to the degree that it became possible to eliminate one potting station. Fernando and Marco Antonio were transferred to other work. Fernando made no protest but, he later told me, he was unable to sleep that night. "Why have they done this to me? I always try to be helpful, as our Father in heaven directs," he said. "I tried to teach the boys everything I know. I respected my assistant, because I wanted to merit his respect. Now they have sent me off, I don't know for how long." Marco Antonio, who was assigned to other temporary work, went to Fernando and told him he wanted to go with him to the mixing department. When I asked Atilio about this transfer, he shook his head sadly and said, "Poor Fernando is just not up to it." Rodrigo took over his work station. He was embarrassed when I asked him what he was doing there. "It wasn't my idea! It wasn't my idea!" he repeated. "They put me here." Fernando wore a baseball cap, like the other potters who made plates.

Héctor, 39, had the least tenure of the potters and was the most eager to please. He too was the son of a factory worker and, although he had eight children of his own, still lived with his wife's father. He was Samuel's brother-in-law. During the breakfast period, he occupied himself with a little biscuit business that he had instituted in the room. This kept him active but rather excluded from the social currents in the potting room. When he did have time, he circulated freely but was never accorded a leading role in the conversations. He sought social contact but was not sought after. When I asked the boys if Héctor was simpático or bravo, they puzzled for a while; finally one of them used the diminutive, *bravito*, to describe him. They usually called him *don*. He wore tinted glasses and a beret like Don Noah's.

Héctor came to my room on the plaza several times for long discussions and to buy me a drink. As we chatted, he puzzled over the precise definition of the phrase *hombre completo*, a term frequently used with different meanings when the potters talked about themselves.

In the factory setting an hombre completo was a man who could do a range of tasks. For Héctor the three potters who could make all types of dishes—Don Noah, Atilio, and Rodrigo—were hombres completos. Carmelo and Fernando, who made only saucers; Samuel, who made only dessert plates and could not polish; Ramiro, who was strictly a bowl maker; and Don Pablo and Héctor, who made cups, were not. Traditionally, an hombre completo was a man who fulfilled his destiny at home and in the plaza. Don Noah subscribed to this view and classified himself in that category. Atilio advocated a still further broadening of the term to include performance of "good works" in helping one's associates on the job in addition to having technical proficiency in the roles prescribed by destiny. He told me that an hombre *incompleto* was one who was noble but did not do good work. The term was also used to designate a son who, while still living with his parents, paid his way through his own earnings. The differences in these definitions troubled Héctor, whose work location at the midpoint of the potting table symbolized his usual position as a moderate on social issues.

Ramiro, 38, was the tallest of the potters. His father was a factory worker. Ramiro worked in a pottery in the village when he was young, but at age 20 he decided to see the world. He went to Bogotá, where he also worked in a pottery. Later he was employed for several years in a pottery in Medellín. When it went out of business, he returned to Santuario, married a local girl, and settled down to village life. "You make sacrifices to return," he said, "but you gain tranquility." Ramiro had come to work for Don José two years before my visits and was first assigned to work at the kilns. While there, he became president of the union. Don José described him as a "quiet, serious type, not difficult to manage." He responded generously and intelligently to my inquiries.

After the electrification, Ramiro moved to the potting area, but the other men found him difficult to know. He still returned to breakfast near the ovens with his friends among the bakers who were active in the union. The other potters and polishers did not consider him gruff but as a person to be treated with respect, somewhat of an enigma. He was the only potter who made bowls, which exempted his output from comparison with the others. There was never any talk about shifting him to work on other products. He was the only one at the table who went bareheaded. The boys usually addressed him with the title don, but they did not classify him as bravo. They found him difficult to talk to; he did not initiate conversations, although he responded readily enough to others. "We are terribly backward here," he told me, "and we suffer from excessive individualism. There is a great deal to be done, but no one has confidence in his associates. Only Atilio will speak up, which makes him the most important man in the room."

Rodrigo, 39, like Don Noah and Atilio, was a plate maker with a work location at a corner of the table. He was Atilio's best friend and ally; they had been born in the same small settlement. Sometimes the two of them came together to talk with me in my room at the plaza. Rodrigo accepted temporary changes in his work and held strong feelings against the men who resisted such changes. His father had been a farmer, and he had never lived in the city. In general, he shared Atilio's views and followed his lead at a lower level of visibility. He wore a baseball cap.

Atilio, 34, worked at the location farthest from Don Noah's. He was also the worker farthest removed from Don Noah's orientation to village traditions. He shared with Don Noah differentiation in dress, for he wore a military-style cap his wife had made, which was the only one of its kind in the room. Also, like Don Noah, he was a plate maker, but he accepted temporary transfer when a neighbor was absent or overburdened. Like Rodrigo, he felt strongly about the potters who did not change their assignments. He was short and lithe with a dark, leathery complexion.

Atilio was one of the few workers who had no relatives in the factory. Few families had moved into the village and few had moved out, and people joked about the fact that almost everyone was related. Atilio was the exception.[2]

Atilio grew up in an outlying settlement that had earlier been an Indian *pueblo* under the protection of the Church. Though Atilio and Rodrigo shared a common origin, Atilio had worked briefly in the city. He returned to the village a restless individual without a focus for his energies and at first took up with shiftless elements.

When he came to visit me at my room, he brought his wife, an unusual departure from village protocol that was explained by his personal history. He told me, "You wouldn't believe it, but we carried on a courtship for four years in this village without anyone knowing what was going on. Then she declared her love for me. I told her that any permanent relationship was impossible, that we were of different social classes. When I left to look for work in the city, she begged me to take her along.

"When I returned, her feelings had not changed. Such love should not go unrequited. I sought her father's permission to marry her. The father's response was twofold. He had a relative beat me up outside a tavern, and he sent the girl out of the village to learn to be a seamstress.

"A year later she returned. She found me in a tavern, barefoot, unshaven, drunk. Her feelings for me still had not changed."

Out of respect for their privacy, I will not tell the rest of their story. It was both dramatic and romantic, filled with confrontations with civic and religious leaders as well as with her parents. It included abductions, separations, and joyful reunions. They were finally married, but Atilio told me, "Our relations with her family are still strained."

Atilio was the most articulate, gregarious, and empathic member of the group. During work breaks he circulated easily and took a leading part in the conversations in the groups that he entered. He loaned money and joked with his neighbors at work. Sometimes he let his assistant run his machine. He also cheerfully dispatched his boy to the other side of the table when a polisher complained that the potted pieces were not coming across right.

In his successful joust with authority and in his unconventional marriage, Atilio effectively challenged his destiny. Some public disapproval over this may have carried into his social situation at the time of the events that I am reporting. His work location, the station farthest from Don Noah's, may have been intended as a public indication of the lower status accorded him because of his nontraditional values. In any event, Atilio sought affiliation where he could find it, typically with new elements not identified with tradition. He also sought opportunities to challenge tradition; indeed, this had become the principal aim of his life. It was as though, having once acted in defiance of Santuarian tradition, he needed to validate repeatedly the conclusions about life at which he had arrived. The post-electrification ferment in the potting room provided such an opportunity, and Atilio exploited with obvious relish the focus that it gave his energies.

Whatever the intent behind its original assignment, Atilio's remote work station became a symbol of a viable alternative to the traditional propositions favored by Don Noah. Atilio accomplished this by cultivating visibility and social centrality. Perhaps to preclude managerial attention, which might have distracted him from his social activities, he kept his output high. But it was on the hombre completo issue that he mounted his principal challenge to the values of the older potters. He wanted to make service to associates, not faith in ascribed status, the basis of the designation. "Someone has to speak up," he maintained. "Ramiro will speak up in general terms but not for his own group."

The men appreciated Atilio, but they had reservations about endorsing the values he espoused. Their responses to him varied. When I was first introduced to him, I was told, "This is Fidel, Fidel Castro!" Atilio was central to the new climate in the potting room, which the boys enjoyed, but most of the men expressed doubt about his behavior. They believed that Atilio, while likeable, was not always predictable and responsible.

Traditionalism versus Modernity among the Potters
As I saw the potters' society and its dynamics, at one pole Don Noah was the head of the potters, the court of appeal that decided

any issue having to do with the values of the group. But he was a restless, uneasy head who watched his lifetime investment in a particular set of values waste away as the result of processes and events over which he had no control. Don Pablo and his young protégé, Carmelo, supported him.

At the other pole, Atilio thrived on the newer and easier modes of interaction that recent changes in the plant and the community made possible. He obviously enjoyed being the center of attention among the younger potters, the polishers, and the boys. Rodrigo followed his lead. Samuel and Fernando were relatively isolated from the flow of events. Héctor, though alert to opportunities for improving his position, was somewhat restricted by his biscuit business. Ramiro, hatless, reserved, enigmatic to the others, was off to visit his friends in the union in another part of the plant whenever he could get away.

I called Don Noah and Don Pablo the traditionalists in the group. As the oldest, they best represented the traditional values of the community. I classified Carmelo with them, even though he was younger. At the other extreme were Atilio and Rodrigo, the activists. I called Samuel and Fernando isolates, for lack of a better term and also because it was descriptive in many ways of their position. I called Ramiro and Héctor moderates, situated between the extremes of tradition and change.

Table B.3 in appendix B gives the age of each potter and rates him on his attitudes toward change on six factors: whether he had been exposed to city life, had joined the union, was addressed by the title *don*, spoke up in discussions, was rated simpático by the boys, and accepted transfer. I totaled the scores arithmetically to arrive at a "change orientation" index for each potter. On this scale Atilio ranked highest, scoring in all six factors. Rodrigo was next highest, scoring in all the factors except "exposure to city life." Don Noah was lowest with no score in any of the factors. Don Pablo, Samuel, and Carmelo each scored in one factor. The other potters scored in between.

I also rated each potter (appendix B, table B.4), on five factors related to their differentiation or visibility in the group: whether they worked at a corner of the table, made only plates, were high producers, wore hats that were nonstandard for their positions, and resisted being assigned to products other than the ones on which they usually worked. I totaled these scores to arrive at a "differentiation" or "visibility" index for each potter. On this scale Don Noah scored five and Atilio four. Samuel, Fernando, and Carmelo scored zeros, and the others were in between.

I then plotted these two indexes against each other, with the result being the approximately parabolic curve shown in appendix B, figure B.1. Crude as these measures were, they clearly showed the latent polarization of the potters' group along the dimensions of traditionalism versus change or modernity. Don Noah and Atilio stand high on opposite sides of the curve. Don Pablo is next to Don Noah on the left-hand side, and Rodrigo is next to Atilio on the right. Samuel, Fernando, and Carmelo are at the bottom, and Ramiro and Héctor somewhat above on the right.

My conclusion was that the potters' social system was in a state of fragile equilibrium. Don Noah and the traditional values of the community maintained a steady state, but the forces for change, symbolized by Atilio, were also strong. I judged that the stability of the department could be easily upset.

The Potters' Output and Pay

Discrepancies with respect to output and pay among the potters were an additional force working for change among them. Most of the potters received the highest of the three day rates used throughout the factory. Samuel and Fernando received the middle rate, and Carmelo the lowest. Injustices existed in that these rates of pay correlated poorly with the men's output. Carmelo, for example, was one of the highest producers and Samuel the lowest. The rates did not even reflect a ranking based on age and experience, for on that basis Samuel would have been one of the most highly paid.

To study these discrepancies more carefully, I kept track of the potters' output for six weeks before their pay was changed from day rates to piece rates, a series of events to be described in chapter 5. From these data I calculated what the potters' pay would have been during this period if they had been on piece rates. The calculations are shown in appendix B, table B.5.[3]

The data show that four of the potters—Don Pablo, Don Noah, Ramiro, and Carmelo—would have received more pay under incentive rates than they received under day rates; and four—Héctor, Atilio, Fernando, and Samuel—would have received less. The biggest gainer would have been Carmelo, who would have earned 29.5% more than he did on day rates. The biggest loser would have been Samuel, who would have earned 21.9% less. In essence, the four potters who would have had earnings above the average of 77.50 pesos a week, if they had been on incentive rates, subsidized the pay of the four whose output was below the average.

The First Proposal for a Football Team

The events that occurred when Rodolfo and his companions first issued the call for players to form a football team provide an example of how ready for change the potting-room workers were. At the same time the social forces in the potting room maintained a steady-state situation.

The idea for a factory football team was Federico's; he sold it to his friends over chocolate in Rodolfo's cubbyhole. To the young mechanic, athletic association was how one expressed social concern and commitment, at least in the city. The young men in the potting room were inclined to respond positively to the call when it was issued. Playing football would bring them out from under their fathers' scrutiny into active contact with their peers and with young men outside the village not subject to its particular codes. Atilio kept prodding them to take matters into their own hands, but many of the potential players still breakfasted with their fathers by the kilns, where they received opposite signals. In addition, practice was scheduled to take place behind the factory, and the prospect of foregoing the habitual drive to the plaza when work was done was unsettling. Moreover, Don Noah disapproved, and his imposing presence had to be confronted.

The establishment of a football team required a minimum number of players. In Santuario the potting room was the only place of assembly where there were young men in sufficient number to answer the call, but the number responding to Federico's first invitation was inadequate.

The creation of a football team was precluded less by active rejection than by the young plate makers' inability to defy established opinion. There was no time for so novel a plan to season, and its advocates did not know how to bring the idea to maturity. After an appropriate interlude, the proposal was shelved.

Thus the new values running free in the community outside the factory had their counterparts in the restricted community of the plate room and in the small group of its leading citizens, the potters.

I wondered what events would bring the issues into the open, who among the potters would take the initiative in settling them, and what the resolution would be. I did not have to wait long to learn the answers.

Change and Its Consolidation in Santuario

Don José unintentionally set the stage for the next act in the sequence of change. His intervention came at a point when the football issue was dormant, although it was still being discussed with discomfort because no final decision had been reached. At this time, six months after electrification of the factory, Don José had the increased kiln capacity in place and additional space to store inventory. With the Christmas season ahead and excellent prospects of being able to sell all that the factory could produce, he needed increased output from his potting room. To achieve it, he decided to put the potters on incentive pay. This step was not unprecedented, for over the years the payment system in the department had been changed several times from day rates to piece rates to build up inventory for the Christmas season. In the past the change had been satisfactory to the workers, for whom the end of year was the heaviest in terms of expenses. Don José's father told me, "José would like to use piece rates all the time, but the workers get sloppy about quality. When they do, he goes back to day rates to discipline them."

Don José's Proposal and the Potters' Initial Response

The customary procedure would have been for Don José to confer with the senior potters—Don Noah and Don Pablo—and then to wait for these key individuals to confer with their juniors before reporting back to him. I could not ascertain why Don José chose to ignore protocol in this instance. The chances were that he was preoccupied with the operation of his expanded plant and thus somewhat out of touch with conditions in the potting room. To be sure, Atilio and Rodrigo had visited him some two months previously to tell him that they were having trouble living on their wages; hence he knew that at least some of the potters would respond positively to an opportunity to increase their earnings. He may also have felt in some unarticulated way that the time was appropriate for him to change his relationship with the workers. He may even have picked up some ideas about participative management and MacGregor's Theory Y from conversations with me.

In any event, Don José proceeded differently from the way he had in the past. He called all the potting-room workers into his office and told them that he needed more output to expand his sales. To help attain it he intended to introduce an incentive pay system. He guaranteed them their day-rate earnings and a share of the earnings from the increased output they produced. He asked them to form a *junta* (committee of peers) to discuss with him the rates for the individual products under the new system.

I was on a short trip to the United States when Don José made this proposal, but I heard about it immediately when I returned a few days later. The request put the potters in a quandary. The prospect of a junta to negotiate so delicate a matter as payment for the comparative performance of the members of a hierarchically organized society represented a clear threat to its established practice. What Don José asked them to do was not within their traditional repertoire of responses to their patrón, nor was it congruent with their concept of their destinies as workers. The request opened the door to their taking responsibility for important aspects of their own lives. I asked if the potters had held a meeting to nominate a junta. The reply was, "Not a single meeting, Don Carlos, but a lot of little ones."

The potters' opinions on the wisdom of Don José's request varied. Don Noah, I was told, sat silently at the meeting in Don José's office. Only Don Pablo and Atilio had anything to say—Don Pablo trailing off into his customary complaints about poverty and Atilio raising questions about the workers' stake in the change. Tobias, the oldest polisher, who subsequently sought and was granted transfer to the baking room, nominated Don Noah to organize and head the junta. Don Noah refused, and he later went even further in an attempt to uphold the status quo. He visited Don José at his home on the plaza after mass on a Sunday to urge him to abandon the idea of piece rates or at least of negotiating them by means of a junta. Don

José did not act on either suggestion. The traditional decision-making mechanism of the department, controlled by Don Noah, thus broke down when pressure was mounting.

I suspect that Don Noah was caught in a dilemma that affected him deeply. His opposition to Don José's request was based on unswerving devotion to traditional protocols as defined by "destiny." To respond positively would have thrust him into what he perceived as an improper collaboration with his patrón. Don Noah told me, "Don José solicited our ideas on the change and asked us to form a junta. We are very badly prepared for such things, Don Carlos. We've never been able to make such arrangements. We are a very incapable people. We have only those things that the patrones initiate for us. Setting pay rates is a matter for a patrón, not a junta of the potters."

Atilio, on the other hand, favored the idea. It fitted with his belief that workers should speak up. He told me, "Getting a junta together is simply a matter of finding a few workers who can and will speak up. I believe that a worker who can should speak up for his companions. Don Noah refused to serve. He has two sons to help him out, but he must be afraid of losing his job. He's not even in favor of incentive pay.

"Samuel is useless in these matters, even though he's a bachelor and makes money outside the factory working with his father. Ramiro is capable of speaking up, but I'm not sure that he will. Héctor might. He has eight children and is concerned about his job, but he's also new in the group and wants to make a good impression.

"Rodrigo, Pablo, and I are the only ones you can count on to speak up. Rodrigo and I went to Don José's home a couple of months ago to tell him that we couldn't live on the day-rate wage. Now we have a chance to do something about it."

Ramiro also told me about the discussion in Don José's office and continued, "Finally, Don José said, 'Why don't you turn this over in your heads for three or four days? Then I will get together with the junta.' Since then, we haven't been able to form a junta. We're poorly equipped to do things among ourselves. Here we have a great deal of individualism. No one has confidence in his companions. The people in the potting room are very timid. Only Atilio, Rodrigo, Héctor, and Pablo will speak up. But I'm still optimistic that we can form a junta."

I asked each of the potters whom they recollected as having been nominated to serve on the junta (appendix B, table B.6). Héctor recalled first that the nominees were Atilio and himself; later he changed his answer to Don Pablo and Don Noah. Ramiro, who first named Don Pablo, later named Don Noah. Taking into account these corrections, Don Noah received the most nominations, and Atilio was second. Rodrigo and Ramiro were not nominated.

In the period that followed, no one moved to resolve the stalemate. Rather the period was characterized by intensified expressions of each potter's regular views. Don Noah, for example, continued to resist any action other than rejection of Don José's invitation. Don Pablo used what occasions he could to relate the impasse to his familiar themes of poverty and misery. Carmelo was anxious to restore events to their previous order by having Don Noah and Don Pablo agree to serve as the junta, which their patrón had, after all, requested. Héctor argued for a junta composed of hombres completos, perhaps in the hope that his neighbors would see fit to include him. Ramiro remained silent and enigmatic. Atilio prodded his associates toward action with increased intensity as time dragged on. When the impasse persisted, the men's expenditure of energy on the issue increased and tended to become more frenetic, with Don Noah resisting, Atilio pushing, Don Pablo protesting, Héctor vying, and Carmelo seeking the comfort of a closure arrived at by traditional mechanisms. Still no one moved toward an act of leadership that would resolve the dilemma.

The situtation was thus unstable, but it held implications for resolution of underlying issues. The intensity of the polarization that developed between Don Noah's traditional views and Atilio's new ones served two functions. First, the debate that it generated helped to educate the socially less literate, uncommitted workers to the issues involved. Second, as this schooling was accomplished with no marked reduction in anxiety and tension, it increased the desire for closure on some basis.

As I have said, up to this time the potting community was accustomed to Don Noah acting as the closure agent for its members. Although he was reserved, the men valued him as an associate and had some appreciation of his dilemma. An initiative from him would confirm the status quo and postpone, not accelerate, change. The men also enjoyed Atilio and appreciated the fellowship he provided. They valued him for being the odd one among them. He would have dearly loved to provide the closure agency for them, but they were not sure that they wished to endorse his values. They sensed, perhaps correctly, that to move from Don Noah's to Atiolio's view would be too great a departure from the potting room's traditional orientation. Samuel and Fernando, the isolates, had no following and were thus not likely to take the initiative as leaders. Don Pablo, second to Don Noah as a traditionalist, Rodrigo, second to Atilio as an activist, and Carmelo, Don Pablo's protégé, seemed equally unlikely to do so. That left Ramiro and Héctor, but as moderates they had little visibility. I could not see one of them as likely to initiate change. The situation thus continued in a kind of stalemate, with issues being settled by inaction and with frustrations mounting.

The Formation of the Junta

As the days passed and the debate continued, the men became prepared to endorse an intermediate closure formula. On the tenth day Atilio and Héctor were working at their stations with Ramiro between them. They were discussing the proposal for the new payment plan, when Héctor commented in the semijocular vein of their discussion, "Why don't we just go see Don José and get the incentive rates established?" In the context of their conversation his question was a remark that called for an introspective answer rather than a suggestion for action. Atilio responded in the same vein, "Why don't we?"

But Ramiro said, "Let's go!" Whereupon he shut off his machine, removed his apron, and wiping his hands on his apron, set off in the direction of Don José's office. Atilio and Héctor took a moment to recover from their surprise before they followed suit. Don Noah was left behind. Don José had the junta he had asked for and with it the support of the potters for the incentive rates he wished to establish.

The timing of Ramiro's intervention was critical, although I do not attribute to him any insight in accomplishing what he did. He acted with intuitive spontaneity in an action that was to a significant extent determined by the development processes of the group. He could not have intervened on day two of the restructuring any more than he could have refrained from intervening on day ten. On day two the social forces making for change had not matured, nor was there clear evidence that deep, transformational change was possible. An overture by Ramiro at that point would have been misinterpreted and would have failed for lack of general endorsement. On day ten, however, the pervasiveness of what was happening was apparent to all parties. In addition, there was an intense desire on all sides for the release that an acceptable resolution would bring. Thus when Ramiro headed for Don José's office with Atilio and Héctor trailing along, he stepped forward with the approval of all the potters.

"Spontaneity" and "stepped forward" are terms that are perhaps too strong to describe his action. He was as much pulled into action by the requirements of the potters' social system as he was pushed by his own psychological inclinations. Recall that up to this time Ramiro had been a somewhat enigmatic character to the others in the plate room. The boys were unable to determine whether they should address him as *don*. The men were not sure of his orientation toward traditional values. In matters of task, dress, and work location, the marks of social differentiation in the symbol-poor potting room society, Ramiro remained ambiguous. Yet he was not blemished by Atilio's history of challenge to the social values that Don Noah represented. He maintained a more intermediate and inclusive posture than the one Atilio pushed for himself.[1]

There were a number of reasons why the question of incentive pay was an issue that the traditional system, already weakened by expansion, could not survive. In the first place, it was a powerful issue, which, when implemented, highlighted the results of individual effort among the potters and thus presented a ranking of individuals that was an alternative to the one that was established by ascribed destiny. The issue was posed in a nontraditional manner by a patrón who, preoccupied with technological possibilities, ignored the customary social amenities. It came at a time when the traditional contract mechanisms in the potting room could get little reinforcement from congruent elements in the baking room which were effectively screened out by the new physical arrangement of the factory. And it came on the heels of the first proposal for a football team, which, although rejected, had also confronted the traditional mechanisms with a serious challenge that left the old value system vulnerable without time for regeneration and reconstitution.

Don Noah's attitude about Federico's first proposal for a football team had been decisive and in the traditional pattern. But when

Don José raised the issue of a change from day rates to incentive pay without consulting him initially, he was unable to provide the closure that the group expected from him. This break in his traditional capability was unsettling to the potters, and cracks appeared in the old structure.

The final step in the sequence was a period of "working out," which served to verify the existence of the new pattern. As Ramiro and his associates left the room, it must have been apparent to Don Noah and his neighbors that the restructuring interlude had come to an end. Although the resolution may not have been completely acceptable to Don Noah, it was certainly more palatable than the one offered by Atilio, with whom he had been locked in public controversy. For Atilio, on the other hand, although the resolution failed to satisfy fully his objectives, it nudged the system closer to his beliefs about how things should be. For the others, the compromise resulted in there being once again an ordering to their universe that allowed them to return their attention to issues concerned with output.

Don José and the junta shortly established a table of piece rates that ran from 1.10 pesos per 100 pieces for the saucers that Carmelo and Fernando made to 2.00 pesos per 100 pieces for the dinner plates that Atilio, Rodrigo, and Don Noah made. Even though the rates were settled more or less arbitrarily rather than on the basis of time studies or other objective methods, they represented a change from pay based on age and social standing to something approximating compensation based on productive performance. As a result, junior men acquired the potential to earn more through their own efforts than their seniors and thus to rise above the level that their destinies assigned them. These social implications gave the change its special significance.

Effects of the Change on the Potters' Pay

To assess the outcomes of the change, I kept a record of each potter's output and earnings for another six-week period.[2] These data reflect substantial increases in both the potters' output and their pay (appendix B, tables B.7 and B.8). In addition, there was a substantial redistribution of pay among the potters, with the result that those who produced the most earned the most, irrespective of whether they were old or young, experienced or inexperienced. This redistribution of pay corrected the injustices that characterized the day rates. The changes reinforced the new values that were coming into the community. These changes are summarized in what follows.

The potters' total output increased 35.6%, from 553 pesos' worth before the change to 750 pesos' worth afterward.[3] The total of the wages of the seven potters for whom complete data were available increased from 540 pesos to 750 pesos or 38.9%, 3.3% more than the increase in their output.[4] The fact that the potters' wages increased more than their output meant that they received relatively more pay for their effort in making tha additional output than they received for their effort before the change.[5]

As individuals, all the potters increased their output, some more than others (appendix B, table B.7). Atilio increased his the most, by 50.0%, Carmelo was next with 43.6%, and Samuel third with 40%. Ramiro was lowest with 21.3%.

Some of the potters increased their earnings even more dramatically (appendix B, table B.8). Carmelo, whose pay before the change was at the lowest of the three day rates, increased his earnings by 86%. Don Pablo increased his by 50%, second highest, and Don Noah increased his by 41%, third highest. At the other extreme, Samuel, the lowest producer, increased his earnings by only 9%, even though the amount by which he increased his output was third highest.

For a short time after the change Carmelo's output and earnings exceeded those of Don Noah and Don Pablo. Thus for a short period, the output of the youngest potter, still considered a protégé of one of the oldest, surpassed his mentor's output. Later Carmelo slowed down, and over the long run his output and earnings dropped so that he no longer exceeded Don Noah and Don Pablo, though he continued to match them. A young polisher in the department had a similar experience. He increased his output after the change to an amount well above anyone else's. The matter was called to his attention, and he soon dropped his output to a level in line with the others.

Even with these adjustments, the redistribution of earnings among the potters resolved the polarization that had occurred among them and established a new order. This order was not based on age and experience; rather it reflected each man's output. Not only did the potters who produced the most now earn the most, but also the ones who changed the most gained the most: their rank in the two dimensions was the same (appendix B, table B.9). Even Don Noah and Don Pablo, the two who most clearly upheld tradition, helped no doubt by the long production runs for the products on which they worked, were among the three whose output changed the most. Thus they indicated implicitly in their behavior, if not explicitly in their talk, that they too accepted the new values, an acceptance that allowed them to maintain their belief in their destinies as persons of importance among the potters. And Atilio, freed from the need to agitate for the new values, gave his energy to production, which he increased more than anyone else among the potters. His output ranked fourth. Thus the outcome of the change in the payment system reinforced new values that supported the ability of individuals to affect their own lives through their own efforts.

The succeeding period in the plate room was accompanied by the collective sense of relief and achievement that Kuhn[6] says often follows the acceptance of a new pattern. Released from their concerns and preoccupations about how they stood with each other, the potters turned their attention to production and their relations with the world outside the factory. Their total output rose just under 40%, from 41,000 pieces of chinaware a week to 57,000. There remained a need for evidence that would underscore for all concerned the fact that a new circuitry existed among them for processing events and making decisions. The opportunity to provide it was not long in coming.

Communication of Change in the Community

Within weeks Rodolfo's group issued a second invitation for a football team. This time the workers responded in sufficient numbers. Included among them were eight from the potting room, four polishers and four assistants, each of whom, not altogether coincidentally, customarily wore a modern straw hat. The team, which began to practice at the end of the day in the meadow behind the plant, augmented its ranks with a few players picked up at the plaza, a step that helped additional agents spread the changes throughout the community. Within a few months there were eight teams competing against each other in the village and seeking games in other villages and in the city. As reform activities dispersed throughout the village, they reinforced each other, and changes in the activities organized by the workers and their associates became irreversible. Within two years the village's social rationale was transformed, and for the first time Santuario possessed nontraditional decision-making processes and a new basis for confronting its most serious external economic threat.

A few weeks after these incidents Don Bernardino passed away. His funeral was a major event. The plaza filled as the hour for the service approached. Although the factories had not been closed for the occasion, the workers were free to participate, and many of them chose to.

The funeral provided a dramatic expression of the old sentiments. Don Bernardino's remains were laid out overnight in his parlor, and the whole village came for a final visit. Fifteen minutes before his body was carried to the church, the pastor arrived to bless the body and close the coffin. While prayers were being said, street urchins jostled for position with relatives and neighbors. In death as in life, Don Bernardino belonged as much to his village as to his family.

The procession was marked by a spreading silence that extended from the plaza to the cemetery and reached out to incorporate a housewife slowly blessing herself in a doorway and a roofer standing bareheaded on his ladder. During these last moments, everything that had been Santuario centered in the swaying file that stretched as far as the eye could see. The unity that broke when the graveside prayers had been concluded would never again be achieved.

The village priest told me, "With Don Bernardino's passing, an era comes to a close. He was a true relic. He invented machinery in his own mind and created it with his own hands. He taught all of the other patrones in the village. He was their father. However serious the problem they brought to him, he would say calmly, 'Let's look for the solution.' He died nobly and well, a true Catholic. For me he is completely irreplaceable."

An era had indeed come to an end in Santuario. Don Bernardino's funeral gave the people of the town the occasion for a public ceremony in which all could mourn the passing of the old era, just as the football games provided visible ceremonies in which they could welcome new values and the new era.

Additional Community Changes and Their Significance

It may seem unjustified to assign so much significance to a series of small events that occurred in a community as dispersed and complex as Santuario, but the changes that followed these events are incontestable. I continued to visit the village frequently, and during the next two years I watched its transformation from a traditional society with values that "call for fatalistic acceptance of the world as it is, respect for those in authority, and submergence of the individual in the collectivity" into a twentieth-century community whose values "are rational and secular, permit choice and experiment, glorify efficiency and change, and stress individual responsibility."[7] If, as Hagen[8] says, the definition of a traditional society is one in which members of the younger generation behave in the same ways as the older generation and a nontraditional society is one in which they do not, then what I witnessed was the transformation of Santuario from a traditional to a nontraditional society in its male sector. The female sector did not change to the same extent, at least not during the period of my visits.[9]

The plaza again proved to be the principal locus of change. Before it had served a screening function; now it was the center of the community's intercourse with the outside world. On Sundays a fleet of automobiles lined up on one side to transport Santuarians to Rio Alto and beyond. As these travelers left the village, they met a line of Sunday drivers coming in. The control mechanisms of the plaza fell into disuse, and visitors felt more comfortable. All kinds of people came, including traveling salesmen to tout their wares in the open market and student poets and musicians from the city to entertain and instruct the young. Outsiders trooped into town for the annual fiesta, the management of which now passed from the priests to the merchants. The restriction against dancing passed away, as did the symbolic Sunday stroll that had joined the pastor and the senior patrones in a public manifestation of adherence to traditional values.

The new activities in the community reinforced the new behavior patterns in the factory in two ways. First, some of them provided new opportunities for the sale of plates, cups, and saucers and thus provided new markets for the factory's increased output. Second, the acceptance of the new behavior patterns in the community and of the values underlying them provided support for the patterns in the factory and made them legitimate.

During these years the patrones departed from the village. Both Don José and his father moved their residences to Medellín. Since their patronal services were no longer required in Santuario, they hired a manager from the city to take over supervision of their factories. One of the manager's first moves was the attempt to merge some of the production processes of the two plants. Supervision changed in quality. It was now the work group that satisfied most of the workers' social needs, a capacity that was nurtured by new manners of interaction at the factory and at the meeting rooms, taverns, secondary plazas, and playing fields that sprang up in all parts of the village. A second labor union was formed, independent of the priests. Out of the ensuing rivalry grew the first authentic management-labor confrontation. On one visit I chatted with a group of striking workers, who had literally sealed shut the factory gates and camped in front of it in tents erected under the national banner.

When it came time to write up my data, I debated at first whether I overestimated the significance of the episodes involving the football team for the process of change in the community as a whole. I decided that I had not, even though the episodes with the team were in some ways less important than the arrival of electricity in the village and Don José's decision to expand the output of his pottery.

The interest in football emerged from a subgroup of the factory's management. Three young members—the truck driver, the gate-keeper, and the mechanic, all with experience outside the village—developed a subgroup that had its own values and routines. They originated the proposal for football, an activity with which the village had no previous experience. The members of the group also proposed their alliance with the young workers in the potting room, the location in the factory where, for different reasons, other structural changes were taking place. The first proposal failed but was successfully revived when these other changes had run their course.

Football had a potential for deep significance in terms of social change.[10] It provided a durable, dramatic, and institutionalized framework for experimentation with new organizational relationships. It demonstrated for participants and spectators alike that there were other modes of association than those prescribed by the concept of destiny. To be sure, the talk before and after a contest might be in terms of one team or the other being "destined" to win, but the players did not participate in the contest as though its outcome were determined.

A football game in Santuario was thus a form of playacting, not yet reality itself but presaging what reality might become. It provided a kind of morality play or folk drama in which new styles of relationships not yet part of the local culture were acted out for all to see. Since the activity was drama and not reality, the participants were protected from undue risk in moving beyond conventional behavior. Players were able to test new modes of relationships under circumstances that freed them temporarily from customary signals of disapproval.

Thus football was a safe escape from the domination of the plaza phenomenon. Furthermore, it brought young Santuarians into contact with outsiders not subject to village codes. Prechange Santuario was highly predictable to a Santuarian; the outcome of a football game was not. Players had to learn to predict the thought processes of their opponents and to devise conditional strategies for countering their opponents' initiatives. The exemption of the playing field from the sanctioning protocols of the plaza supported them in doing so. It is little wonder that Anderson and Moore thought of organized play as "constituting the theoretical arm of a society's prescientific culture."[11]

At the time that electricity arrived and Don José made his move, Santuario had many organizations. It had a church, schools, charitable and civic societies, a labor union, and 14 small factories. Yet it had only one organizational style and format.[12] The village was organization rich but style poor, an arrangement that had worked admirably in the past. It precluded speculation, misgiving, and recrimination about how action should be initiated and work organized. It offered the economies of effort that attach to a single design that has general application. But it could not support production activities on a larger scale, such as would permit the acquisition of electrically powered machines and the employment of mechanics, and later, engineers. External competitive developments, however, now required that the historical ceiling on factory size be exceeded. The village either had to invent domestically the new social apparatus that would support larger enterprises or fall behind and have a new social apparatus imposed from the outside. It succeeded in fashioning a culture that was capable of supporting the larger organizations that modern industrial practice requires.

Don José, compelled by both rational and emotional motives, gambled that his factory community would be capable of inventing the social technology to support new machinery and plant technology. This move set off a chain of events that eventually resulted in an organizational style without precedent in the village. As this new style survived and gained legitimacy, it provided a second model for Santuarians to use in association with one another for productive purposes.

The difference between the first model and the second was that the second gave group support to members acting in terms of their individual interests, needs, and capabilities. It was not without its limits: Carmelo, who had the dexterity, strength, and interest to produce more than the other potters, stayed within group norms. Nevertheless, although members had previously conformed with their destinies, the group now supported its members in the pursuit of their individual interests and needs. It is often assumed that group values and individual values are antithetical—that acting in terms of one is thereby acting in opposition to the other—but this is not what I observed among the potters in Santuario. The workers in Don José's plant tested a new social model that challenged, first in the factory and later in the community as a whole, the powerful and broadly supported concept of fixed destinies.

At the end of my studies, Santuario was entering a difficult period. For the first time its people would come to know criminality, delinquency, and intergenerational conflict. There would be individual casualties, and many would long for the prechange quiet. Yet as a result of the changes Santuarians were moving into their futures, supported by social arrangements that gave them an understanding of themselves, their history, and their needs. They were able to negotiate their own places and positions in the company of their peers rather than having their fates ascribed to them by the dictates of inherited destinies. Each person, at least among the men, could test the limits of his potential; if he chose to do so, he was supported by social circumstances that permitted and even endorsed such testing. The triumph of Santuario was that out of a complex of technical and social events, one small community moved perceptibly toward change and in doing so created institutions that would support further movement.

The findings that interested me most from my studies at Santuario concerned the speed and pervasiveness with which the behavioral changes of the potting-room workers occurred and were transmitted to the community. I knew that Rostow[13] spoke of the initial period of change in a culture as the period of "takeoff" and that Kahl[14] referred to it as a "spurt toward change." Mead documented an instance of rapid change in her study of the Manaus in the South

Pacific.[15] But the general view of social change that I encountered in my studies in New England was that it took place gradually at a slow and steady rate. In Santuario social change occurred rapidly, in a burst that spread from the factory and engulfed the entire community in a short period of time.

The changes in the competitive aspects of the market for china-ware in Colombia, the availability of electricity from the cable dangling unused outside the village, and Don José's decision to electrify his factory were events outside the potters' work group. These and similar events were perhaps necessary to bring about changes in the workers' behavior but were hardly, it seemed to me, sufficient to gain their commitment to the changes. For that to occur the workers themselves had to initiate a response. At Santuario the first step in this connection occurred when Ramiro, Héctor, and Atilio left their machines to meet with Don José. At that time their roles in the social organization changed. New patterns of membership and leadership emerged in the group and linked them with the technological and other changes that were affecting it.

Don José could have established the new rates by himself and announced them to the potters, as he had before. If he had, production might have increased in the factory, but it is not clear that commitment to the changes would have occurred in the potters' behavior. Without those changes, there would have been none to spread to the community.

The second step in the workers' response to the changes occurred when the young men and boys, out from under their fathers' supervision at the kilns, finally agreed to form a football team. Their action connected the changes in the potting room with the community.

McGregor's Theory Y would explain the changes in the potters' behavior by assigning credit to Don José's initiative in asking for their participation in establishing the new rates. An explanation of this sort seems inadequate. It neglects the tensions that developed among the potters from the time Don José made his request to when Ramiro, Héctor, and Atilio met with him. Don José's request could be said to have pushed the potters to change their behavior, but there was also the pull from inside their group that developed while they discussed what action to take. Other tensions developed between the fathers and sons at the kilns and helped to propel the sons from their fathers' supervision to the potting room and the football field.

These processes include issues of productivity, satisfaction, growth, and learning, and changes in behavior that lie at the heart of organized human endeavor. They include questions about relations between leaders and followers in work groups and about relations among group members. Although these relations are interdependent, they are not the same. What I observed at Santuario was that leadership, contrary to the views of those who have written on the topic, was not a unitary phenomenon, an attribute of the personality of a single individual or of a position at a high level in a bureaucracy. Rather it was a many-faceted phenomenon in which many persons participated, the members of groups as well as their formal leaders.[16]

In what sense could it be said that Don José was the leader of these changes? Certainly the changes were of a character that transformed the community into one with different norms, different values, and different relationships among its members. By taking account of the potters' needs for extra funds during the Christmas season, Don José looked for potential motives for change among them. By asking for their views about piece rates, he made it possible for them to satisfy some of what is sometimes called their higher level needs, that is, their needs for respect for and standing with one another. In these ways he secured their full engagement as persons in the process of change.

Don José's behavior thus matched the three criteria that Burns established for leadership that transforms a society from one kind into another.[17] An important element of that kind of leadership in Burns's conceptualization is the intent on the part of the leader to change the members' behavior. It is not clear that Don José intended to do more than increase La Nueva's output. Although he may have intuitively sensed a readiness among the potters to change their behavior, the changes that ensued after his action were not in any real sense part of his goals. Fortuitously, as the changes meshed with his intentions, they stemmed from other factors in the situation, primarily the readiness of both the fathers and the sons to assume new responsibilities in their lives.

In connection with these processes of change and leadership, the significance of the group's response to Don José's initiative in bringing change to La Nueva caught my attention. The response of the potters set the conditions for the effectiveness of Don José's leadership. Most of the workers in the potting room had a hand in framing this response. Even the young boys who left their fathers by the kilns had a part in the workers' response to Don José's initiative. My question was whether these circumstances were unique to Santuario or whether at least when changes in behavior are at issue, the responses of the members of a group always limit the leaders' initiatives. If the latter is true, must it be said that a leader's actions are prisoner to the responses of his followers? What implications would this have for ideas about the behavior of leaders and members of work groups in organized settings?

I decided that I needed to understand better the conditions that supported change in a work group and that transmitted it to the community outside the factory. I thought that understanding those conditions and the social structures and leadership patterns that accompanied them might make it possible for me to say something about the circumstances that favored rapid social change. I was confident that analysis of the data I had already gathered at La Blanca would allow examination of these questions, for the data were rich in these respects.

View of the Santuario plaza and church.

La Nueva.

A water wheel at Santuario.

Decorators and polishers at Santuario.

Don Noah (right), Santuario potter.

Don Pablo (right), Santuario potter.

Atilio, Santuario potter.

Ramiro, Santuario potter.

Héctor, Santuario potter.

Plate-room assistants and local boys during a lunch break at Santuario. Marco Antonio Sanchez is on the right.

II

La Blanca: A Time of Consolidation

6

The Coming of the Doctores

La Blanca, a town of 2,500 people, is an hour's drive up a winding river canyon from Medellín. The village is nestled in the canyon where it widens briefly on its ascent to the cold mountain passes. Across the mountains are the broad plains of Colombia's southward extension. A visitor's initial impression is of bright sunlight on adobe dwellings, a plaza, and a church that presides over what appears to be timeless rhythms of tradition. The small houses with iron grilles over their windows are attached to one another and thus create a single line on each side of the street. Only different pastel colors differentiate one house from another. Beneath this tranquil face, a subtle ferment of social change was taking place that gave the village a special utility as a site where I could pursue the questions I wanted to study. It was a halfway town, a by-station on the migration route from the region's past to its future.

Historically, the village was a final stopping place for mule trains embarking on the two months' journey to the south. On the road from the plaza was a shrine at which the muleteers paused to say a final prayer before attempting the difficult ascent. A narrow-gauge railroad was put through the mountains to the village in the 1930s, and a highway was constructed in the 1940s. But still a tiring, overnight journey along gravel roads through crag-hugging villages was required to reach the southern plains.

During the time of the mule trains, La Blanca was a compact village that seemed to huddle before the massive church in the plaza. Its only manufacturing establishment, a pottery that made chinaware, came into existence at the turn of the twentieth century and slipped almost unnoticed into the village scene. The first may-ordomo was a colorful character known as Pablito. He was noted for the white sandals that he wore and the secrecy with which he mixed production formulas. His son kept the books, and his nephew Don Antonio, still employed in quality control in the 1960s, helped him supervise.

The tile-roofed adobe factory on the edge of the village had little to differentiate it from the other buildings in the area. The same congruence was to be noted in the social arrangements a worker encountered once he entered the factory. Like his counterparts in Santuario, Pablito decided who came to work, and once a worker was employed, he dealt with a family through its principal male.

Don Eduardo, head of La Blanca's most important family, later took over the business through a bank transaction, more out of civic concern than out of any plans for expanding it. By temperament he was a banker rather than an industrialist, but as a leading spirit in the village, he could not permit the loss of its principal industry, then employing some 40 persons.

Don Eduardo's home, Linda Vista, commanded a view of the plaza from a bluff above the canyon (figure 6.1). Set among royal palms and hung with orchids and geraniums, it served to comple-ment the imposing presence of the church, which it matched but did not surpass in size and significance. On the plaza side of the building was a three-story cupola built over a veranda from which the family had a view of all the village. The villagers came on Christmas Eve to pay their respects and receive gifts of food and clothing. Don Eduardo's three sons, Adolfo, Ramiro, and Alfredo, spent their childhood and later their school vacations at Linda Vista, riding with neighborhood boys through the orange groves out back and among the pines and poplars on the steep mountain slopes. Later they went to the United States and Europe for university training.

Linda Vista's reassuring presence was especially notable at night. The moon, splashing down through the rustling palms that sur-rounded the villa, gave unaccustomed shapes to the village in its narrow canyon below. At dusk, Don Fusto, Linda Vista's elderly handyman, mounted the cupola to set burning a light that could be seen from all parts of the village. The people of La Blanca shut-tered their homes early against the evening chill. Wrapped in woolen ponchos, they recited a rosary, sometimes two or three, while chil-

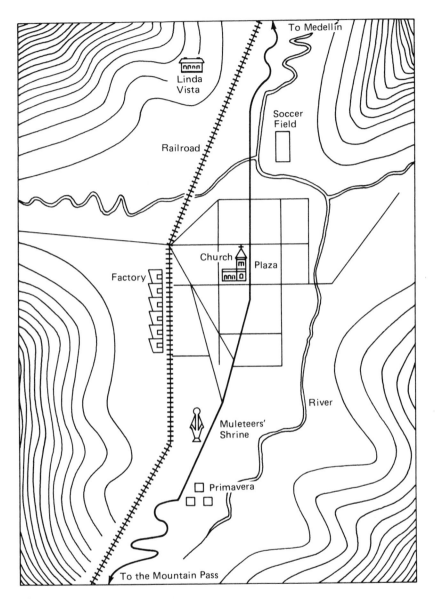

Figure 6.1
Map of La Blanca village.

dren dozed on hard wooden benches. Later, over steaming bowls of chocolate, the father might regale the youngsters with tales of the "violence," the time when La Blanca had been touched by a nationwide bloodletting, or of the "moss-covered man," a frequently heard but rarely seen figure who trod the empty mountain trails at night. The night might be fearful in La Blanca, but there was security in the family circle and the promise of support symbolized by the beacon on the bluff.

The coming of the train, highway, and factory broke the tranquility. The younger villagers, particularly, acquired new points of reference. The children ran to the tracks when they heard the train laboring up the canyon. Their imaginations translated its sound into "Mucha plata, poco peso; mucha plata, poco peso" (lots of coins, few bills; lots of coins, few bills). Even when they were climbing in the hills that flanked the canyon, they monitored the traffic on the highway and could identify by the sounds of the motors the automobiles of the patrones and the trucks heading for the pass or bringing job seekers from the mountain settlements.

La Blanca became a major destination for migrants from the high coffee country driven by the loneliness and the banditry that plagued the remote uplands and also by prospects of employment in Don Eduardo's factory. The arrival of these gentle montañeros was augmented by a smaller stream of migrants, who were more articulate and aggressive, from the city and the hot river valley beyond. At the beginning of my visits, La Blanca was experiencing the divisions that accompany transition into pluralistic society.

The divisions were readily apparent in physical changes in the village. Don Eduardo's Linda Vista continued to serve as one reminder of the valued past, but the house was now empty. Don Fusto kept the master bedroom ready in hopes that one of his beloved patrones would pay an unexpected visit. Don Paco, the personnel manager at the factory, did what he could to perpetuate the old symbolism by having the children in the factory school brought to Linda Vista several hours a week to cultivate vegetable gardens there.

A powerful center of offsetting symbolism had also come into existence. It was located, appropriately enough, on the opposite side of town, where the road continued to the pass. Known as Primavera (literally "first truth," but more commonly "springtime"), it consisted of several thatch-roofed and open-sided dancing and drinking establishments that housed activities entirely new to La Blanca.

Primavera was the gathering place of the *camahanes*, a regional word to be found in few dictionaries. The term was used to designate young men whose affectations included tight trousers, bright-colored shirts open at the neck, long hair and jewelry, and a distinctive public posture. A hint of the sexual, the illegal, the deviant attached to the term. In English, both "zoot suiter" and "young punk" convey shades of the meaning.

The central plaza served a mediating function among the village's social divisions. I remember an occasion when some of the town fathers engaged in a long and friendly conversation at the plaza with an outsider who had driven into the village in an old wagon. It was not until after the traveler had gone on over the mountains that I learned he was an evangelical minister taking his coffee at an overwhelmingly Catholic plaza that had yet to number among its citizens a devotee of a Protestant religion.

On Sundays the plaza filled for a long series of masses at the church, which were attended by all elements of the village. The men attended the last mass, after which the older ones entered a nearby tavern for refreshment and a game of dominoes; their sons headed for Primavera and the rituals of the camahanes.

At first La Blanca had few true camahanes, but interest in their activities was widespread among the younger men. By midafternoon on Saturdays and Sundays, Primavera was crowded with young people who came more as spectators than as participants. The jukeboxes played modern music and sometimes there was a band from the city. Dancing was continuous, but the dancers were few in number and not locally known. Blanquero girls never visited Primavera, and the few who came from Medellín were in constant demand as dancing partners.

The principal function of Primavera was the spectacle it provided. It was clear that the villagers did not consider themselves a part of the activities they witnessed, activities that stimulated intense conversation in which established values about masculinity and femininity, companionship, and authority were subjected to critical review. Despite their apparent disdain, the villagers obviously valued Primavera as a place for taking stock, for evaluating over a glass of beer or aguardiente the traditions that had come down to them. The impressions acquired there still had to be sorted out, combined, and incorporated into the more powerful social processes and traditions of the village as a whole. With old Don Fusto's nocturnal beacon fading and Primavera's loud rituals providing an insistent backdrop for cultural reevaluation, what disposition would the Blanqueros make of the changes that pushed them? With this background I entered the factory, which in La Blanca was the arena where the accommodation drama was taking place.

The Factory at La Blanca

La Blanca's single-story factory building sat lengthwise along the western wall of the canyon. It was unlike anything that the country people had seen. It was longer than the church, but lacked the church's grace and openness. The face it presented to the village was not a pretty one but a long blank windowless wall capped by a series of sloping roofs with skylights. There was no landscaping or green area. The workers sometimes called the factory the Ark and the managers who drove them in its narrow confines Noahs.

An office building stood next to the factory and was separated from it by an alley. During Christmas festivities, the alley was decorated with lights. Small boys, not permitted to enter the production area, waited in the alley with their fathers' lunch pails. Don Paco, the personnel manager, stood by his office door to call in a worker he wanted to see, and supervisors sometimes passed through on their way to chocolate or coffee at the plaza.

Access to the plant was restricted, so villagers had only secondhand information about what went on inside. Those hired into the factory encountered strange taskmasters promoting a stranger way of life, one for which their previous experience had not prepared them.

It had not always been that way. In earlier times, a young man would adjust to factory work in the comforting context of the sustaining bond between family and patrón. Later, there had been the hope that somehow that patronal bond symbolized by Don Eduardo would survive the disruption of expansion and mechanization. "I dealt with Don Eduardo in the patronal context," an old-timer recalled wistfully. Don Eduardo's sons slipped easily and gracefully into this context, applying the deft touch at appropriate moments. One worker reported, "Don Adolfo would meet Fulano in the factory and ask, 'Fulano, how is your wife?' 'She is in need of an operation.' Then Don Adolfo would take a large bill from his pocket and hand it to Fulano on the spot." Another recalled, "I was 12 when my father was killed by bandits in the groves above the village. After the funeral my brother and I were consoling my mother, who was worried about the family's prospects, when Don Alfredo drove up to the house. 'I want both of you boys to report to the factory for work tomorrow,' he ordered."

The Doctores and the Changes They Introduced

The factory already employed some 200 workers at the time of Don Eduardo's death. When his sons assumed leadership some years before my visits, they shared the hope of continuing the patronal system. It was the style of industrial organization that they knew, and they enjoyed the role of patrón. Moreover, this was the arrangement that had brought their business to its position as the nation's leading chinaware producer. One worker said to me, "Don Alfredo told us when he returned from a trip to Brazil a few years ago, 'Look, if the Brazilians can produce 30,000 pieces a day, we Blanqueros can do better.' We replied, 'But, Don Alfredo, we would have to move this, that, and the other thing.' He instructed, 'Then get busy moving them!' We produced 30,000 pieces, but we had to work late at night the first few days to do so."

Yet the factory's success doomed the patronal system. As at Santuario, increased size proved its undoing. The system thrived only in the context of intimate contact, and that was becoming increasingly difficult for the patrones to sustain. Now reaching their early and middle forties, they were being pulled out of La Blanca by expanding business interests in Medellín. They were also being pushed out by the difficulty of fulfilling the patronal relationship with the increasing number of families that moved into factory employment. In the mid 1950s, some seven years before my visits, with the work force exceeding 500, management of the factory was in the hands of professional doctores, the title used locally to address university graduates. The patrones did so with the hope that somehow their replacements would find a way to fulfill the social terms of the traditional employment contract.

Figure 6.2 shows the management organization of the factory at the time of my visits. The brothers who were the owners, Don Adolfo, Don Ramiro, and Don Alfredo, were at the top. The doctores all had titles that included the word "manager," whereas Don Paco in personnel and Don Antonio in quality control, the only two men

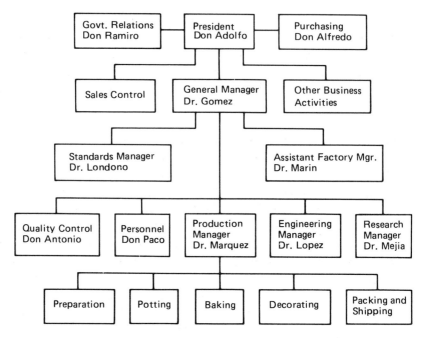

Figure 6.2
Simplified organization chart of the La Blanca factory.

in the leadership group who were not doctores, did not. Dr. Gomez, the general manager, Don Paco, and Dr. Londono, the manager of the standards department, all had private offices.

The doctores turned to the system of industrial management developed in the United States by Frederick Taylor and taught at their university in the city. When Don Alfredo, who had not been trained in Taylor's methods, instructed the workers to produce 30,000 pieces, he asked them to use whatever methods they could contrive. In contrast, the doctores, the oldest of whom was younger than 30 at the time he was hired, believed that the intuitions of workers were not to be trusted in the organization of work. What was required, they maintained, was detached observation by trained observers for the purpose of spotting and eliminating inessential motions in traditional work cycles.

The doctores' approach was based on the premise that increased compensation would overcome the workers' identification with the traditional, less efficient, and less rational routines. In addition, the doctores rejected the legitimacy of distinctions between workers on any basis other than output. They assumed that pay should be the only form of recognition for good work and that differences in pay should be based on output.

Thus, in the customary manner of industrial engineers, the doctores broke up the production sequences in the plant into their component tasks. The workers were instructed to specialize in these tasks with standardized movements. An hourly "bogey," a standard for how much work was to be done in an hour's time, was assigned to each job, and workers were compensated according to how well they did in comparison with this bogey.

In implementing their new system the doctores gambled that the prospect of increased earnings among the workers would be a substitute for the forces of the old social system. The patrones' contact had been with family teams through the padres de familias, not with individuals. Because these fathers had both a technical role as work leaders and a social role as family heads, their preferential treatment on the factory floor served dual purposes. It reinforced their ability both to resolve disputes and issues that arose among the team members and to originate actions that helped members with their work. They were the persons through whom a patrón communicated with workers during his visits to the factory floor. Team members accepted this arrangement without damage to their personal prestige or future prospects, for this behavior reinforced the leadership role of the padre de familia, to which each member of the team aspired.

Thus each work team was equipped with a built-in leadership mechanism that a patrón activated in his contacts with its principal member and that members of the family team also activated in dealing with issues that arose among themselves of which the patrón was often unaware. This mechanism received strong confirmation from its environment, for it was replicated in adjacent work groups, in activities in the village, and in the family structures of the workers' homes.

An older worker recalled the earlier times as follows: "In those days a potter was a man of importance. He was paid for the work that his group turned out. Out of what he received, he paid his helpers and the boy who turned his machine. We did the potting on Mondays, Tuesdays, and Wednesdays, and the rest of the week we polished the pieces we had made. If a load of clay arrived at the factory door, we all pitched in and unloaded it. If it was a particularly pleasant afternoon, we might all take off and go swimming, but when work was needed, we might stay until two in the morning."

Under these arrangements, making the pieces of chinaware was clearly the most important task, and the potter, as a padre de familia and leader of his group, was clearly the most important person, even though he also polished the pieces he had made whenever the cycle of work called for him to do so. Both the wage rates of the different jobs and the method of payment recognized these social facts.

The doctores' new program changed these relationships in several ways. Most important, it separated the task of polishing from that of potting, so that each was done by a different person. Though the new system continued to recognize potting as the more skilled task by paying for it at a higher rate, the system encouraged polishers to reject inferior work coming to them from their potters. The purpose was to get defective pieces out of production as rapidly as possible, before they picked up additional cost through added labor and storage. Under the system, a polisher was paid for all the pieces on which he worked, whether or not he chose to polish them. A potter, on the other hand, was not paid for the pieces he produced that his polisher rejected. The polishers' new authority over quality control thus represented a threat to the status of the potters.

Under the new system each potter retained an assistant who prepared his clay for him. Each polisher also had an assistant, whose work was designed so that it could be done by a woman. The social mechanisms that the work teams had used to stimulate work and to process social issues were thus undercut and changed.

La Blanca's new managers may have had no choice but to opt for the new rationale. Patronal responsibilities were inherited, not acquired. At La Blanca the role was open only to members of Don Eduardo's family. It was based on their residence in the village and a special style of participation in its ceremonial routines, roles for which professional managers had little appetite or aptitude. The new leaders had been raised by tradespeople, teachers, and civil servants who had managed to provide a university education for their sons. As professional managers, they were testing a role new to La Blanca, one based on organizational reform and the rationalization of production procedures.

This role had social as well as technological components with consequences for the doctores and for the workers. It acquired legitimacy in the activities of the university's alumni engineering societies, to which all the doctores belonged and which were central to their future prospects. Good standing in these societies required behavior as managers that was clearly differentiated from the traditional behavior of the patrones.

Workers' Response to the Doctores

At first the workers hoped that the doctores would address themselves to correcting problems they had unintentionally created. This, however, did not happen, for in the period that followed their arrival, the doctores and the workers spoke to each other in different languages. The workers continued to use the language and communication channels of the earlier age, but the doctores did not recognize what was being said. Their ideology restricted them to a narrower work-place language. In the doctoral scheme of things, workers were expected to adhere to the new methods. That they were doing so, as evidenced by higher productivity, was the only important communication for them to make. Moreover, the doctores were overwhelmed by the task of technical revision, and they were committed to preventing their own number from lapsing into patronal forms of behavior.

Older workers especially resented the changes that the standards program brought. Expressing the general feeling, one of them said, "We liked it the way it used to be. We enjoyed being in touch with the patrones. The doctores ask us to turn out the work, but when we do, it is they who get the credit and respect."

Another said, "It was better working for the patrones. There was more understanding, more compassion when they were here. The patrones used to pass the time of day with us. Now everything is standards. The doctores don't ask you, they tell you! But what can they learn at the university? When they first arrived, they asked us questions. We taught all of them. They walk around with eyes for nothing but the work. 'Fix this! Change that!' they say. We stayed until midnight the other day to put up Christmas decorations. The doctores didn't even comment on what we had done. They rush in with defective pieces to fight with the people."

Don Antonio, Pablito's nephew turned quality control manager, fought to preserve the family-based team system. "I battled the doctores to leave things so that the potter could motivate the others," he said. "In this business you have to have a man's head working for you as well as his hands. But for the doctores, every problem has to have a mechanical solution. If something goes wrong, they look to the machines, the materials, the incentive rates."

Another worker told me, "I can't make out the way my machine has been located. They've got me backed up against some pipes, so that I work hot in back and cold in front. I'm an honorable worker, but how can I make my rate when I'm always sick? Things were better before job standards."

Noting the doctores' preoccupation with the worksheets on their clipboards, the workers labeled the new managers *polillas*, or "paper-eating moths." Their attitude became, "If you want to talk with a polilla, you talk polilla. It's the only language that he understands." The workers saw no alternative but to withdraw from all but highly stylized interactions with their new managers. All problems, whether psychological or economic, had to be converted into the language of productivity: a machine was too low, the clay was too dry, a job rate was too tight.

Thus, for the human concern that the patrones brought to the factory, the doctores substituted inquiries about job methods and individual output, an approach the workers saw as meddlesome and offensive. They felt alienated from their new managers and misunderstood by them. They longed for the old regime to return. The workers saw the doctores acting, in Octavio Paz's words,[1] as sons of the machine, and they felt that the doctores expected them to act that way too.

Doctores' Response to the Workers

The workers' reactions hurt and confused the doctores, who expected the workers to appreciate their higher earning opportunities under the new arrangements. They resented the workers comparing them unfavorably with the patrones. At first the workers tried to convert the doctores into patrones, the only kind of leaders they knew. The doctores, of course, resisted these efforts. When a young worker addressed Ramon Garcia, a new manager, with the patronal title, the latter replied, "I am not Don Ramon. I am Doctor Garcia." Dr. Garcia did not intend his response as a reproach; he was simply signaling the worker that he was in no position to respond to the expectations that attached to the patronal designation.

The narrowed range of communication between the workers and the new managers validated, at least at a superficial level, the understanding of worker motivation that the doctores had learned at the university and brought to the factory with them. The new leaders, confronted by such rejection of their innovations, began to cut back on their visits to the factory floor. Not only did the content of manager-worker interactions become highly stylized, but also the frequency of their interactions was reduced.

The doctores probably understood the early alienation that the installation of the job standards program produced. Although the human implications of the system ran counter to the warm interpersonal traditions with which they as Latins had been reared, they were prepared to outwait these first results. Nevertheless, the workers' rejection stung them. They turned inward to their own ranks for support and solace. They formed a tight fraternity marked by high internal controls that regulated their behavior on and off the factory floor. Their norms included a strict commitment to Taylorist doctrines and a prohibition of the patronal style of interaction with workers. As one of the doctores expressed it, "If there is too much friendliness, there will be too little productivity."

The doctores boycotted La Blanca on evenings and weekends. Dr. Garcia, the general manager, rented a house for a while on the edge of La Blanca, probably at the patrones' urging; but he soon abandoned it and moved back to the city. Thereafter he commuted the 20 miles from the city daily, as did all his associates. One evening a doctor loaned me his jeep to take some workers to a village festival up in the mountains. It was only at the last moment that I realized that he was not coming with us. The loan of a car in this setting was a handsome gesture, but a long evening of drinking and dancing in the company of workers was more than his social identification would permit. The doctores assigned Don Paco the task of representing them in village and family affairs, whereas they and their wives shared each other's company in the city. One of them commented to me privately, "There should be more friendliness in the factory. Perhaps with more friendliness the plant would run better. We depend on Don Paco for this sort of thing, but this doesn't provide for enough understanding."

The doctores devised a clever social mechanism to enforce their norms. Its primary setting was the luncheon table in the company house where they gathered at noon. Only the managers who enjoyed the doctoral designation lunched together. Don Antonio ate at his home nearby, whereas Don Paco, obviously nettled by his exclusion, ate alone in the early afternoon and attributed this to the fact that he had to be available to the workers during their midday break.

The doctores punished infractions of their norms with jokes that centered around a biblical name-calling game devised by one of them. They called the plant manager the Father, the assistant manager the Son, and the production manager the Holy Spirit. They poked fun at Don Paco by labeling him Saint Vincent, Apostle of Charity. They underscored the standards manager's leading role in factory reform by designating him Martin Luther. Names like Pontius Pilate, Herod, and Judas were assigned temporarily to anyone whose behavior became suspect. The terms were used in the jovial, intimate spirit of fraternity that the doctores maintained when they were by themselves.

These daily rituals supported the doctores on the course they had charted for the factory. Taylorism became more than a method for organizing factory work; it became the emotional center of their world, the mortar that held it together. If the doctores felt themselves confronted at La Blanca by "a cult of the patrones," they themselves came to constitute "a cult of the doctores," a specific ideology of industrial reform.

The doctores' insensitivity, although it created frustrating and apparently insoluble misconceptions about the workers' motivations and behavior, also helped them accomplish their purposes. The doctores were, after all, technical innovators in La Blanca. They had embarked on an unsettling and socially disruptive mission, and the outcome of their efforts was by no means clear. Their leadership, sanctioned by the patrones, was based on their knowledge as experts about efficient methods of production, of which they were advocates. Although the rationale of their leadership was in conflict with the values and complexities of their workers' social organizations, it provided them with a clear goal for their actions. Thus Taylorism at La Blanca, although wrong or at least incomplete as a view of the workers' motivations and behavior, served temporarily useful purposes for the doctores. As one of them put it, "Tradition is on all sides of us and in each of us. If we open ourselves to it, we risk losing the ground we have gained."

Cut off from the social reality of the workers by their Taylorist ideology, the doctores were out of touch with the shifting contours of worker opinion. To some extent the patrones realized what was happening, and occasionally they would get into their cars and drive to the village. But when the patrones entered the factory, they exposed themselves to signals that had already been distorted. At first they would touch base with Don Paco and the senior supervisors who were members of a social committee. Then they would walk through the plant and talk, naturally enough, with the older supervisors and workers with whom they were familiar. In the course of exchanging pleasantries in this way, they convinced themselves that things were as they had been and that the doctores misread the signals that were coming to them. The old potting-team heads were happy to play through the familiar routines with their beloved patrones, but both parties were playing to an empty house. The social restructuring of the factory deprived the old leaders of their centrality.

During these visits the patrones sometimes granted requests and petitions from the workers. This was unsettling to the doctores, who had set up formal procedures for dealing with such matters. "But of course I had to help that man," a patrón would say in response to criticism from a doctor. "My family has known his for years." The patrones were disappointed that the doctores did not adopt their own manner with the workers. One of the patrones told me, "Sometimes the doctores treat the workers like cows. We are a proud people."

Thus their early years in the factory were difficult ones for the doctores. Their expectation was that, once their new system was installed, the workers would appreciate their new earning opportunities. This was not yet the case. The workers persisted in comparing the doctores unfavorably with their previous managers, and their subtle hostility to them endured. Later, the spirits of some of the doctores began to break. One developed stomach trouble. Another drank too much. Two others left, one suffering a nervous breakdown, the other to go into teaching. The workers said of one of them, "We cried when he left. He was *muy madre* [very affectionate]."

Problems Resulting from the Changes

The departure of the patrones from La Blanca and the efforts of the doctores to substitute less personal hierarchical relationships created a social vacuum. Patrones, doctores, and workers entered an uneasy interlude of alienation and standoff. With the weakening of the role of the padres de familias, misunderstandings and other problems of communication became apparent among the workers as well as between the workers and the leaders of the enterprise.

Clearly the factory and its community had arrived at a critical stage in its journey toward industrialization. The venture had succeeded until this point because the patrones had maintained the social practices that the villagers valued in their preindustrial experience. Both parties had taken solace in familiar interpersonal arrangements when experiencing the strains and ambiguities of earlier technical advance. In the period of expansion, however, the familiar protocols were withdrawn at a time when, if anything, even more powerful social devices were needed to process the issues that demanded attention. Problems that threatened the well-being of the plant community went unresolved, and tension mounted.

Specifically, during this period the problem of hiring new workers in order to expand the factory became acute. The flow of young campesinos from the high mountain settlements continued at an accelerated rate. These arrivals required the sensitive conditioning to factory employment that had been provided by the now-weakened system of family work teams. In addition, women were moving into employment in significant numbers. To compound the difficulties, the families migrating to La Blanca from Medellín and beyond brought with them contrary and unsettling orientations.

There was also the matter of the potters. The elimination of their special status threatened the interests of the family heads, the former padres de familias, who currently occupied these positions. The separation of the polishing function gave the polishers a potential advantage over the more senior potters. How would the potters' sensibilities be attended to during the transitional period? Who would pick up the social mandate they had held but were now blocked from fulfilling?

Clearly the doctores needed help in interpreting their new system to the plant community. The old motivational triggers, part of an intricate social complex, were neither comprehensible nor accessible to the doctores, committed as they were to Taylorist ideology.

Prechange Santuario worked because it had hammered out tenable social formulas. The concept of destiny and the plaza phenomenon, although anachronistic and sustained at times at high personal cost, provided a viable basis on which villagers could relate to visitors, fathers to sons, and patrones to workers. What would hold the new social components in place at La Blanca? It was good for a society to develop new social elements by a process of differentiation, but how were these to be combined to provide leadership as a unified whole?

It may be that for each industrial undertaking there comes a critical point when the original impulse of the founders has spent itself and secondary, motivational and integrative apparatus comes into play. Taylorism aspired to fill that role, but whereas rationalization filled one vacuum, it created another less visible but more pervasive one.

To study the resolution of these problems, I moved to the factory floor, where I could observe the potters' experiments with new social structures. This experimentation laid the foundation for a later confrontation between the workers and the doctores over the doctores' proposal to form a football league for the workers. The resolution of that confrontation decided the social fate of the factory and of the village.

7

The Social Organization of the Plate Room

At the time of my first visits the factory at La Blanca employed some 500 workers. In later years it grew to nearly 1000, over half of whom had not worked under the patrones. Inside the building, an observer's first impression was of rows of machines to which lines of workers addressed themselves with such apparent concentration that they did not look up until the visitor had passed. "Work in Silence," one sign admonished; another said, "No Games Permitted." It was thus easy for the casual visitor to take away an impression of regimentation, with the workers alienated from their neighbors and relating only to their machines. This impression was encouraged by both the doctores, because it was central to their logic, and the workers, because it provided some protection for their social order. Yet earlier studies suggested that the ways in which workers relate to one another are too resilient to be overwhelmed by systems of technological organization. The workers knew that there was more to the factory than the diligent industry that first struck a visitor's eye. When I asked one of them why they did not dust off the glass windows that enclosed the shrine in the plate-making room, he replied, "We don't keep the glass clean because we don't want Our Lady to be shocked by all that goes on below Her."

During my first days in the plant, responding perhaps to the same discomfiture that the doctores felt when they found themselves on the factory floor, I busied myself with the task of charting the plant's production sequence. The workers took me for another polilla and addressed me with the title *doctor*. They offered me the kind of response they thought a manager would expect, complaints about working conditions and pay rates. When I started interviewing, I used a small storage room that opened off the factory floor; it was immediately labeled "the confessional." As my visit extended, the workers began to reveal deeper dimensions of factory experience to me as their "Father Confessor" and, finding me willing, started to drop the protective coloration of their initial responses. I became Don Carlos and was provided access to a rich world from which doctores and casual visitors were excluded.

Factory Layout

The layout of the production area was not difficult to understand (figure 7.1). Fifty men worked in preparation. They mixed and shoveled the clay into machines that squeezed it out in ribbons of various diameters; the ribbons were then lopped into slices. The small-diameter slices went to the cup-making room and the large-diameter ones to the plate-making room. The two rooms together made up the potting department, but the cup makers and the plate makers thought of themselves as distinct groups. Each group had its own supervisor. Almost 100 workers were employed in cup making. Many were women, because forming and attaching the handles was delicate work. There were 40 employees in plate making, six of whom were women.

The baking department was separated from the plate-making area by a large storage area. Thirty men worked at lacquering and baking the greenware. Fumes and heat replaced dust as the unpleasantness to be endured in this department.

The decorating department filled the rest of the main area of the plant. Two hundred girls and young women worked in this department. They painted lines and floral designs on the finished chinaware. Their work was light and easy. There was little noise and the air was clear. They worked seated at tables. The supervisors were older women, who were addressed by the title doña. The atmosphere they created was similar to what the girls experienced at home and at school.

Off to one side 40 men and women packed and stored the finished goods. The women did the inspection and packing, and the men made the crates and piled them up to await shipment. The balance of the plant force was occupied with inspection, record keeping, and maintenance.

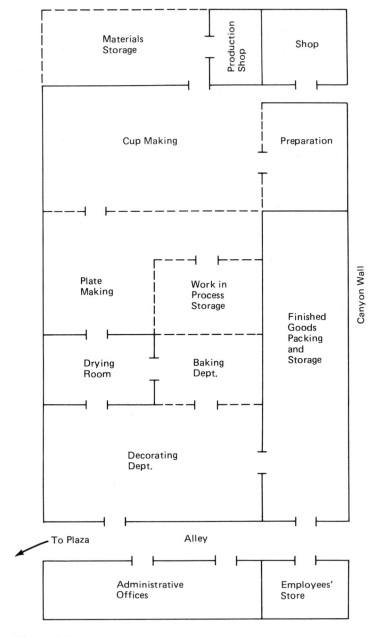

Figure 7.1
Layout of the La Blanca factory.

A small union, which had not been central in plant affairs, was active in the factory. Its president worked in the storage department.

Work in the Plate Room

I needed an operational base from which to survey all that was going on in the factory, and the doctores suggested the plate room. The young managers knew that Arturo, the supervisor, would prove an attentive host. Moreover, they may have had an idea that something special was happening there.

Working conditions in the plate room were relatively pleasant. The machine noise was not so excessive as to preclude normal conversation. The walls were solid and windowless. Light came through the roof. There were also electric lights to be turned on when needed. It was cool in the morning, mildly warm in the afternoon. The dust was so heavy that it fell to the floor without hanging in the air, although it also covered the workers' hair and clothing. Most of the men wore aprons and changed their clothes before leaving the plant. The potters wore gloves. One man worked barefoot. The men exchanged a great deal of banter at work. Arturo's desk faced into the main production area but was behind a pile of bins, so the view from it was restricted.

The two main operations in the room, potting and polishing, were the same as at La Nueva in Santuario, but the layout and many of the detailed arrangements were different because of the larger scale of operation. Looking up the main aisle from Arturo's desk (figure 7.2) on the left was a series of short production lines, each with four work stations, called puestos. The products moved toward the aisle and the center of the room. At each puesto, a potter, a polisher, and their assistants worked. The potters' assistants were boys, but the doctores had recently brought in women as assistants to the polishers.

Because potting took twice as long as polishing, there were twice as many potters as polishers in the department. The extra potters worked at the end of a long conveyor that crossed the far side of the room and at one of the two carousels located at the side of the conveyor, somewhat apart from the main production area. The conveyor and the carousels served the same functions as the production lines, but work in process on the carousels moved in circles instead of in straight lines. The conveyor and the carousels were designed to store a backlog of work in process, which the assistants brought

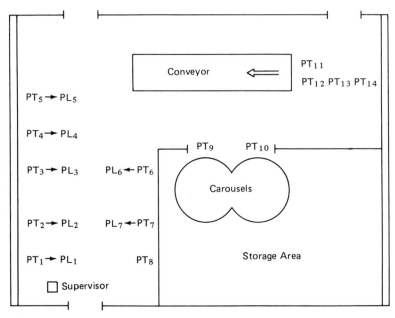

Figure 7.2
Layout of the La Blanca potting room. PT stands for potter and PL for polisher. The numbers refer to work stations.

to the polishers when there was none coming to them from the potters on their lines. On the rare occasions when a polisher exhausted both his normal and his backup supply of work, he assisted a potter who worked alone on special items not under job standards.

A polisher was never assigned, even temporarily, to work as assistant to another polisher: this was considered to be women's work. The assistants worked around the edges of the central aisle. The two quality control inspectors, also women, restricted themselves to the same areas and communicated with the workers on the plate-making lines only through the women who served as polishers' assistants.

A sense of cohesiveness was apparent in the department, particularly among those who worked along the main production aisle. This cohesiveness was reinforced by the group's clear separation from adjoining areas. There were solid walls on two sides of the room, and racks of work in process screened them on the other sides. The plate-makers had their own religious shrine, and they planned and executed the decorative motif for their department at Christmas.

Each morning the factory office informed Arturo about the number of plates, bowls, and saucers he was to schedule for production that day. Some of the items had such limited demand that a potter could turn out in a few hours enough to supply the market for a long period. He had then to tool up, a simple matter, for the production of another item.

The doctores introduced their standards program in the plate room. The work that they estimated a worker could produce in an hour's time was converted into a standard score of 60. Each afternoon Arturo received and posted the score sheets for the previous day's work. If a worker's output had fallen below 60, it was marked in red.

The Potters

As I became acquainted with the department, I realized that the plate room was a highly competitive place. Striving for position was intense and the outcome unsure. The central aisle was the plate room's plaza; its centrality was important both socially and in terms of work flow. The potters who occupied the work stations near the aisle were the main persons in the department. For this reason I came to call them *nucleados*. The potters who worked at the far end of the big conveyor were isolated ones who did not observe the norms of the central group; I called them *aislados*. Between these two groups, spatially as well as socially, was an intermediate group of young potters. They worked at or near the carousels and were vying for regular positions; I called them *candidatos*.

Social standing in the department was based on several factors. Perhaps the most important had to do with the possession of a *puesto fijo* (fixed work station). The work stations most valued were the ones numbered 1, 2, 4, 6, and 8 in figure 7.2. The potters who worked at these five stations, the nucleados, rarely moved to any other location and then only temporarily to fill in for an absent worker. Candidatos worked at stations numbered 3, 5, 7, 9, and 10. They moved from one station to another much more frequently than the nucleados. The positions numbered 11, 12, 13, and 14 were the aislados' stations.

Nicanor, known by the nickname La Montaña (the Mountain) and employed at station 1, stood at the pinnacle of this society and was in some ways its leader, for he best represented the values that were important in it. His machine was the first one to be ready in the morning because it was the first to be supplied with raw materials. He did not initiate nonwork activities in the room, but whoever did always came to his station and cleared them with him. When the group met with management, he was the one addressed first, and the others waited for him to reply.

The potter at work station 8 worked on special production items that had not been placed under incentive pay. This circumstance exempted him from the social pressures that attached to questions of productivity. He played a supportive role as godfather in both a literal and figurative sense. He had 22 godchildren, three times as many as anyone else in the room. The night that many of the workers stayed after hours to put up Christmas decorations, it was he who went out for food.

Another factor that determined social position among the potters was the *referencia* (production item), on which each man worked. Of the referencias that were made in the plate room, only a few had enough market demand to permit continuous production. To shift from one to another took no more than a few minutes to change jigs or to move to another station. Furthermore, the short-run items were often the ones that required the most skill. Nevertheless, an informal poll that I took among the potters indicated that they considered the long-run referencias the desirable ones on which to work, for continuous production enhanced the possibility of protecting a permanent work station. Also the fact that there were only a limited number of long-run referencias made them prestige items.

By keeping track of which potters had puestos fijos and noting the popularity of the referencias on which each worked, I made an approximate ranking of the social standing of the potters in the room.[1] La Montaña scored highest. In addition, I found that during a six-week period the potters who were nucleados worked on only six referencias, whereas the candidatos worked on fifteen. Five of the six referencias on which the nucleados worked were among the products that all the potters selected as most desirable. Only six of the fifteen referencias worked on by the candidatos were as popular.

Given their longer production runs and their greater skill and experience, the nucleados consistently outproduced the candidatos and had lower rejection rates; hence their earnings were higher. During the six weeks that I kept records, the nucleados had an average output of 66 units against the standard hourly rate of 60, whereas the candidatos had only 49. The rejection rate among the nucleados was 7% and among the candidatos 17%.

At first glance it might appear that the candidatos' low scores reflected simply their lack of dexterity and the fact that they, as persons with less experience and skill, were working on the more difficult products. The difference also had social significance and expressed the group's belief that it was appropriate for persons with high standing to have high output and for persons of low status to be kept in their place with low scores.

To keep track of how they were doing, most of the potters kept a running total of their output during the day. They exchanged information frequently, especially in the groups called *fogones* (literally, "family hearths"), which they formed near their machines for coffee. The fogones were an important site of social interaction in the department.

Each afternoon shortly after Arturo posted the score sheets for the previous day's work, most of the workers found a reason to go over and look at them to find out how they had done. Most of the candidatos hurried over as soon as the sheets were posted. The older men waited until the first rush had subsided. Then they too found a reason—a bandage from the first aid cabinet, a word with Arturo—to pass by the bulletin board where the sheets were posted.

The aislados did not take part in these activities. "If somebody asks me how I am doing," one of them told me, "I will tell him, 'Enough! Enough!' It's not a fair question. If a man wants to work rapidly, that's his business!" And the one who was called "the Marxist"—in the local sense of the term, meaning one who is against the old values—reported, "There's no pressure from others on matters of productivity. If a man has a good day or a bad day, that's the way it goes. We never discuss output."

An additional value in the plate room was the belief that a worker should not aspire to a place or position other than ones in the department itself. The nucleados had surrendered, at least publicly, aspirations to advance to positions outside the group's own scheme of things. Some of them had foregone opportunities for further education for fear that it would jeopardize their place in the shop-floor competition. They were careful not to appear to cultivate their superiors, either the patrones or the doctores, lest this be construed as evidence of hope for promotion in the factory organization.

In one way or another, all the aislados rejected promotion. Luis, the oldest, was a former padre de familia who had been unable to make the conversion to the new system of work as a supervisor. He spoke with affection of the earlier days. His work station was one at which the patrones touched base on their information-gathering forays in the plant. Luis was the only potter who admitted that he wanted to be a supervisor, but he knew that even this opportunity had slipped away from him: "Once I aspired to be a supervisor. I don't have that aspiration anymore. I don't deal with people in my work anymore. I've lost the knack. I deal with no one."

Another aislado came to La Blanca from a large hacienda where he had engaged in unskilled labor not usually found in the region. Two, Roberto and Pedro, were students who publicly acknowledged that they were preparing themselves for office work in Medellín. The remaining one, the Marxist, had worked in the city and still spent his free time there. The reluctance of the villagers to take their affairs in their own hands struck him as mensos (foolish), and he did not hesistate to say so. For such nonconformist convictions, the aislados paid the price of social isolation. They did not join the other plate makers in decorating the department for Christmas. The others decked the aislados' machines with tinsel.

The candidatos were the youngsters in these social ranks. Their personal histories did not reveal the strong orientation to established Blanquero values that the nucleados held, though their statements and behavior sometimes exhibited surface identification with these values. They visited Medellín from time to time, something the nucleados seldom or never did. The candidatos also participated in the activities of the camahanes at Primavera, where I never saw a nucleado. The candidatos were prominent in the nonwork activities of the plate room that the aislados eschewed.

The candidatos were the social climbers in the system. Their situation was unresolved, for the outcome of their efforts was by no means assured. The interviews I had with them indicated that they were studying the alternate routes of the nucleados and the aislados to see which offered the greater promise of fulfilling their needs.

The work arrangements of the department provided a social mechanism that fostered the process of a candidato making a choice about the group's values. As a candidato shifted from station to station and from referencia to referencia, he was exposed to social warmth along the aisle on one day and to the isolation of the aislados at the big conveyor on the next. He could not fail to be impressed by the spatial and social exclusion that was the price of pursuing the aislado option, but he still may have been drawn to the independence of this path.

Umberto, known as El Camahan, presented a case in point. A handsome, strapping Indian, he had passed his boyhood on his father's *finca* far from La Blanca until the family was driven out by "the violence." Then followed two years of work in Medellín while he was still a boy. When I interviewed him, he readily identified his friends in the group, an action in contrast to the typical response of the nucleados, who answered, "We're all friends, all!" His friends were other candidatos; he also named one of the two student aislados. With these friends, he occasionally visited Medellín and took part in camahan activities at Primavera. When I asked him about his plans, the immobility that resulted from his unsettled orientation showed through: "I'd like to live and work in Medellín, but I wouldn't go out and look for work there. If an opportunity to work or study there came my way, I'd take it but I can't study nights like Pedro. He's got the constitution, I haven't. I exchange figures on output with the others during breaks. We find out from each other how we're doing. These are good people here, and it's a good deal for a bachelor, but I don't think that the work prepares you for anything outside the factory."

During the six weeks I monitored the nucleados' and the candidatos' output, Umberto's relations with the group underwent a change. At the beginning of the period, he was clearly in the transient status that was the lot of a candidato. Later, however, it became possible for him to work a permanent production item. At this point his average hourly production rose from 42 to 60. "I can be an old boar, too!" he commented when the score was posted. He used the word *berraco*, which had a connotation of active sexuality. He seemed to mean that he had made his decision to move into the nucleado world.

The Polishers

Though potting took much longer to learn than polishing, the polishers had achieved a social standing in the room nearly as high as the potters. They too had achieved the fixed work stations that all aspired to. To move a polisher, even briefly, to another's station was an unsettling experience that all parties sought to avoid. Once when one of them, Zambariffi, had to be away from his position for a few hours, another was asked to move there to finish some work. He went grudgingly and complained vociferously that he was feeling *maluco* (sickish). Finally he sent Zambariffi's assistant away, called over his own, and went about the work with obvious displeasure.

During the period when I was seen as a polilla, I asked the polishers why they disliked moving. At first they talked of variations in the speed of the polishing machines. Later they admitted that they were more comfortable at their own stations and, taking me into their confidence, showed me where they had scratched their initials or some other personal markings on the undersides of their jigs and fixtures, hidden from sight so as not to violate the group's value against personal visibility and self-promotion. Of their work stations they would say, "Es mi puesto! Es mi casa!" (This is my station! This is my home!).

Because of reject allowances and other adjustments, it was difficult for the polishers to keep a running tally of their personal output. Yet all of them, especially the younger ones, were sensitive to any high daily averages that they ran up. The youngest, Orlando, known as El Policia, (the Policeman), one day ran up a score in the 90s, well above average. When I commented on his achievement, he waved off the compliment. When I mentioned it a second time in the presence of his neighbor Mario, know as La Vaca (the Cow), a steady worker with a placid temperament, Orlando pointed to Mario, who was older, and said, "Mario is the better polisher!"

All the polishers had strong orientations to the factory and the village. None had roots in the potting-team era or a history of relationship with a patronal family. That they were reasonably content was underscored by the fact that there had been no turnover in their ranks in recent years.

When the doctores gave the polishers the responsibility of rejecting the defective pieces that came to them from their potters, they unintentionally threatened the social values in the plate room. As

I noted, the doctores instituted this change in the interests of getting low-quality work out of the production sequence as early as possible. When a polisher rejected rather than reworked a defective piece, he gained time that he could translate into either a more leisurely rate of work or increased personal earnings. At the same time, the potter who made the defective piece was not paid for it. Thus the technical arrangements gave the polishers a mechanism that they could use to raise their earnings above the potters'.

In practice, the potters' output scores generally ran in the low 60s and the polishers' in the low 70s. However, the potters' standard hourly rate in pesos was 1.25 (equivalent to U.S. $.10 at the time of my study) and the polishers' 1.10. The take-home pay for both groups of workers therefore tended to be roughly equal.

The plate makers wanted to keep things that way, and they carefully monitored who was available to fill any openings that developed among the polishers. Anyone in the position of polisher who behaved inappropriately posed a threat to the whole group. Mateo, a floorboy who moved racks of plates from the plate room to the baking department and did other such work, was the next obvious candidate. He had worked in the plate room longer than any of the assistants, was older than they and married, and had relatives in the room. Furthermore, he aspired to be a polisher. The doctores thought of him as a candidate and assigned him to the work whenever a position was temporarily available. But Mateo was caught between conflicting desires to impress the doctores with his productive capacity on the one hand and to conform to the group's values against promotion on the other. The group, not without sympathy, sensed Mateo's dilemma, but there were larger issues at stake.

One day I observed Mateo, somewhat rattled by his dilemma, fill in for an absent polisher. He worked rapidly, took no time out for relief, and ran up a high score. His neighbors made jokes about him and threw pieces of scrap in his direction. They used his nickname, which was an unflattering one. When he went back to his regular work, his distress was obvious. He slammed his carts around corners and left them blocking aisles. He told the other workers that he was going to look for work as an independent tradesman, strong language in the group whose values held that young men should not have external ambitions.

Among the polishers, Pancho was the one most favored by the doctores to become a potter. He was also the one who occasionally gave the other workers cause for concern. They called him Molleja (Chicken Liver) and accused him of rejecting their work "without mercy." His potter would put his foot up on a bin and wait until Arturo came over to decide whether a rejected piece was defective. Pancho was highly sensitive on these occasions. He tended to back away from such confrontations and even accepted pieces of work with borderline defects.

These, then, were the means to forestall the potential disruptive social consequences of the innovation the doctores introduced in the relations between the potters and the polishers. The polishers were allowed fixed work stations, and they achieved take-home pay approximately equivalent to that of the potters. In return, they did not employ the technical leverage inherent in their position to raise their earnings above the potters'. The social controls that sustained these arrangements included informal screening devices that allowed advancement only to those whose allegiance to group protocols was above question. Subtle social sanctions were also used to remind even the established polishers of the group's concepts of proper work behavior.

The Potters' Assistants

The relationship of a potter's assistant to the department's affairs was determined largely by the interests and social priorities of the potter with whom he worked. The assistant depended on his potter for the speed of his work and for instruction on the job, including an occasional opportunity to try his hand at potting. For this kind of dependent relationship, young campesinos from the lonely coffee fincas in the high mountains were well suited. Don Paco said that, in the agricultural work they had carried out with older relatives, they had already become accustomed to working with older men and had learned "the law of work."

One of the assistants told me, "The pueblito where I lived is still without a road. It was an hour and a half to the coffee grove, so I had to leave the house at five in the morning, six days a week. Sometimes I worked alone or with two or three others. The sun was hot and the rain was cold. Frequently I was hungry. Here, there is shade and warmth, better guarantees, and more companionship."

When the campesinos first arrived at the factory, they were likely to be bewildered, and they made what sense they could of their surroundings by employing familiar systems or social status. Thus they sometimes called their young supervisor, patrón or Don Arturo. One new arrival commented, "There was little talk when we work on the finca. Here I find it hard to get use to the chatter, and the vulgarities that I hear on the streets bother me."

In any case, the task of orienting these young men was one that the potters liked. It helped maintain their sense of social usefulness. They made jokes at the young men's expense to try to ease them out of their country ways. One thoughtful potter reported, "When they first come from their little settlements, they wear sombreros and ponchos and go about without shoes. They don't talk much because of the solitary life they led on the fincas, and they never use bad language. The men kid them a little and call them montañeros (mountain boys); but it's just a way of talking. Some of them get upset, but they get used to the factory, put on shoes, and leave their sombreros at home."

Out of this joking usually emerged a nickname—Little Bird, Horse, or Bandit—used among the men but not with Arturo. The act of finding a nickname had a symbolic importance. It was a firm sign that the recipient had been accepted for membership in the plate-making community. One young man recalled the induction procedure to which he had been subjected: "At first I thought the work was maluco, all of these machines crowded into so small a space. I was afraid that all the others were talking about me, laughing at me. 'What mountain did you come off?' they would ask me, although not with unkindness. After a while they got to know me. They settled on a nickname for me, and then things went better."

The potters gained the respect and reassurance that was important to them from their conversations with their assistants. In return for this support, the potters gave instructions and protection to their assistants. They even risked managerial displeasure and reduced their own earnings to let their assistants take over the potting machines from time to time. Once a potter and an assistant had an established relationship, the assistant was seldom moved to another potter.

The Women

The women's presence around the central aisle of the plate room dated from the time when the doctores introduced the revised and standardized layout. The women called the area their asylum.

The arrangement that limited women to working as polishers' assistants had been breached only once and then only briefly. On that occasion the doctores invited a young woman to try her hand at polishing. Technically the experiment should have worked. Polishing was light work and required manual dexterity. In the United States, it was common for women to perform the task. But at La Blance a social boundary of importance to the workers had been crossed. As one of the plate makers reported, "We knew this was not suitable work for a woman, but we said nothing. We just waited and sure enough, what we knew would happen came about. The girl was transferred out of her polishing position and out of the plate-making room."

The special status of women was underscored in other ways as well. None of them, for instance, had nicknames. Instead, all, whatever their age, were addressed as vieja (little old one). Nor were the women permitted to use the men's nicknames. They were excluded from the men's fogones during coffee breaks and made their own arrangements in an out-of-sight space behind the storage bins at one end of the department.

In the words of one plate maker, a woman's role was to be "quiet and respectful." When one, a new employee from a family that had recently moved to La Blanca from the city, protested her transfer to a less popular polisher, she received little support from either the men or the other women.

Women in La Blanca played a powerful role at home, but their public participation in village life was carefully prescribed. The matter of naming a queen for the annual fiesta was typical. When La Blanca's fiesta was in religious hands, the queen led the procession to church as a representative of Mary, Queen of the Angels. Even when the fiesta became a commercial rather than a religious event, proscriptions still attached to the queen's participation. For instance, she was not permitted to dance at the ball over which she presided, although the more adventuresome among the younger men used every ruse to get her to do so.

When the men took up a collection to buy Arturo a Christmas gift, they excluded the women. Later, however, the men invited them to stay after work to help put up the holiday decorations. Women not only stayed but took over the task, for it was a householdlike role in which they felt comfortable and in which the men deferred to them. They devised a motif that converted the room into a cathedral of paper streamers and balloons. It was a gay exception to normal practice, and the work went on until midnight. Then the men walked home with the women in a group through the deserted streets.

By working in the plate room, the women were testing a new role, one that had great potential for change in the village, yet one that made them the subject of and vulnerable to village gossip. By restricting them to the central aisle, where interactions could be monitored easily and departures from customary behavior promptly disciplined when necessary, the plate makers conformed with village conventions. Some of the younger women chafed under the restrictions and talked about transferring to the decorating department, where they felt the working conditions were "more feminine," but others, especially some of the senior women, welcomed the detached but amicable arrangements that the plate makers contrived for them. Although these arrangements led to separation, differentiation, and subordination for the women, they also provided continuity between their roles in the village and in the factory until a social apparatus capable of more inclusive arrangements could be devised.

Zambariffi's Role

In a society as segmented by age, sex, and occupation as the plate maker's, the risk was high that the parts would lose touch with one another. In the plate room this risk was lessened by the fact that, except for the introduction of the women, the members had not changed much recently. Thus there had been few interruptions in their working together. In addition, there was one polisher, Zambariffi, who kept in touch with all the sectors as well as with Arturo, the supervisor. He worked at position 5, at the far end of the aisle from La Montaña and Arturo (figure 7.2). He was well located for keeping in touch with the workers on the long conveyor and on the carousels as well as with those whose stations were on the main aisle.

Zambariffi's connection with the patrones and the factory did not extend beyond his own few years of employment. At age 23, small, mild, and sad-faced, he had not built up a stake in the old order that would have tied him to the traditional work-team system. He was active in union affairs but was considered a moderate, opposed to strong courses of action and willing to wait for the emergence of natural forces. The Marxist said of him, "He is without blemish." His allegiance was clearly to La Blanca, the village of his birth. Zambariffi subscribed to most of the village customs and left La Blanca only on specific errands. Yet he was intellectually affiliated with the aislados. I brought small gifts from the United States for those with whom I established special relationships, and Zambariffi expressed interest in books on economic or current affairs, although he had not completed more than the first few years in the village school. Zambariffi said of the potters, "I think that in all honesty they deserve better pay. After all, it is the potters who do the basic work and give the product its final shape. They are the most dissatisfied, and I believe that they have justification for being so."

Thus Zambariffi was centrally involved in departmental affairs, but his involvement was a special one. As prime minister to La Montaña's king, he enjoyed universal respect but had no intimate friends. He was the only worker in the plate room who did not have a nickname. He was addressed simply by his last name.

Zambariffi also worked with Arturo when, for instance, Christmas decorations were being put up and when a farewell party was being arranged for me. For most workers there were limits to associations with supervisors, but Zambariffi's collaboration with Arturo was outside the dimensions of personal friendship. He cooperated with him as an agent of the group rather than as a friend. Arturo reported that it was Zambariffi who came to him the day that the mother of one of the women died: "Zambariffi told me that the men would work only until three that afternoon because they were going to the funeral. They went together to the woman's home. The family wanted to hire a car, but the men said no. They hoisted the coffin to their shoulders and carried it the half mile to the church. Later they carried it out of the village to the cemetery." Before any such undertaking, Zambariffi moved to La Montaña's station and consulted him. On such occasions I would see him signal to the others by means of a facial expression or a flick of his hand.

Workers who made their peace with both their group and management were free to accept the advantages of company housing and other fringe benefits. Such a course was not open to Zambariffi.

Doing so would have made him unacceptable to the members of groups that were not so rewarded. The students and others whose aspirations were linked to the city and the promise of careers outside the factory could put up with a certain amount of tension arising from their disassociation from the rewards that the group and the company provided; they took solace in their hopes for the future. This too was denied Zambariffi so long as he contributed to the services that his role entailed. The little world of the plate room needed its high society as represented by La Montaña and by the other high-status members whom it held up to its constituency as evidence that the effort required to gain the status was worthwhile. Attaining this status would have limited Zambariffi's maneuverability because it would have restricted his rapport with the groups in the plate room whose members opted for rewards outside the society.

A period of rapid structural change in the social organization of a group of workers is a time of dislocation and personal pain for many of the members. At such a point an organization is able to preserve its integrity better if there is a central figure who shares in the suffering of those most affected by the change. Zambariffi was eminently qualified for this role in the plate room. The strains of carrying out his role, which went well beyond the nutritional and job-related sources to which he sometimes attributed his worries, was evident in his face and manner.

Zambariffi thus possessed a set of relationships, sensitivities, and personal experiences that permitted him to offer the different groups a set of specific leadership activities. Accepted by all but closely identified with none, he carried out this role by keeping in touch and communicating with all the group's sectors. His service was an important explanation of the stability that the social organization of the plate makers achieved during this period of intense change.

These arrangements gave the plate makers' social organization its internal structure. They prescribed how the members of each occupational group related to each other and to the other groups in the room. The organization legislated low visibility for its members and prohibited self-promotion. In return it provided for their task, membership, and leadership needs. By virtue of these arrangements, it restrained potentially unsettling influences at a time when their release might have had a disastrous impact on both the department's output and the needs of its members.

These structural developments affected the organization's capacity to survive. When an organization has methods for indoctrinating newcomers in the behaviors that its existing members consider appropriate and methods for promoting and rewarding those who conform to its ways, it achieves a degree of independence from its surroundings. It can accept a variety of changes, including technological and personal ones, without losing its stability, provided of course that the changes are not so great or so rapid as to overwhelm it.

The structural changes at La Blanca allowed, among other things, the plate makers to meet the needs of a modern society for higher levels of productivity and of work groups with members of diverse backgrounds. The changes resulted from fortuitous circumstances, not conscious control. These structures were tenuous and vulnerable, easily subject to external pressure. Indeed, in terms of Taylorist premises about how a work group should operate, the department's social organization represented an anomaly that should not have existed. If some supervisory and management support other than the leadership that group members generated internally had been available to the group, it would have helped preserve the society's integrity. Arturo, the young supervisor, provided this service by acting as a bridge between the plate room's internal and external circumstances.

8

Change and Its Consolidation at La Blanca

Arturo was the son of Don Chico, the first worker Don Eduardo employed when he acquired the factory. The story went that before working there, Don Chico had done carpentry and odd jobs for Don Eduardo. One day he was whitewashing his house when the patrón came down the street. "Get down from that ladder and come to work for me, *viejito*," Don Eduardo called. "I've just bought the factory."

In the 20 years before I first visited La Blanca, the factory became Don Chico's life. During the most recent years he had restricted himself to the construction and maintenance of plant equipment. Don Chico liked to teach the younger men, and they responded by calling him El Maestro.

Don Chico sent Arturo for secondary studies to a seminary in the city with the hope that his son would become a priest. Arturo, however, proved more adept at making friends and playing football than at studying. One of Don Eduardo's sons spoke to Don Chico about Arturo: "Look, the factory will be the boy's life. Take him out of school and bring him here, where you can teach him yourself." He knew a young man with Arturo's connections could be useful to the doctores, who were searching for a way to run the factory.

By the time of my visits seven years later, Arturo's mother had passed away, and Don Chico had remarried and was raising a second family. Whenever I visited La Blanca, I spent a few minutes chatting with Arturo and his wife at their home, which was across the town from his father's. The conversation usually turned to events in the factory and the status of its football team, which Arturo had organized several years earlier. Arturo would insist that we cross the plaza and call on Don Chico. A visit with the two of them was a lively event. They were both tall, alert men who listened in the same way as they talked, with all parts of their bodies. They broke into laughter easily. During these visits Arturo addressed his father as El Maestro. Although Don Chico was no longer employed at the factory, he still went there from time to time and worked alone among the mixing vats and tanks. Looking across the factory, he would say to me, "This is my life, my life!" He also sometimes expressed concern about Arturo's lack of total allegiance to the old values, for although Arturo still went to Sunday mass, he had stopped attending midweek services. Don Chico chided him by calling him Communist, but he used the term with toleration and deep affection to mean only that Arturo followed new values.[1]

Arturo's Role as Supervisor inside the Plate Room

Arturo progressed rapidly in the factory from one position to another. He started as a potter's assistant and became successively a potter, an assistant supervisor, and then a supervisor in the plate room. At age 20 he was the youngest supervisor in the factory; he soon became one of the most influential. He related easily to the older elements that shared his father's orientation. He also became a moving spirit among the younger workers who were recruited to staff the company's expanding operations.

For La Blanca the period of expansion was a time of intense jousting, contained and confined by the tradition of interpersonal tolerance that was at the heart of the village's values. Vibrant new strains were in competition with older ones to establish the emerging tones, habits, and priorities that would command the allegiance of the work force. Arturo was able to play a bridging role between the two without being subservient to either. He developed trust with both the patrones and the workers and was able to provide the plate makers the breathing space they needed to fashion a social structure that helped them maintain a sense of their own integrity.

Arturo's fluency in the several idioms and his capacity to respond to the different protocols was perhaps most evident in his dealings with the potters. I had an opportunity to interview each man in the plate room on at least two occasions. Arturo set up the first interviews. It was not coincidental that he arranged for me to meet first La Montaña, Zambariffi, and the Godfather, in that order. Nor was it surprising that his best friend and football companion was La Montaña, who was field captain while Arturo was manager off the field. Through football Arturo was in close contact with other young supervisors and workers throughout the plant. He knew the nickname of each worker in the plate room, but he never used it in speaking to one of them. "I have a group that is *muy unido* [very united or cohesive]," Arturo told me, "but others consider it a source of trouble!"

Arturo demonstrated his understanding of the workers' values in the way he assigned work to individual potters. As I studied this matter, it became clear that the potters' work locations could not be attributed to seniority or skill or to any other factor that managers traditionally use as the basis for such decisions. Rather, work-station assignments were the result of a continuing process of negotiation between the workers and Arturo, both negotiating within the bounds of what was possible given the production requirements of the managers and the social values of the workers. The major determinant seemed to be the dynamics of social rejection and personal preference among the potters rather than management logic.

Thus Arturo let the nucleados have the long production runs that allowed them to stay at their fixed work stations, to turn out more pieces than the candidatos, to earn more take-home pay, and to maintain their standing as the most prestigious group in the plate room. He did not do this all the time, and it was not necessary that he do so. There were times when the production situation in the room as a whole, often involving a rush order for a particular customer, required that a nucleado work on some other referencia than the one he preferred. Yet Arturo did not ask this so often that the men thought he overlooked the values that were important to them. He easily could have. As I pointed out in chapter 7, the values of the plate makers' society resulted in the youngest, least experienced, and least skilled of the potters working on the referencias that had the shortest runs and required the most skill. It was therefore not clear that the values of the plate makers' society resulted in job assignments that were the most efficient from the point of view of the department's output. Nevertheless, Arturo's supervisory skill at integrating the technical and human aspects of the society allowed the plate makers to produce their present levels of plates and saucers and of human satisfactions.

Arturo's ability to accomplish this was reinforced by his affinity for the values of the different groups that he bridged. Like Nicanor and Zambariffi, he was clearly of La Blanca and unencumbered by external commitments that might have limited his local maneuverability. The image of his father's affinity with the patronal families carried over to Arturo and obviated any questions about the new styles of comportment that he condoned. Paradoxically, because of his commitment to tradition, Arturo could on occasion disregard historic protocols without penalty. He was the first person to take me to Primavera, where he played the camahan without raising questions about his basic allegiances.

Arturo also avoided the kind of extreme commitment to a particular set of values that limited the flexibility of the more senior participants in the restructuring process. The older supervisors were referred to by the workers both as *vigilantes*, a somewhat dated term, and as patrones. They were also addressed with the traditional prefix *don*. Their orientation was clearly toward the old family-work-team system. The doctores found these older supervisors inflexible in adjusting to the standardization program. In contrast, Arturo gently rebuffed the attempts of new workers to address him as *don*. A skilled practitioner of the middle course, he provided a delicate brokerage function that the doctores valued, even though its real nature escaped their understanding. The doctores, after all, were the ones who recruited Arturo into a supervisory position. To support their position, they were prepared within limits to close their eyes to the measures that Arturo accepted as a means for softening the sharp edges of the standardization and other programs that they were implementing.

In no way does it downgrade Arturo's leadership role to suggest that his mediating contribution to the social structure of the plate room was possible only because of certain attitudes and tolerances already present in the culture of the region. Arturo was a leader because he expressed and defined values that had popular support in that culture: values about work and how it sustained a man's right to be an individual and to subscribe, if he wished, to opinions not generally held; values based on the expectation that the future would turn out well, whatever the current misery that surrounded the workers; values deeply rooted in strong family and village institutions, cherished to the degree that it was possible to submit them confidently to scrutiny and review; values about individual behavior and social affiliation that had stood the rigorous test of an inhospitable terrain and an ungenerous history. It was to such values that Arturo responded with genuine respect for the people whom he served and for their ability eventually to find a way to accept their divergent orientations despite their differences.[2] In Burns's terms[3] Arturo was a transactional leader who exchanged with the plate makers his support and goodwill for their conformance to the factory's work rules.

Arturo's Role as Leader outside the Plate Room

Arturo carried out the same middleman role as an agent of exchange in his interactions with supervisors and managers outside the plate room. By putting his understanding of the workers' sentiments at the disposal of the doctores, Arturo and a few other supervisors like him in other sections of the plant won the trust of the doctores. This trust allowed the middle-level supervisors and managers, who worked between two sets of values—the doctores' and the workers'—to experiment with styles of upward communication for which there was no precedent in the plant. The following were among the reports I received of meetings where these new patterns were tested.

One supervisor told me, "Dr. Gomez called us into his office and asked, 'What's the matter with production?' Nobody replied. He got up, shut the door, pounded his fist on the table, and admonished, 'Nobody leaves this room until I hear from each one of you a statement as to what is holding up production.' Arturo got up and opened the door and said, 'You're talking to men, not children!' "

Another time Dr. Gomez invited all the supervisors to his home. One of them told me later, "He gave us drinks and sat down on the floor himself with a pad of paper in front of him. 'All right!' he said, 'I want you to talk. Give me all of your problems.' At first he got the routine answers, machine breakdowns, poor material, and so forth. Arturo took a couple of shots of whiskey just before Dr. Gomez pointed to him with the exclamation, 'You! Talk!' Arturo replied, 'If you really want to know the answers to the questions you ask, your Señora will have to leave the room.' Señora Gomez, who had come into the room, asked, 'Are you going to fight?' 'No,' said Arturo, 'but I'm going to say some things that you won't want to hear!' Then he told Dr. Gomez, 'There is no one to talk with us, listen to us, or for that matter direct us. You doctores have no respect for us, you don't treat us like people.' At that point one of the doctores applauded and cried, 'Go after him, Arturo!' We really had it out that night. The older supervisors were shocked."

Arturo told me of still another occasion when he had stood up to Dr. Gomez. Dr. Gomez, who had been on a trip to Argentina, returned unexpectedly and made an unannounced tour of the factory to check on the work being done. Arturo told me that he asked him, "Who do you think you are? Perón or somebody?" Dr. Gomez replied, "What do you mean by that?" Arturo said, "Well, one day you are here, then you are gone, and then you are back again. We never know that you are going, or that you are coming back, or what you learn while you are away. We are never told anything!"

Such encounters were evidence of a new stage in the dialogue between the new, externally derived technological ideas of the doctores and the slowly evolving social reality of the workers. Supervisors and supervised were testing broader dimensions of authority relationships. The time was ripe for a rapprochement on new terms, but it was several years in coming, a short enough period when one considers the time required for the evolution of the easily shattered structures I have described. Arturo and the football team he started had a crucial role in the events that led to the new arrangement.

The Proposal for a Factory Football League

In addition to the meetings the doctores held with the supervisors, there were two factions in the plant that competed to fill the vacuum created by the passing of the patrones and the reluctance of the doctores to fill their leadership roles.

One was the factory's social committee, which Don Paco started and which he and Don Antonio headed. Its members were the older supervisors. It offered the plant community a traditional brand of paternalism with which all sectors of the community were familiar.

After the doctores' arrival, the social committee became the company's visible instrument for employee relations. Its principal activity was running the annual fiesta in honor of the Virgin, who served as protectress of the factory. Interest in the event diminished over the years, but a first communion ceremony for the children of factory families, with many of the costs subsidized by the company through the committee, served to maintain interest in it. The patrones still came from the city to march with the members of the committee to the communion mass in the church. Nevertheless, it was obvious that the committee had been playing to a shrinking constituency, at least until the most recent celebration, when the supervisors campaigned quietly to have the workers regain control of the annual fiesta from the commercial interests into whose hands it had fallen. More than 150 workers not directly involved in the activities of the service responded and took their places in the procession behind Arturo and the soccer players. They left the Virgin's float and their banners in the hands of the members of the social committee.

The second faction that competed for social leadership consisted of the young supervisors and workers who rallied around Arturo. They used the factory football team as their point of contact, building the core of the new order around the team's daily practice sessions after work and its weekly excursions away from the village for games. Relations between the two factions were at first more tolerant than competitive, although they were marked by some disapproval on both sides. The members of the social committee referred to the soccer players as camahanes and were referred to in turn as *pájaros*, literally "birds," with the connotation of subordinates who "sang to" their superiors.

The younger group was a new force in factory affairs and was just beginning to come into its own. Its members were interested in breaking new ground, and they embarked on innovation and experimentation in matters of social organization. They had no intention of moving backward, even though they were not sure what, if anything, they had to propose.

At about this time one of the doctores suggested to Dr. Gomez that the company should support the organization of a football league for the factory. The plan called for ten teams, eight composed of workers and two composed of managers and office employees. The proposal included having a playing field leveled at company expense near the primary school that now flanked Don Eduardo's Linda Vista. The company was to provide equipment and trophies to be awarded at a company-sponsored fiesta at the end of the season.

At first Dr. Gomez was reluctant to implement the proposal, for it would relax the rigid divisions that he believed accounted for a large part of the success his staff had achieved in rationalizing the factory's production. He believed that his staff had accomplished a great deal in redesigning the flow of work and in standardizing jobs, but he thought that more needed to be accomplished. He hesitated before putting a doctor in any position that would make it difficult for him to take actions that would disrupt established work routines and displease workers. Dr. Gomez was also convinced that the old patronal style of leadership was doomed but that even some of the most dedicated doctores had a hidden desire to return to the old ways. He did not wish to undermine the "objectivity" they had achieved at so much cost by relating to workers on the basis of measurements of performance. A football league with teams on which both managers and workers played would initiate new styles of encounters between members of the two groups.

Dr. Gomez was more optimistic about the workers' reactions to changes than he had been a few years earlier. He was encouraged by the number of young workers who participated for the first time in the recent fiesta. I also learned later that he and his staff believed that the first draft of my report on my observations, which he circulated among them, was critical of the doctores for not associating on a friendly basis with the workers.

The doctores discussed the proposal at some length in their own ranks. Those who supported it believed that it would help develop company spirit, improve communications, and strengthen the identification of workers with the company as distinct from the patrones to whom the workers had previously given their loyalty. Don Paco opposed the plan on the grounds that it would have limited appeal and would generate only a small response. Finally, the doctores presented the plan to a group of supervisors and workers. They need not have bothered. The group, which included Arturo and La Montaña, sat respectfully throughout the presentation. Then Arturo, the football devotee, founder and first captain of the factory team, responded for the delegation, wagging his finger in the Latin signal of disapproval. "No," he retorted, and—note the pronoun—"futbol es de nosotros" (football is ours).

The spontaneity and abruptness of Arturo's rejection indicated that the proposal touched an important nerve in the social life of La Blanca's industrial community. The doctores, in the position of negligent fathers who found that their adolescent sons did not wish to attend the circus with them, were astounded. Arturo, for his part, recognized that the football team and its principal supporters represented a social nexus that both expressed and contained the multiple patterns that had developed in the plant since the traditional ones had been withdrawn. They were not about to surrender this to control by the doctores, however well intentioned they might be. The workers did not want to revert to a patronal system in a modernized form. To underscore the point, the members of the football team canceled all games scheduled for the upcoming season. There was no football in La Blanca for one full year.

Once the point had been made, it was unnecessary to make it a second time. A year after the rejection of the proposal, a delegation headed by Arturo appeared in Dr. Gomez's office. "Now we are ready to go ahead with the football league," they told him. The playing field was soon leveled and the teams recruited. All sorts of people volunteered to play, including sad-faced Zambariffi, who had previously been considered too small, and fathers of large families, previously considered too old and heavy. The members of Don Paco's social committee declined to participate, despite much chiding, as did the aislados in the plate room. The candidatos trailed along. Competition by the old single factory team attracted only a handful of fans, but games of the new league—there were two each Sunday afternoon—were well attended. One of the teams made up of doctores and office employees was called the Punta Negra, literally "Black Point." The spectators seemed to get special pleasure out of hooting at the doctores' mistakes, applauding their successes, and seeing them, when the game ended, locked in hearty *abrazos* with the workers, something that could not have happened even a few years earlier. A team made up of the best futbolistas represented the factory in matches with teams from other factories and towns. A fiesta was held at the end of the season at a local tavern, where the outstanding players and teams received trophies. Arturo told me, "The doctores used to walk around with faces like Perón. No more!"

Subsequent Events

The factory's football league lasted for only three seasons, but it made its point. Arturo was promoted to the post of chief of social welfare for the plant. In this position he shifted attention from football to basketball, organizing both a women's and a men's league. He also moved the action out of the factory and into the community by establishing volunteer social action groups that built a school, planted gardens, and conducted evening courses. Workers from the factory organized the groups that carried out these projects and encouraged others from the town to participate in them. These activities ensured that the new behavior patterns spread throughout the village.

In addition, Arturo's football companions—El Policio, for example—began to replace the older pájaros as the ones who received promotion to the rank of supervisor when openings were available. Don Paco withdrew to the more technical aspects of personnel administration in the factory, and the plant social committee became more a ritualistic tribute to things remembered than an effective force in its own right. It eventually ceased to exist.

When I last visited Arturo, I wondered if the wheel had come full circle, for after ten years the former revolutionary had become surprisingly conservative. My visit came at the time of the annual fiesta in honor of the factory saint. Arturo was in charge of the festivities, which honored Don Paco; several doctores, veterans of the plate-room wars but no longer active in the factory, provided the symbolic centrality.

Two other events of some significance occurred during this later period. First, a number of doctores decided to buy a large plot of land on the edge of town and to construct their homes there. The possibility of their presence in the community being confused with that of the patrones no longer existed. Their own identity was established and accepted.

The second occurrence had equally interesting undertones. The patrones decided to donate Linda Vista to a religious order that was interested in training rural leaders. The light finally went out in Don Eduardo's cupola. Old Fusto, who had tried to maintain the empty rooms, was bought a house by the plaza. It hurt him even to look up toward the bluff by the canyon's mouth.

I had the occasion to walk down the road that leads past Linda Vista and circles under what had been the center of the social values that at one time had controlled village life. I was looking for a bus to take me to the city. Arturo's son, a perceptive lad of ten—his mother had counted his age in months when my study began—came along to carry my bag. I asked, "Who lives in that big house up on the bluff?" He replied, "The priests." I pursued the matter, "Didn't anyone else ever live in that big house?" "No," he reported, "the priests have always been there."

The postpatronal interlude at La Blanca thus featured both clear breaks among the patrones, doctores, and workers and personal pain over the inevitability of these breaks. It is not easy for anyone to endure alienation for one's associates, especially if one is convinced that one has a special contribution to make. One feels cheated when the more general appreciation that one considers as one's due is not forthcoming. At La Blanca some became casualties of these breaks and withdrew. Those that remained used the interlude to create among themselves and their leaders the social structures that I have reviewed. Now feeling themselves less welcomed at La Blanca, the patrones shifted their attention to the secondary business ventures they had established in the city. The doctores gave up trying to understand, let alone win over, the workers and occupied themselves with their biblical name-calling fraternity and their professional activities. The workers concerned themselves with the social mechanisms of the plate room.

At some point in time it became apparent that the breaks had positive as well as painful aspects. The longing for the past as represented by the "cult of the patrones" became distant music appropriate to an age that was cherished but over. Although additional changes would undoubtedly occur—Mateo, for example, was likely to become a polisher at an early date—the burst of change that affected behavior in the community as a whole had run its course. A new stage of toleration and acceptance took root and was supported by durable social apparatus. As the structural integrity of each group ripened and set, the threat that they might be overturned or undone diminished, for who really wanted to go back?

In this connection, it is fair to ask whether the changes at La Blanca were away from one form of dependence, patronalism, toward independence or toward paternalism, another form of dependence. If the social welfare programs that Arturo instituted grew in influence, the community might come to be dominated by company values and interests. My view was that the changes toward independence were sufficiently well established before Arturo's programs began that the risk of their diversion was minimal. Also, Arturo's leadership reduced the danger of paternalistic dependence. When he rejected the doctores' proposal to establish a football league, he showed that he understood that it was important to the workers that their activities and values be respected by management. But because his understanding was intuitive and implicit and therefore without conceptual support, it is necessary to raise the question, even though its answer is beyond the scope of my research.

The Plate Makers' Society as a Whole

The measures that the plate makers contrived for governing their affairs in the postpatronal era incorporated a range of personal orientation more varied than the patrones had known.[4] At the heart of their new system of governance was a code that specified the essentials of good citizenship: how much work a man should turn out, and how he should relate to his neighbors, to women, to new arrivals from the country, to older citizens, and to visitors. The elements of the code were not stated systematically or explicitly, but each worker carried them within himself, learning by personal experience and by observation how the group dealt with infractions. The newcomer learned, as his work station oscillated between nucleados and aislados, that observance of the code resulted in place and position consonant with his social standing and the servicing of his personal needs. He also learned that infraction brought public rebuke and punishment.

The system of governance included a clearly defined and easily accessible leadership structure, with the senior and most respected member of the group, La Montaña, symbolizing its principal values and with Zambariffi acting as its agent of internal communication.

The doctores, locked into their narrow perspectives, did not sense the plate room's codes or trace the subtle restrictions that the codes placed on the plate makers' behavior. They tended to interpret any behavior of the workers not covered by Taylorist premises as random manifestations of perversity. One of the doctores told me, "As individuals the workers are great people; but as a group, impossible. If I ask one of them to do something, he'll be very helpful; but if I make an appeal to the group, I get irrational responses."

How different was this world from the fictions of the Taylorists and the intellectuals in which the wisdom of the day customarily wrapped it! One day toward the end of my visits to La Blanca, I slipped away from a boisterous despedida that showed no signs of abating. I crossed the plaza to the factory and went through the aisle of machines to the plate-making room. It was Sunday and the plant had the haunted mood of an empty cathedral, a theater after hours, or other temporarily unoccupied sites of human congregation. At such times the solitary visitor is alone with his thoughts and sees, as though for the first time, the half-remembered outlines of physical objects standing on their own and not merely as the backdrop for human association. Yet it was human association that gave these objects their special character. I went over to the machine used by Nicanor, the big gentle La Montaña. It was on this machine that I had tried my hand one day at the intricate skill of potting, so that Adolfo, Nicanor's polisher, drawing on his considerable talents as an actor, could loudly reject the pieces that I turned out, to the great amusement of the workers. Across the way, Pedro had raffled off a hen on a Saturday at noon. And at the end of the floor, one of the workers operated a small store during work breaks, selling biscuits, cheese, bread, and cold drinks, and endured the sharp-tongued teasing of his young customers. Today he would have caught the early truck up to his parents' village to take them groceries, as he did each Sunday. This was the gap in communication that Arturo bridged, with the result that there were effective channels of communication between the doctores and the workers in the plate room through Arturo, La Montaña, and Zambariffi.

Among these machines, willing Bertulfo had wordlessly courted shy Teresa. Young Guillermo, the high school graduate the doctores had hired from the city as assistant supervisor, had tried without success to establish rapport with the village people. El Cachaco they called him, an unflattering designation used historically for dandies who had come from Spain.

"You have to love the factory. It has to be like a family for you or you don't succeed," Arturo told me. Now that my days in this setting were running out, I had some sense of what he meant.

The patterns of behavior that I observed in the plate room showed how the workers held in check the forces from outside the department that could easily have disrupted their society. The accommodations that they developed allowed them to maintain the values important to them and also to meet the production needs of the factory.

Some Preliminary Findings

By the time I had finished the intensive periods of my fieldwork at Santuario and La Blanca, I believed that I had answers to at least some of the questions with which I started my research as well as some new questions about how social change develops.

First, the intellectuals' view of workers as automatons who were faceless in their alienation was wrong. The workers whom I met at both Santuario and La Blanca were richly human with romantic and tragic personal histories and experiences to match those found in literature. This was so even at La Blanca, where initial impressions were to the contrary. Once I pierced the veil that protected their privacy from intrusion by casual visitors and misunderstanding managers, the social richness of the workers' small society was fully apparent.

Second, the Taylorists were wrong or at least not entirely right. Rational patterns of behavior were apparent among the workers but so were nonrational, nonlogical social patterns. To restrict attention to the first was to perpetuate the error of the Taylorists and other intellectuals, namely, that the actual behavior of workers was the same as the intellectuals' views of it. On the contrary, I found rich, though small, communities developing around workplace encounters at both Santuario and La Blanca. That these communities were unexpected in both management theory and philosophy underscored their importance and the ingenuity of those who created them.

The social structures of these societies solved a number of important problems for their members. They were sturdy yet fragile creations. They developed fortuitously, without explicit attention or conscious understanding of how they formed and functioned. Once formed, their influence was pervasive and their members fought for their survival. In the absence of understanding, they needed time to consolidate. That, as I understood it, was what happened at La Blanca during the year in which there was no football. During that period the structure of the society in the plate room was consolidated and strengthened to the point where its members were willing to risk their new behavior patterns in the wider community.

I had not expected that these societies would develop such complex patterns of membership and leadership nor that they would solve such a variety of problems. Even less had I expected that they would be the initial sites for structural change in their communities. What I found was that, once new behavior patterns were established at work, they led to changes of behavior in the plazas and recreational activities in each community as a whole. At La Blanca, as at Santuario, it was the workers who carried these new behavior patterns into the community. The formal personnel programs of the company, eventually under the direction of Arturo, supported the spread of these patterns of providing an organized framework for them. This formal support helped consolidate in the community changes that began among the workers in the plate room.

The differences in the character of these groups before and after the changes raise interesting questions about what is transformed when social change occurs. Among the potters at Santuario, as among the plate makers at La Blanca, the changes were not in the population of individuals in the room but in the values that governed their behavior. That is, when Ramiro, Héctor, and Atilio went to see Don José about the incentive rates, the change was different from what would have happened if, let us say, Don Noah had retired and Don Pablo had succeeded him as the most highly respected person there. That change would have been a change of the elements *within* the system without a change *of* the system as a whole.[5] Both Don Noah and Don Pablo, different though they were as individuals, represented the same social values: respect for tradition, age, and unchanging ways of doing things and belief in fixed destinies. The action of Ramiro, Héctor and Atilio, on the other hand, symbolized a different distribution of values in the potting room and the emergence of a different orientation toward work and life; young persons were allowed to act in ways that they themselves decided. Thus the changes were in the values that governed how the potters related to each other, to their leaders, and to their society as a whole.[6] Clearly these were significant changes to the individuals who participated in them, and they are important for students of social change to understand.

In this connection it is worth noting that some students consider behavior at this level of intimate, interpersonal relations to be relatively stable and less subject to change than at other levels, even in such all-encompassing processes of change as those of social revolutions. In his classic study, Brinton wrote that the effects of revolutions "seem slightest" with respect to "the social arrangements that most intimately and immediately touch the average man. . . . The grand attempts at reform . . . try to alter John Jones' relations with his wife, his children, try to give him a new religion, new personal habits. . . . [I]n the end John Jones stands on [these] matters about where he stood when the revolution began."[7] In contrast, the changes at Santuario and at La Blanca affected behavior at this interpersonal level, including changes in the relations among workers as colleagues, between fathers and their sons, and between workers and their managers. These changes thus presaged important questions about the relationships between individuals and their societies.

Homans addressed these questions by contrasting the social contract theory of Hobbes, in which individuals are considered primary and society is viewed as the resultant of their characteristics, with Durkheim's social mold theory that emphasizes society's role in forming individuals, "like a mold forced over hot metal." Homans wrote[8] that the social contract theory emphasized "(a) . . . certain characteristics of mind and certain sentiments (needs) [that an individual brings to his group]. These sentiments are at once biologically inherited and socially instilled. (b) His group has a method of cooperation for satisfying these sentiments, which makes natural and appropriate certain forms of behavior in certain situations. (c) But while these forms of behavior may be natural and appropriate, the group has also reached the idea that they *ought* and *must* be adopted in these situations. (d) If an individual does not behave in these ways, the relationships in the group are such that he will be punished. Moreover, the norms, or if we prefer, the culture, will be taught to new members of the society, which brings us back to statement (a), that the needs of an individual are at once biologically inherited and socially instilled. . . . The social contract theory emphasized (a) and (b); Durkheim with his social mold theory emphasized (c) and (d)."

Certainly both the impulses of individuals and the expectations of groups were present at Santuario and La Blanca, but during the period of my visits their communities became more like the ones described by the social contract theory of Hobbes and less like the ones described by the social mold theory of Durkheim than they had been in the past. The changes that occurred were in the direction of giving individuals, particularly younger ones, opportunities to make choices—contracts in Hobbes's and Homans's terminology— that had not been available to earlier generations. At La Blanca, for example, the opportunity that the candidatos had to experience the lifestyles of the nucleados and of the aislados before making their own commitments had not been available previously. Santuario certainly had its isolates, such as Marco Antonio Sanchez, but his isolation was a matter of destiny—or so he and the community believed—not a matter of his choosing to live differently from others in his group. Indeed, he desperately wanted to live as they did. In contrast, at La Blanca Roberto and Pedro, the students who were preparing themselves for office work in Medellín, made the choice themselves to work as aislados and thus to make the kinds of social contracts with their colleagues and supervisors that that role implied.

Having the opportunity to make one's own social contracts did not of course guarantee that that individual would get his choice: Luis, the oldest aislado, who aspired to be a supervisor but failed to be promoted and then longed for the earlier days, was an example of such an individual. But Luis accepted as a personal responsibility, not as a matter of destiny, both that he had had the aspiration and that he had failed. "Once I aspired to be a supervisor," he told me, but "I've lost the knack [of dealing with people]." He did not say, "Being a supervisor was not my destiny" or "My destiny was against me."

At Santuario Ramiro, Héctor, and Atilio created similar opportunities for themselves and the other potters to work out new social contracts and ways of behaving with each other and with their leaders when they formed a junta to negotiate new wage rates. Eventually the changes in the potters' social contracts with each other and with Don José spread through football games and in other ways to affect behavior in most sectors of the town.

At La Blanca the process had gone so far that workers, doctores, and patrones had different expectations of each other and behaved and lived differently than they had before. The doctores moved to La Blanca and the patrones to Medellín.

The social changes that I witnessed at Santuario and at La Blanca thus increased the opportunities that individuals had to make contracts with each other through their behavior in ways that they chose, in contrast to their society molding their behavior by assigning their positions on the basis of an ascribed destiny inherited from a distant past. It became socially appropriate for younger persons to do things differently from older ones.

The changes were especially noticeable in relations of authority— between fathers and sons, patrones and workers, leaders and followers. The effectiveness of the leaders' actions was not independent of their organizational setting nor solely determined by the leader's charisma or by his position in the hierarchy. Rather their effectiveness depended on their acceptance by those to whom they were addressed. At Santuario, many people participated in these acts, which were diffused and scattered throughout the group. In contrast, at La Blanca the roles were specialized among individuals. La Montaña symbolized the social values of the group; Zambariffi acted as the agent of internal communication; and Arturo, the accommodative formal leader, saw to it that the values of the workers' social organization meshed with the doctores' values and vice versa.

As a result of these observations, my interest was clearly centered on a set of questions about how structural change occurs in a society. Rather than being a gradual and continuous process, my observations showed that structural change at Santuario and at La Blanca occurred in rapid bursts over fairly short periods of time. Furthermore, my observations showed that the members of a group as well as its leaders helped to establish the conditions that supported structural change and made it permanent. I wanted to study the processes of change—including relations among members of groups and those between followers and leaders—in a situation in which the process had begun earlier and lasted longer and in which the movement from a traditional to a modern society could be expected to have gone further than it had at either Santuario or La Blanca. For this purpose a site in Medellín seemed ideal. Although adjacent to both Santuario and La Blanca, technological change had started earlier there. At the time of my visits, Medellín was an industrialized, cosmopolitan city. I continued my reasearch there eagerly, though hardly prepared, it turned out, for the contrasts that I found.

The factory (right) at La Blanca.

Market day at the La Blanca plaza.

Delivering breakfast to La Blanca workers.

Distributing milk at the company store at La Blanca.

A group of La Blanca doctores in a relaxed mood.

Inspectors at La Blanca.

A potter making a dish at La Blanca.

A polisher sponging a plate at La Blanca.

Zambariffi, La Blanca potter.

Nicanor (La Montaña), La Blanca potter.

Work in the La Blanca plate room.

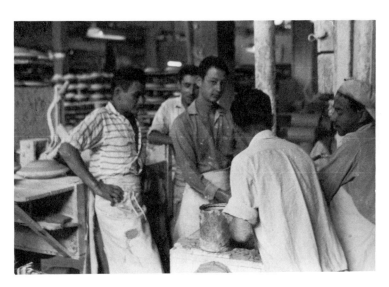

Los fogones at La Blanca.

Una vieja at La Blanca.

Arturo, supervisor of the plate room at
La Blanca.

The La Blanca factory football team.

III

El Dandy: A Time of Conflict

9

Dr. Medina's Dream for El Dandy

Medellín stretches along the length of a cool mountain valley. Coming from La Blanca, the traveler approaches it over a high mountain lip, fragrant with flowers. If the day is as clear as it usually is, greens, blues, and adobe whites predominate. Jet airplanes land on the other side of the valley. There are tall office buildings and a divided highway lined with modern factories that manufacture machinery, chemicals, and textiles. The city encompasses all the joys and miseries, Marxism and mysticism, conflicts and collaborations of any center of large organizations.

In Colombia rural banditry of obscure origins added to the problems that accompany rapid industrialization.[1] The banditry was especially violent between 1948 and 1953, though its activity was not limited to those years. It pushed the plight of many village families beyond tolerable limits and sent waves of displaced youngsters to the cities. Antioquia escaped the full force of this massive bloodletting and might have avoided its consequences almost entirely, but for the development of its transportation facilities. The same roads and rails that took its goods out brought elements of social unsettlement into Antioquia. Each train and truck that labored through the canyons and across the mountains to the marketplace of Medellín came equipped with a human complement of refugees: youngsters aged 12 to 20, each carrying a small bundle of clothes, on the run from villages that could no longer support them psychologically or economically. Around the depot in the center of the commercial area, there emerged a community espousing an amalgam of values such as the region had not previously

seen. It was populated principally by footloose vagabonds who traveled from city to city as the spirit moved them. Here blacks from
the coast mixed with Indians from the cool savanna and with
youngsters from Antioquia's many Santuarios.

Life in this city within a city required little of those who lived
there. There was always company, ways to pass the time, food, and
one's group to defend in return for the protection from outsiders.
The center had its own social structure and methods for admitting
new arrivals. When the train arrived at night after its long trip from
the river, it brought a cargo of boys who were fleeing from home
with no preparation for city life and no place to go.[2] The leaders
of the street gangs (sometimes called Fagin gangs after the Fagin
who organized boys into groups of petty thieves and pickpockets
in Charles Dickens's Oliver Twist[3]) and the madams from the houses
of prostitution went to the station to look over the new arrivals
and to offer temporary arrangements to the more promising. The
others found places to sleep in the parks or on the streets and
eventually, if they were lucky, some niche in the complex web of
the city. Members of the leading families had the boys collected
from time to time and deposited in juvenile homes, but the boys
found life there boring and soon returned to their own way of life.

A rich cast of characters peopled Medellín's drama of the night:
drunks, prostitutes, cripples, bewildered waifs, locos, police who
patrolled in pairs, knife artists, and drug addicts who stumbled or
strutted on the stage. The wide-eyed country boy entered this world
through his Fagin gang. Sometimes he sat by a tavern table while
his seniors exchanged tales of intrigue and views of the decent
world, the "outside" society beyond the center's immediate
perimeter.

The leader of a gang was a young adult of perhaps 20 years.
Having an apprentice or a helper to run errands gave him a certain
prestige; if he could hold several or even half a dozen, so much
the better. The members of these gangs sold magazines, newspapers,
and marijuana, shined shoes, and committed petty thefts. Belonging
to a gang was transitory, but the arrangement provided a home and
some security for the migrant who joined. The leader had a room
without windows in a flophouse and a bed where two or more
people could sleep. A new member was provided with a shoeshine
box and a companion. He delivered his earnings to the leader but
received enough to eat, to go to the movies, and later to buy mari-

juana. If the police arrested him, the leader tried to arrange his release. If his parents came in search of him, he would be alerted, hidden, even spirited off to another city, thus maintaining a way of life from which there were few exits. With luck a boy might find a cobbler, a trucker, or a tailor who would reclaim him for society by apprenticing him to his trade. The other exits were the prison and the morgue. The central part of Medellín had no senior citizens.

If the youngster was fortunate, he drifted into a chulu (street tailor shop) and gained tentative acceptance as an apprentice. This too was an emotion-filled experience. At first, the boy ran errands, carried lunch pails, swept out the shop, and slept at night on a table in a room behind the shop. He did not receive a salary, but his companions shared their meals and cigarettes with him. His maestro might give him a few pesos at the end of the week, more as a sign of affection than as compensation.

These shops at one time produced most of the men's clothing sold in the city. They had no fixed hours. Monday was sometimes a day of rest after too many weekend hours spent in a tavern, but when a maestro had promised a suit to a client, a worker might stay until the early hours of the morning. The men worked in a circle, smoking as they sewed. Their conversation was intermittent but wide-ranging, tuned to the rhythm of their stitching and the movement of anyone who entered the shop. It also defined a view of life that exerted a strong influence on the group.

A youngster entered this small circle fresh from the traumatic break with his home and his village. He had first immersed himself in the pleasures of the city streets, and once apprenticed, only the most tentative bonds separated him from the excitement of that life. A few feet away, plainly visible through the open front of the shop, lay the brash spectacle of a Medellín street, which beckoned him. He also knew that a second break would mark him as a refugee forever, working out his brief destiny in one or another of his country's several large cities. A strong mutual affection was needed to keep him in the shop during the long, tedious hours and years that an apprenticeship required. Most maestros appreciated their boys' unspoken dilemma. They were also skilled in its resolution. They used the group's easy joshing as counterpoint for their own gentle ploys to move the boys into the world of work and discipline.

An apprentice held the lowest place in the work group and was the target of jokes and pranks. If he responded with good humor and respect, he would one day be allowed to hold a piece of cloth on which a tailor was working. Then he might be given a cutting to trim. Later he would get a chance to make a cutting from a bolt of cloth by following a pattern a senior tailor chalked for him. Sewing the cuttings into a pair of trousers was the high point of an apprentice's preparation. Making a coat, including the difficult business of hanging the sleeves on the body of the jacket, was reserved for a *sastre completo* (master tailor). The technical preparation required to enter the tailoring fraternity sometimes consumed ten years of a man's life.

In later life an apprentice did not forget his maestro. One tailor told me, "Sometimes I go back to help my maestro with a jacket, and sometimes I just go back to see him." He invited me to accompany him on his next visit. The affection that he held for his maestro and with which he greeted him was apparent when he introduced me.

Life in other parts of the city was different—for some, very different—from that in the center. But for all the center was an ever-present reminder of the precariousness of their own existence. The barrios, where workers such as the tailors lived, were on the outskirts of the city. They were composed mainly of row houses with eight to twelve children in many of them. Few families had money for recreation or entertainment, not even for buying drinks, except when *machismo* required. Many of the children did not complete grammar school. The few vacancies available in the high schools went to children of the most aggressive parents. To get one of these openings a father had to take valuable time off from his work to make the rounds of the schools, medical clinics, and other government bureaus from which it was necessary to get papers in order to enroll a child in a high school. A worker who had taken the day off and put on his best Sunday suit to visit such a school felt uncomfortable while he waited outside the director's office, sometimes for hours, to establish his boy's credentials, something a father who was better off could do casually in the course of a social function or a business contact.

The children of working-class families who did not go to high school supplemented the family income by selling lottery tickets and newspapers on the streets. As a result, the father who managed to get his boy admitted to a high school deprived his family of income that neighbors with working children received. And from his street contacts a boy soon learned values other than the strict and disciplined ones that he had been taught at home.

These circumstances accentuated the conflicts that in any case were likely to develop between adolescent children and their parents. Working-class fathers, burdened and harassed by economic problems, placed their hopes for lifting their families up the social ladder on their sons, who had to earn money or get an education. The sons, as the fathers well knew, could escape these pressures and lead their own lives, protected even from parents who came looking for them, by going to the center of the city to join the young people who were arriving from the country. Fathers and sons were reminded of this refuge every day by reports in the newspapers and on the radio, both of which provided free public service announcements of missing sons. Families took advantage of the service to exaggerate their stories and strengthen their petitions to their wandering children: "José Mario, 16 years of age, ran away from home two weeks ago. It is urgent that he return. His mother suffered a nervous breakdown as a result of his leaving and will recover only if he returns to his place in his family."

Thus for the parents of working-class families, the central part of Medellín was a heartsore. Even as they policed their homes with strict disciplinary ethics, the radio brought them the distraught appeals of other parents who had policed too well. For their sons the center of Medellín was an option to be exercised if life pressed too hard, a sanctuary into which escape was possible if family discipline passed tolerable limits. The sons knew that they could find in the center new dimensions of adventure and community. Life might be short, but it would never be dull.

The residences of the successful professional and business men in Medellín overlooked the rest of the city from high in the mountains, where the wealthy had created their own luxurious surroundings and private clubs, schools, and values. They dedicated themselves to graceful living and the arts and maintained uninterrupted connections with the outside world by traveling, reading contemporary literature, and sending their children to foreign schools and universities. They had only egocentric and stereotyped views, based on their own values, of the city center and the workers' barrios, just as those who lived in those sections held stereotyped views of the upper class. The residents of the different sections lived by themselves without direct knowledge of the other parts. An industrialist told me, "I have never entered the central part of Medellín, not even during the day." He finally agreed as a gesture of hospitality to accompany me on a visit but only after he had removed his jewelry and borrowed a handgun for the occasion.

He need not have been concerned, for the leaders of the Fagin gangs and the madams wanted nothing but to be left alone. The threat that they posed lay not in any initiatives they might take but in how their neighbors perceived them. Their values showed from time to time in the radical politics of student and union activities and reached the city's factories through the workers.

The industrial community was ill prepared to respond to these values. Some industrial leaders denied that any threat existed. Others sought to isolate the dangers by increasing security around their compounds and country clubs in the hills. Religious schools in particular became sensitive about accepting applicants other than those from the city's best families and devised subtle methods of eliminating others. At some schools it became necessary to pay a year's tuition in advance; at others bonds for the school's development programs had to be purchased.

But the industrialists could not insulate the people who worked in the factories. The sensitivities they acquired through their exposure to life in the city, together with their hopes and dreams for escaping the precariousness of their existence, came with them to work.

Dr. Medina's Dream for El Dandy

Dr. Manuel Medina, chief executive of El Dandy, a textile and garment factory that manufactured both cloth and men's suits, was unusual among the industrialists of the city. He spent his boyhood on La Blanca's quiet plaza and attended one of the better high schools in Medellín. He graduated with honors in civil engineering from a university located a stone's throw from the site where he later built his plant.

Regional custom dictated that outstanding young men enter either the church or a manufacturing enterprise; Dr. Medina chose the latter. He took up his vocation with fervor and rapidly advanced to a management position with a textile company. Just before his thirtieth birthday, some 20 years before my visits, he was invited to take over the management of El Dandy.

Dr. Medina maintained his home on the central plaza of Medellín, where his family was exposed to the rhythms of the streets and the throb of urban reality. He opted for local university training for his sons and offered his services as an occasional lecturer. As the confrontation deepened between the old values and the new, he began to take part in the activities of the national association of industries and the Catholic employers' society. The government granted him internationally recognized awards and honors for national service. He knew, nevertheless, that the critical encounters were not taking place in these activities. "Our social problems will be solved on the factory floor," he told me, "if they are to be solved at all."

No patrón, Dr. Medina preferred the professional title of *doctor* to the honorific one of *don*. He considered his role in presiding over the consolidation and expansion of El Dandy to be the greatest achievement of his life. He proudly escorted visitors through the plant. His own office was a cynosure of Latin taste and restrained elegance, decorated with local sculpture and paintings, a rich setting for a pleasant chat over black coffee served in the best La Blanca porcelain. When he arrived at the plant, Dr. Medina usually puttered for a few minutes in the orchid gardens through which the workers entered the factory. Dr. Medina himself designed these gardens with an eye to "raising the sights and comforting the spirits of a sad worker who arrives here depressed from his unhappy and gloomy environment." On one occasion when Dr. Medina was working in the garden, a delivery truck carelessly grazed a tree as it rounded a corner. He called to the driver, "Take it easy! No one is going to destroy what I have created."

Dr. Medina's dream ws to create an efficient and just industrial society in which the best of the new could be married with the best of the old. "To sow the Christian seed of understanding," he once wrote, "we have undertaken the extraordinary adventure of creating a climate of peace where we might build a perfect company, the company we all dream of some day being associated with, a comnpany molded by our aspirations." He almost succeeded.

Products and Management Organization

El Dandy was established in 1944 to manufacture men's garments— heavy- and lightweight woolen and gabardine suits, sport jackets, and slacks in a variety of styles. It was an offshoot of an older firm that made woolen textiles, and it represented the first serious attempt in Colombia to manufacture men's wear on a mass-production basis. Previously the market had been supplied by a number of small plants and by the chulus in the city's center. Dr. Medina rapidly brought El Dandy to the forefront of the industry, and the company came to provide nearly half of the ready-made suits sold in the national market. Its competition was with the chulus, not the small factories. It soon took the lead from the chulus as well, many of which were customers of the company's cloth-making division.

In 1953 El Dandy's cloth- and garment-manufacturing operations, which until then had been carried out at separate sites in the city, were combined at one location in the suburbs in a large, modern, one-story factory surrounded by lawns, gardens, and fountains. Each division of the company had its own section of the building and its own work force, supervisory personnel, and superintendent. The divisions shared other administrative functions, including engineering, maintenance, sales, personnel, and accounting. The company's clinics, store, restaurant, and conference rooms were spacious and well patronized. According to the garment division's fashion designer, Guido Zambretti, the plant was superior to any clothing factory in Europe or in the United States.

At its new location the company turned out 30,000 garments a month, and employment rose to 450 in cloth making and to 1,175 in garment making. The workers in the cloth division, mostly women, were represented by a union that was affiliated with the Catholic church; about half of the workers in the garment division belonged to a large national labor federation that most observers considered to be militant and many to be Marxist. The company provided office space at the plant for both unions.

Dr. Medina retained the services of Guido Zambretti to improve the styling of El Dandy's garments. He was an Italian-American designer of men's clothes and was well known in the United States. At El Dandy, he was known as Mister—not Señor—Zambretti. He told me how his association with the company came about. As he talked, he was fitting a jacket on his assistant in the little room that he used to work out his styling ideas.

"Look at this coat. It's a disgrace. It hurts me to see poor work. People believe I'm a clown or a fool. I can't help it. I can't stand bad work." In a dramatic manner he tore the sleeve from the coat.

"I started to work in a clothes shop when I was 16 years old. My boss discovered that I was enthusiastic about my work, and I started to rise in the business. When I was 21, I had 11 others working under me, but I did my share, working at their side. At night I studied designing in my room.

"When I came here, I would stand on street corners and look at the clothes the passersby were wearing: pants with cuffs like bells, coats that came halfway to the knee, shoulder pads three inches thick. Then I traveled around the country, urging them to change their clothing habits. How I suffered in those small-town hotels with the hard beds, the lice, with no good bread or spaghetti! But the new styles started to catch on. We raised prices, we increased wages, we built this beautiful new factory. There is no factory like it in the United States or in Europe. The clothing industry in the United States and Europe is a disgrace. The tailors work so close to each other that they have to work their needles up and down instead of sideways." He demonstrated.

"But who is going to replace me when I am gone? I can't inject my enthusiasm into my assistants. One has to be born with it. I try to teach them how to wait on customers, to make them feel important, to do it in such a way that the tailor's special ability is not diminished."

In retaining Mr. Zambretti's services, El Dandy gained more than a style consultant. The company employed experienced tailors directly from the chulus rather than providing training, and when a tailor first came to El Dandy, Mr. Zambretti helped him to make the difficult transition from the easy informality of the chulus to the structured world of rationalized production. One of the tailors told me how he resolved the dilemma: "At first the supervisors tried to push me, but I am an independent type and too old to be scolded. Now I work in a way that does not attract attention. I work slowly, but the inspectors never return a jacket that I have sewn. This way I demand and get good treatment." Mr. Zambretti's presence provided a backdrop for such resolutions, an effective symbol of the world the tailors had come from.

Dr. Medina also cultivated the technological efficiency of the production activities at El Dandy. He insisted that his staff make every effort to keep in touch with new developments in garment manufacture, especially new machinery. In accomplishing this, Dr. Medina was a leader of the modern style who practiced delegation of authority. He avoided direct intervention in his factory's day-to-day affairs, but he was not an aloof or absent chief executive. Although he himself maintained a low profile with his work force and surrendered direct supervision to his production and personnel managers, they knew that he was to be called, even at home, whenever the situation required it.

The superintendents of the plant's two divisions, the technical superintendent, and the manager of standards for the plant as a whole were all graduate engineers, although the personnel manager of the plant, Don Fernando, and the production manager of the garment division, Don Antonio, were not (figure 9.1). Don Antonio, who was single and a hunter and sports fan, devoted a good deal of time to El Dandy's football team and maintained close relations with the players. Don Pépé, his assistant, had been a tailor and had many acquaintances in the plant. Don Antonio and Don Pépé got together every morning to review the progress of work and to make plans for the day. The floor bosses under them in each workshop received these plans and carried them out. Don Pépé and Don Antonio handled most of the specific questions about worker motivation and discipline as they arose.

Dr. Medina wanted something different for El Dandy, not the highly personalistic jockeying for favor that marked many of the local companies, especially during the period when they were outgrowing their patronal origins. Like the patrones at La Blanca, he was convinced that Taylor's system for making decisions, based on standardized work measurements to determine the compensation and advancement of workers, was superior to the subjective judgments of supervisors. He invested heavily in a job standards department to make these measurements possible. He believed most workers wished to dedicate themselves to sustained work in order to take advantage of the earning opportunities that Taylorism gave them. He sought to create a setting in which they would be protected from the chatter and disruption of the idle few. He designed an open plant in which all work areas were clearly visible, and he encouraged his supervisors to be out on the floor to motivate the workers by their presence.

Engineers from the standards department established the standard for an operation by timing a worker with a stopwatch while he performed the operation several times. The average of the times became the standard. When an evaluation was completed, the job

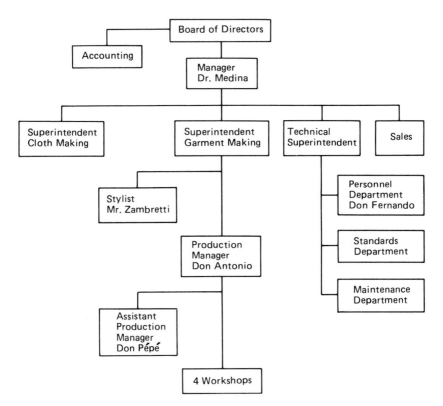

Figure 9.1
Simplified organization chart of the El Dandy factory.

was assigned to one of seven categories on the basis of its difficulty and of the skill required to carry it out. The category determined the base rate of pay for the job. The rate for jobs in category 7, the highest in the shop, was the equivalent of $2.50 a day; an assembler, for example, had to produce 38 jackets to receive that wage. When a worker's output exceeded the standard, he or she received additional incentive pay that increased proportionately with output. A committee consisting of the superintendent of the garment division, the production manager (Don Antonio), the manager of the standards department, and a representative of the workers reviewed the results of each study. Other members of the administrative staff attended the meetings when they had knowledge about a specific job.

El Dandy's personnel programs were extensive by the standards of any country.[4] The programs included tuition aid for workers' children at high-school levels, home purchase loans, a medical and dental clinic, training and recreational rooms, a store, and a restaurant for which the company provided a partial subsidy. The company did not have a training program for tailors. Its managers believed that to obtain the volume of quality production that they desired, it was necessary to hire only experienced tailors who were ready to meet company standards at the time of their employment.

Dr. Medina scheduled weekly seminars at which his employees could raise topics that interested them. Those who chose to participate were later invited to his country place for food, drink, and conversation. Once a year he shut down the plant for a week, so that employees could attend spiritual exercises conducted on company premises by local clergy.

In keeping with Dr. Medina's philosophy of not burdening the workers with activities that would divert their attention from production, the company's top executives managed its personnel programs. The only exception was the garment division's store, which was administered by a joint management-union board. It came to be the center of the protracted struggle that brought Dr. Medina into confrontation with his employees. Before describing these events, I need to say what working conditions were like at El Dandy from the garment makers' point of view. To do this, I describe the garment makers and their tasks in workshop A, where the union president, Hugo Soto, and three other members of the union board were employed as tailors.

The Social Organization of Workshop A

Working conditions at El Dandy were relatively pleasant. The building was cool in the morning but warm in the afternoon. Light and air entered through a series of skylights that ran across its roof. In workshop A the only noises were the whir of sewing machines and the hiss of steam escaping from pressing equipment. Men did the hand sewing, women the machine work. Cutters and pressers stood up, tailors and seamstresses sat down. All of them punched a time clock when they arrived in the morning and when they left in the afternoon. They worked a five-day week. Dr. Medina wanted to change to a six-day week to allow time in the afternoons for seminars on subjects such as economics that he felt would enhance the employees' understanding of work. His managers did not agree, however, and he had not pushed the question.

When El Dandy moved to its new site, the production line in the garment division was designed to extend the full length of the building. The workers sat facing each other at long benches and tables, an arrangement not unlike the ones the tailors had known in the chulus, though at El Dandy they were required to leave the work area when they wanted to smoke. Workers could talk with one another easily. Demand for the different products fluctuated throughout the year, but since all the garments were made on one line, an increase or decrease in the production of one type affected the others.

A few months before I began my study, the management decided to rearrange the production line into four areas separated by partitions that reached across the plant floor (figure 10.1). Each in-

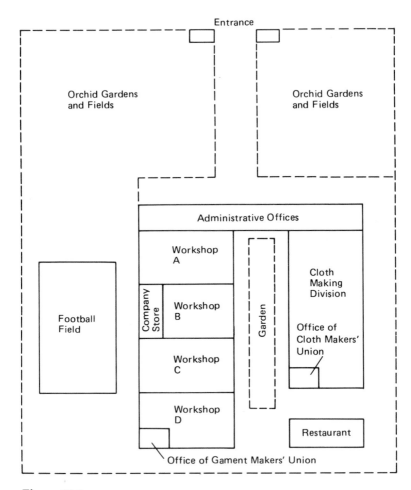

Figure 10.1
Layout of the El Dandy factory.

dependent workshop or department thus established manufactured a single item of apparel. Workers could be added to or taken from a workshop as the market for its products required without affecting the others. The new arrangement thus provided flexibility for management in scheduling production.

At the same time short work tables, separated by an aisle down the middle of the room, replaced the long tables. Under this arrangement workers sat on one side of a table, so that everyone faced in the same direction. As a result, a worker could talk easily only with the persons on each side of him. Don Antonio pointed out that the new arrangement helped eliminate the temptation of constant chatter.

The garment makers learned of the impending rearrangement just before they left for their two-week Christmas holidays. When they returned, each found a neatly lettered card with his name on it at his new work station. Some workers were upset that members of the groups with whom they had previously worked and with whom they had become friendly had been dispersed to other locations in the room. A few complained to management, but their complaints were not acknowledged. Indeed, the garment makers received no further communications from management about the reorganization. Output sagged for a time, but by the time I started my research in workshop A, it had recovered to its previous level. Management believed that they gained from the reorganization the flexibility in scheduling that they desired.

Workshop A (figure 10.2) was bounded on two sides by exterior walls and on a third side by the partition that separated it from workshop B. Along the remaining wall were the production manager's office and the locker and shower rooms. Workshop A's shrine and altar were located between the office and the locker room.

The initial task carried out in workshop A, where men's lightweight suits were the principal product, was finish cutting. A finish cutter trimmed excess cloth from the cuttings for a jacket's body and sleeves. The cuttings were produced in bulk in a room apart from the workshop's main area. Although finish cutting was considered tailor's work, it required less skill than the other tasks the tailors performed. In a chulu an apprentice was often assigned to finish cutting before he was given work as a cutter or trouser maker. Nevertheless, senior men liked the work. Even though they stood up and were thus more visible than most of the other workers in

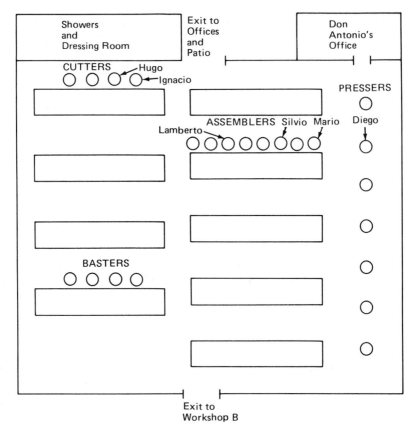

Figure 10.2
Layout of workshop A at El Dandy. Circles indicate work locations.

the room, they said that there was less pressure on them and that they found it less tiring than the other jobs. A cutter could work ahead and then take a break. Furthermore, there were no hot presses at their table to interrupt conversations; neither did they have to lean over a low tailor's stool to converse with someone else.

The trimmed cuttings, tied in packets, went next to women who did preliminary stitching by machine before the next step, which was called shoulder basting. Basting was done by men, who stitched together the pieces for the sleeves and the bodies of the jackets. Special skill was needed to make the sleeves hang in proper alignment. This operation and the final assembly of sleeves and jackets determined a garment's finished appearance. The basters sat on small stools, bent over their work, which they held on their knees. The low table in front of them held bundles of jackets, needles, and thread.

After basting, the garments were taken to the center of the room for an intermediate pressing, which facilitated subsequent operations. This operation was done by women. Then seamstresses undertook the final machine stitching, which consisted of sewing collars, lapels, buttonholes, and hems.

The next task, known as assembly, consisted of adding shoulder padding and doing the final stitching of sleeves and jackets. It was considered skilled work and was done by men who, like the basters, sat on small stools at low tables. The finished jackets were then given a final pressing before being inspected and warehoused. The finish pressers worked at machines that were placed in the aisle at one side of the room.

The remaining space in workshop A was used for making pants, a less-skilled operation, performed entirely by women who worked at sewing machines.

The work of the basters and of the assemblers was more highly valued than the work of the pressers and cutters. Basters' and assemblers' work had job ratings in category 7, pressing was rated in category 4, and cutting in category 3. The work a baster did took less time than the work of an assembler. Thus a baster had to work 6.8 jackets an hour in order to receive incentive pay, whereas an assembler had to work only 3.9 jackets an hour. To balance the production sequence, there were twice as many assemblers as basters. Finish pressing was not considered a basic tailoring skill, and there was no opportunity for pressers to advance in the workshop.

All these tasks were done by men and were considered better than machine sewing, which was done by women. As was typical of their roles in activities outside the home in Colombia at the time, the women did not take much part in departmental activities. Turnover among them was high, and none had more than a few years' service.

Supervision was provided by two floor bosses and two inspectors. These men concerned themselves with the flow of work, production records, and quality control. One floor boss, Pépé, supervised the cutters and basters and the workers who were located on the right-hand side of the room as shown in figure 10.2; the other floor boss supervised the remainder of the workers. Pépé was a tall, soft-spoken, middle-aged individual who had been a tailor all his life. Whenever he was in the shop, he was to be found bending over someone's work station, checking the work in progress. Although most of the workers spoke disdainfully of the supervisors as a group, I heard no negative comments about Pépé. Two floor boys were also assigned to workshop A; they carried packages of materials from one work station to another.

One hundred sixty-eight men and women were employed in workshop A. In view of the limited amount of time that was available to me to make observations in the department, I decided to concentrate my interviews and observations on the men, whom I also visited in their homes. Table B.10 in appendix B gives selected information about them from company records and from my interviews.

The Men and Their Activities at Work

All the men in workshop A, except the pressers, were experienced tailors, but none was a master tailor. Many were the sons of tailors and had trained under relatives or friends at small shops in the city, whereas others had "hung out" as boys around the chulus until a maestro had given them work. All of them knew the central part of the city well, though not necessarily from having had direct experience of it.

In my interviews with and observations of the workers, the men expressed little interest in the work they were doing. Some indicated that they did not think this attitude was right for tailors who worked in a trade that had a long tradition as a skilled craft. I did not hear much conversation about output among them either, but the fact that most of them kept a written record of their output during the day was evidence of its importance to them. Union president Hugo Soto told me, "We should worry more about our output than we do, but we don't. I guess it is of less importance than the other matters with which we have to struggle."

None of the men had anything good to say about the standards program. The pressers especially felt that it was unfair. They said that the texture of some materials made them difficult to work on and that the standards did not take these differences into account.

I was not able to make a detailed study of the output situation in the workshop, although I did record the productivity scores shown in appendix B, table B.10. The men worked hard while it was cool during the morning, from 7 A.M. until lunch time at 10:45 A.M., then slacked off in the afternoon, when it was hot. Even though the day was supposed to end at 5 P.M. some worked until 5:30 or 6:00 to make their quota; some also worked during rest periods for the same reason. I did not hear any resentment about these practices. Some of the men said that they liked to work next to a fast worker, because doing so helped their own pace. One told me, "Some workers are naturally more capable than others, but the less dexterous also have to earn their bread."

Héctor, the high producer among the tailors, discussed his work as a shoulder baster as follows: "The standards people don't appreciate good tailoring. With a little more time I could often improve the appearance of a jacket, but the standards people don't appreciate that kind of work. No one in this department can really judge my work except Mr. Zambretti. The inspectors are trying to impress the management, so that they can be promoted to supervisor. If I bring them a doubtful coat, they say, 'Let it pass, let it pass,' so I pass it. You have to go along, but it preys on my mind. When I feel frustrated from catering to the judgments of other people, I go back to my old shop to talk things over with my maestro, and he helps me.

"I work quickly, and I am the highest producer in our group. When you produce a lot, you are not popular with the others. They criticize you, because you show them up. I avoid friction by coming in late in the morning and after lunch. I take a walk alone in the front park. I take a lot of breaks. Besides, I help the others by making a suit for them once in a while. In this way I keep things under control.

"I can do this in the basters' group, because there are only four of us. It would be harder if I worked with the assemblers. The assemblers are very discreet. There are no high producers among them. Instead, the group is well balanced, so that all the workers produce at the same level. When the workshop was reorganized, I was assigned at first to another workshop, where I worked with three other fast workers. There was always competition, and you worked with one eye on where the next package was coming from. After a few weeks I asked for a transfer, and I was sent here. Things are going better now."

The subjects that interested the men and provided topics of discussion were outside their work and included such matters as football, chess, music, international news, and the unions. With few exceptions these topics were of interest to the members of only one group, so that the topics of conversation as well as work tasks differentiated the groups.

The activities that helped integrate the groups were carried out under the leadership of Silvio and Lamberto, two of the assemblers. They informally organized a mutual help service to assist the workers at times of crisis in their personal and family lives and to pursue complaints and grievances against inspectors and supervisors.

Lamberto pointed out that there were two kinds of people in the department: *los quietos* (the calm ones) and *los inquietos* (the restless ones). He said that los inquietos were city-born and took part in the workshop's activities, whereas los quietos were country-born and did not. My observations bore out his views; I seldom saw any el quieto speaking with more than one other person at a time, whereas the city-born were often active in groups of two or three or even more. Ignacio Porras, who succeeded Hugo Soto as union president, was the exception. Although he was country-born, he was often to be seen engaged with others.

"Actually los quietos, the mountain folk," Lamberto told me, "don't come from the mountains but from the villages. I like to kid Don Alberto [village-born] by telling him that I am going to get him into the union. He knows that I am joking; and he answers me back, saying that we are a bunch of communists. We don't expect these people to take an active part in the union; they are incapable of it.

"The union has to rely on the restless ones. When we find someone who is restless and is a good worker, we propose him for membership in the union. Cheese Face is the most restless of the pressers, but he says that football takes up too much of his time, and he is probably right. The football players try to be useful to their comrades in other ways and thus run a risk with management. Besides, if one of them is injured, he has to quit work and pay for his own treatment. Héctor and Flavio are the most restless of the basters, but they seem interested only in international affairs that do not affect us directly. As the saying goes, 'There are some who want to fight the bull, but only from the stands.' "

The village-born usually spent their nights and weekends with their families, which typically were large. Some of them were working on additions to their homes. Most of them made their children's clothes. On Sundays they took their families for picnics in the fields outside the city. A few had small stalls at the public market, where they sold trinkets of one kind or another. Even so, there seemed to be fewer demands on their time away from work than among the city-born. They never went to the taverns, where the city-born tailors congregated.

From my talks with the workers, I gained the impression that father-son conflicts among the village-born were more intense than those among the city-born. It was as though urban families expected that there would be conflicts, so that when they occurred, they were taken for granted. Reconciliation and return to the family were possibilities not always taken advantage of. If a country-born worker saw his family again, it was his mother he visited; his relation with his father continued strained. One of them told me, "My father tried to prepare me for a life with the soil and in the fields, the only life which he knew. He would not let me learn anything better. He took me out of school to work on the land with him. One day he struck me during an argument. I left the house and lived as a street boy in the city for a while. I started carrying lunch pails for tailors in a chulu. Later they taught me to tailor." Another told me the priest and the mayor in his village had forced him to leave because he was living with a woman without benefit of marriage.

The Finish Cutters

Interactions among the cutters were limited. Hugo Soto, for instance, was often away from the table on union business. He was president of the garment makers' union, a small union that was controversial in the city. It had recently been expelled from its larger parent federation on the grounds that it was communist dominated. Its adherents claimed that it was the only union not subservient to either the Church or the national government. Hugo Soto was also chairman of the committee on propaganda and agitation of the labor federation and one of the workers' representatives on the board that administered the affairs of the company store that the garment makers used. When he was at the table, the workers who came to speak to him came on union business, many of them from outside the workshop. When I first talked with him, he insisted that all the members of the union's board of directors attend our meeting. He spoke of "the class struggle," "the struggle between the exploiters and the exploited," and "the evil designs of capitalist imperialism." Later he told me, "In my business you have to 'make theater' in order to get an audience for your ideas. I may be less a tailor than the others, but I dominate the situation. I write the *Union Bulletin*. Everybody knows where I stand. I don't kid anybody."

When he and I knew each other better, he talked to me about El Dandy and his work as a tailor. "We may be factory workers, but we're also tailors," he told me. "We may not make much money, but we come to work in white shirts and ties, not in overalls. Mr. Zambretti understands this, but the supervisors see him as taking away their authority. They make all kinds of charges against him. It may be true that Mr. Zambretti screams a lot, as Italians will, but he's a good man. When he embarrasses someone, he always comes back later to apologize, sometimes with tears in his eyes."

Hugo Soto was born in Medellín some 40 years earlier. An intense youth not given to the games of the boys on his street, he remembered his father, a construction worker, as a complacent man "without feeling for the large adventure." After a few years of primary school, Hugo apprenticed himself to a tailor and made it as far as *pantelero* (trouser maker) before the army drafted him at the age of 20. Two years of military duty provided him with important new exposure, a sense of mobility, and a belief in his capacity to generate a spirit of camaraderie among his associates. He was a regular attender at nightly meetings at a local tavern, where tailors gathered. He was thought of as a powerful man, not averse to taking advantage of others to get his way.

When he came back to Medellín, he joined the police and became an inspector of gambling establishments. He found that the pay was insufficient to support his growing family, which by the time I knew him numbered nine, some of whom had Russian first names. Twelve years before my visits, he became a cloth cutter at El Dandy.

Hugo Soto said that Ignacio Porras, who worked next to him, was "one of the embittered ones." He thus classified him with los inquietos, even though Ignacio had been born and brought up in a village. His father had been an alcoholic. Gruff but gentle in character, Ignacio told me, "I have an acute sense of social justice. When I find the company treating a fellow worker like an animal, I can't remain quiet. I know that I should, but that's not the way I'm put together."

Hugo's other neighbor at the cutters' table, Favián, was an old friend who had worked with him when he was a policeman. Favián had been the city's chess champion. At one time he had been an officer of the union. Héctor, a baster, sometimes came to the cutters' table to talk about chess with Favián.

The fourth cutter, Roberto, came to El Dandy from a village tailor shop and did not take part in the table's—or for that matter, the department's—nonwork activities.

The Shoulder Basters

The basters were spatially isolated from the rest of the workers. They sat facing the partition that separated workshops A and B with their backs to the rest of the room. During their free moments they read newspapers and discussed international and other affairs not directly connected with their work. Héctor and Flavio, particularly, would get into heated discussions about the news of the day. Both had been members of the football team but had been forced to quit because of injuries. Both avoided participation in union affairs. Sometimes Favián joined them from the cutters' table; and sometimes Héctor, Flavio, and Carmelo visited some of the assemblers and Cheese Face and Eliseo among the pressers. But the basters mostly stayed by themselves, especially Arcesio, who had a lower productivity score and less security than the other three. Arcesio occasionally took long walks by himself through the orchid gardens.

Flavio, a former futbolista who had injured his knee, was a talented singer who had recorded some of his songs commercially. He had tried unsuccessfully to get the company to sponsor a workers' chorus and had come to resent Don Antonio's support of football in general and of Diego in particular. Flavio's father was a well-known musical figure in the city. Flavio presented me with two phonograph recordings of his own vocal solos. Though he was articulate and popular, he had refused opportunities to become an officer of the union.

Carmelo reported that without Flavio's support he could never have survived his transfer to El Dandy from the more relaxed climate of a chulu. He recalled, "The work here was so intense and the inspectors so demanding, that I thought five o'clock would never come. All day I was bent over that little table without an opportunity to straighten up. I was ready to quit after a few weeks, but the men working with me raised my spirits. Flavio said, 'Don't go; we all go through the same thing.' I have a very special regard for Flavio."

The Finish Pressers

Among the pressers, Diego, called Cheese Face, was the most active. He was captain of El Dandy's football team. When he was a boy, there were two professional teams in Medellín that competed actively for the national championship. The boys in his neighborhood formed a team that lasted for many years. Eliseo and Héctor were members of that team. Its trainer worked for El Dandy and helped members of the team get jobs with the company. Later he and Don Antonio founded El Dandy's team with Diego as captain and Eliseo as manager and first aid attendant. He had been asked to serve as an officer of the union but declined because he preferred to spend his time with the team.

Although none of the other men in workshop A went to the team's football games, the team was useful to them, for football players enjoyed privileges not granted to other workers. Don Antonio allowed them to leave early at the end of the day for practice. In addition, they were allowed to move around the plant during work hours to make arrangements for their games. This freedom became important to the workers, for the managers had recently forbidden the practice of taking up collections of money during working hours to buy flowers for someone who was in a hospital or funeral wreaths for someone who had died. The managers believed that frequent collections of this sort placed an unfair burden on the workers. The football players used their mobility in the plant to continue the collections in secret. Diego frequently acted as a representative of the group to call on a worker who was in a hospital or on a bereaved family who was holding a wake.

None of the other pressers, all of whom were village-born, took part in any of these activities. Alvaro, who worked next to Diego, was a talkative man and had been brought up in a town on the outskirts of the city. Diego was his only close friend in the plant. Sometimes the two of them did house painting together at night or on weekends. Alvaro, Jairo (a former futbolista), Edgar, and Léon, though members of the union, were not active in it. Carlos was not even a member. He, Edgar, and Léon had the highest productivity scores in the workshop. Carlos took a paternal interest in Léon and teased him about his courtship of a girl from his hometown whom he wanted to marry and bring to the city. Otherwise, each of the pressers worked standing up at his machine without participating in the workshop's other activities. The pressers and the tailors agreed that it was not possible for a presser to become a tailor.

The Assemblers

Silvio and Lamberto were the main figures at the assemblers' table. The two were close friends. They had grown up in the same neighborhood of the city and had known each other as street tailors. They were both members of the union board.

Even though Silvio was shy and little given to conversation, he was respected by all the workers and was the only one who interacted with workers in all the other groups. He concerned himself with practical issues, such as grievances over the determination of job ratings or the application of inspection standards. He had a modest, slow smile and resisted shows of affection, even the traditional abrazo given whenever friends met. It was no accident that his neighbors at the bench were villagers who stuck to their work and avoided many of the pranks and joking that went on around them.

Hugo Soto said of Silvio, "He doesn't have an appetite for the broader struggle, because he operates in a narrow dimension. In our environment it is necessary to have the will to fight. Silvio doesn't know how to deal with management, when it is a matter of a broader question." But Lamberto told me, "Silvio has trained all of us in how to negotiate with management. He has taught us all that we know. He doesn't speak too often, but when he does, everyone listens."

Silvio was even more constrained in his behavior when members of management were present. For example, as secretary of the union he attended the grievance meetings that were held in the division superintendent's office, but he refused the traditional cup of coffee that opened these sessions. Sometimes he remained standing throughout an entire meeting rather than accept the offer of a chair. He refused to travel with other members of the union board in Don Fernando's car to meetings held in the city. When Dr. Medina invited a group of union leaders to his home for drinks and general conversation, only Silvio stayed away.

Silvio talked to me about his views one Sunday afternoon when I visited him at his home in a workers' barrio located high on the valley floor where it tilted toward the mountain wall. Though he had not expected my visit, he surprised me by greeting me with hospitality and even affection. His oldest son, who was just finishing high school, talked with us while the other children played nearby. Medellín's buildings and streets stood out in the valley below. He talked about his views of his role and of the union: "A labor representative has to be clean, above reproach. For this reason, I won't talk to a manager unless another worker is with me. I have no complaints against those who don't want to get mixed up in union activities. They want to avoid problems. They want to concern themselves with their families. I respect the reasons people give for staying out of the union. The people from the villages don't know what's going on. Only education can help them, and that will take time.

"People like Diego, Héctor, and Flavio are perhaps more intelligent than we are. But they don't want to get involved. They say, 'Look at yourself and Lamberto. You have dedicated so much time to the union. What have you gotten out of it? Nothing. You are worse off now than you were before.'

"We may be lost, but we hope our children won't be. I am not in agreement with Hugo's demagogic approach. I believe we should improve our economic situation so that we can educate our children.

"These are dangerous times for young people. The streets are full of vice, not only at night but in the daytime, not only in the center of Medellín but also up here. Some of the workers' children become addicted to marijuana. Many El Dandy families have been touched by this vice, but they keep quiet out of shame. We have to bring up our children to be decent in a setting of misery, poverty, and insecurity. Around here, that means tight control. I want to know where my children are when they are out. Maybe tight control is bad, but that's what the situation demands.

"You may ask why with nine kids I invest my time in union activity. Not many people agree with me. Sometimes my wife approves of my union work, but usually she doesn't. A union leader has to cut himself off from his family, yet in a way I am helping my family through my union activities.

"Few of the other workers share my sentiments. When they reach my age and discover that it is their connections that count and not their actions, more of them will respond as I have done. They will come to appreciate what I appreciate, and they will try to serve the people with whom they work.

"An employer feels aversion for a union leader and calls him ungrateful. Your boss may know that you are sincere, but the topics that you push are a bother to him. You can't confide in him or talk to him alone. A boss is a boss and can never be a friend. Moreover, a union leader has to be clean. He can't sell himself for penny candy. This makes it look as though he's rejecting his boss.

"I may be worse off; but I hope that my children won't be. I hope that later on my children will appreciate that *compañerismo* [good fellowship or camaraderie] in our day is expressed at work. After the company gets out of you whatever production you have to give, your concern for others remains your only avenue to individuality."

Next to Silvio, Lamberto provided the most help to other members of the workshop. He was also its lowest producer. The workers, including the women, went to him to discuss problems that worried them, to relieve their tensions, or when they felt frustrated or unhappy. He listened in an alert and sensitive way. When a petition was to be processed, a wreath to be purchased for a funeral, or a dispute settled, the matter usually came first to Lamberto, and it was he who eventually issued instructions for resolving it. Before he did so, however, he consulted Silvio, who listened to the problem dispassionately, his needle still at work. A nod of his head sent Lamberto off on his mission, perhaps to ask one of the futbolistas to take up a collection. He had been known to make a loan to a worker who was temporarily hard up for funds. He had many family and business connections in the city.

Among the other assemblers, Mario, a young futbolista, was particularly skilled at assembling jackets. He liked to work quickly and then to take time to walk around and talk to the other men.

Since his place was at the end of the assemblers' table next to the pressers, he was in a good position to act as a bridge between Diego and Eliseo on the one hand and Silvio and Lamberto on the other. However, his restlessness and his easy familiarity with people tended to unsettle his neighbors who were not from the city, especially Alonso and Don Alberto.

Don Alberto, the most respected of the village-born in the workshop, was the only person there who was referred to as *don*. He told me, "I do not like football, and I do not like football players. We never played it when I was a boy. If that Mario slaps me on the back again, I am going to hit him. I cannot stand familiarity, and I do not like crowds. I was brought up in the country in peace and quiet. I do not like to be pushed. I would like to take my family on Sunday on trips on the railroad, but the idea of all those people crowded together scares me. Instead, we pack a lunch and go for a walk in the fields in the upper part of the city."

Alonso was a quiet man who, though he grew up in a village, had worked some years in the city before coming to El Dandy. He was on good terms with both Silvio and Mario and acted as a shock absorber between them. He did not participate in workshop activities; this was also true of Don Alberto, Simón, Ricardo, and Gonzalo. Gonzalo told me, "I do not have anything to do with anybody, only with my work. If a neighbor asks me to make a suit for the first communion service of his son, I reply that I am too tired or too busy. I devote my free time to my family and to working on my house." Simón told me, "Lamberto is always turning around to talk to the girls who bring their problems to him. He hardly ever meets the standard. Gonzalo, on my other side, was very slow when he first arrived. I used to exhort him, 'Animo, Gonzalo!' Now he outproduces me!"

The Social Organization in Workshop A

Figure 10.3 depicts the social organization that the tailors of workshop A devised to order their responses to the forces arising in their environment. The diagram shows the groups of the workers based on their job assignments, together with the topics other than their work activities that interested them. I observed few interactions among them other than the ones that occurred within these groups. The figure also shows who among the garment makers was a tailor, who was raised in the city, and who was village-born.

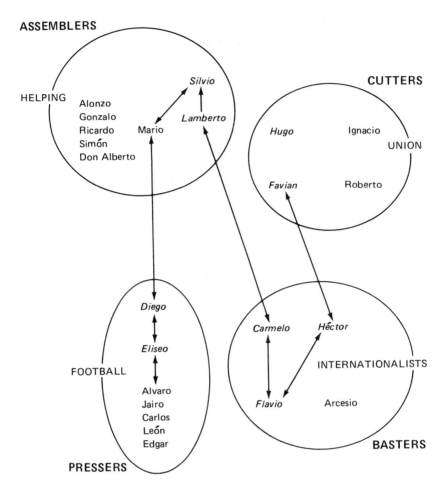

Figure 10.3
Social organization of the men in workshop A. Assemblers, basters, and cutters are tailors; pressers are not. Persons whose names are italicized were born in the city; the others were village-born.

As among the potters at Santuario and the plate makers at El Dandy, the garment makers' stock of order-building, chaos-avoiding materials was strictly limited. The large, open room designed by the engineers provided few opportunities for interaction, reinforcing management's expectations that the workers should not converse with each other. There were no hiding places for private conversations, such as the spaces between the racks of dishes at Santuario and La Blanca. Even the seating arrangements, which initially allowed easy conversation and a warm social climate approaching that of the chulus, had been reorganized because of the management's belief that physical separation and minimal conversation would keep the workers' attention on their work. The floor supervisors and inspectors showed no interest in the workers as persons. The workers' other principal contact with higher levels of authority was with Don Antonio, maintained through an interest in football rather than in the work itself.

Despite the bareness of these surroundings, the garment makers in workshop A devised the means to incorporate individuals with a wide range of personal backgrounds into their community. The workers' lives in the barrios, in country villages, and in the chulus determined the behavior that they felt appropriate and restricted the activities in which they felt comfortable. Their social organization provided human dignity and the warmth of social companionship. It attended promptly to personal problems that arose in their lives. Few management programs could have done as much; none could have done more.

Their social organization also provided a measure of security to those who had suffered the uncertainties of living in the city. The village-born, trained in a social discipline and needing the security less, received less. Bewildered by what they perceived as the disorder and chaos of city life, the villagers' response was to participate as little as possible in the workshop's activities and, like Don Alberto, to long for the peace and quiet of their previous existence.

The garment makers' social organization gave them a measure of security in a field of flux and uncertainty and a sense of control over their way of living. It accomplished this by responding to unique personal histories and shared cultural traditions on the one hand and to technological pressures encountered in the factory on the other. The garment makers maintained this structure in their behavior because it afforded them ways of satisfying their needs for the security of their jobs in their interactions with their associates. In this sense the group's structure created bonds among them as it reached out to incorporate the self-interests of the individuals. At the same time it ensured at least a minimal commitment to and concern with their work. As individuals, they needed this structure to provide them with the means of collaborating with one another, just as the structure needed their individual interests to maintain it.

Silvio was the structure's conceptual architect and leader. Lamberto made its wisdom operational; he served a mediating function, sometimes employing the privileges of Diego and the football players to bypass supervisory scrutiny. The symbolism provided by Mr. Zambretti also helped to blunt the impact of the standardization program as it affected the workers' tentative social constructs. As I will describe more fully in chapter 11, Hugo Soto performed something of a shaman's role as leader of the union.

The strong artisanal tradition nurtured in the street shops could have been an important resource for workshop A, but the behavior patterns associated with it conflicted with management's beliefs about how workers should behave. As a result, the tradition was not availed of. Dr. Medina, transfixed by his dream of a perfect and just society, was unaware of these structures and the needs that they met. If his considerable talents as a manager and leader were not fully up to the achievement of his dream, the deficiency centered on his estimate of his workers' desire to participate. His misevaluation was to assume that he could establish for them a way of life that only they could achieve for themselves.

Unbalanced Character of the Workshop's Social Organization

Clearly the social organization in workshop A differed in important ways from the ones that I found at Santuario and La Blanca. Each of those functioned in ways that integrated the productive purposes of the company with the personal needs of the workers. In workshop A the social structure also reconciled the nonwork interests of the men—in chess, music, football, international topics, personal and family emergencies, and the union—with the requirements of the company. The difference was that at Santuario and La Blanca the interests of the men and the purposes of the company became integrated in a unified whole, whereas at El Dandy the two sets of values, though coexisting, remained largely separate. The accommodation, no small achievement in its own right, did not engage the personal interests of the workers with the purposes of the company. Their work activities did not satisfy their needs for social affiliation, standing, or recognition. The workers looked to interests and activities other than their work to satisfy these needs.

I found the consequences of this difference striking, even though according to Taylorist views there was little that was unusual about the behavior of the garment workers in workshop A. Since Taylorists did not expect workers to satisfy needs other than financial ones at work, they would consider the behavior I observed among the garment makers at El Dandy as the norm and that of the potters at Santuario and the plate makers at La Blanca as unusual.

The questions at issue are ones of motivation. My study does not include data of the kind provided by in-depth interviews and projective tests that psychologists and others use to study such questions. However, Maslow's[1] and McGregor's[2] ideas, used as a conceptual scheme to order my observations of workers' interactions, allow the questions to be considered in relation to the norms and membership patterns of the social organization in workshop A.

Maslow and McGregor suggest that the needs that motivate men's behavior are best conceived as ordered in a hierarchy in which lower-level needs, such as the need for the safety and the security of one's job, must be satisfied before higher-level ones, such as the need for friendship and affiliation, self-esteem, and recognition by others, become operative. If there is also a drive from lower to higher levels, the question then arises, what happens if progress or growth is interfered with? In writing about this question Zaleznik et al.[3] suggested that thwarted needs "do not remain still. They continue to flourish."[4] They point out, however, that the elaboration of thwarted needs "should not be confused with growth; it is symptomatic of the frozen state"[5] and leads to behavioral consequences "in the form of passivity, apathy, refusal to accept responsibility, and sometimes hostility toward the goals of the organization."[6]

In industrial settings the blockage, when it occurs, typically affects workers' needs for membership and belonging. Under Taylorist assumptions, individuals are supposed to work by themselves without interacting with other workers. Their tasks are arranged so that they can do so, and management rewards and punishes them accordingly. By fulfilling production requirements, the garment makers were able to satisfy their needs for maintaining and protecting the security of their jobs. Beyond that level, despite management expectations, the blockage was not complete. The garment makers found ways in nontask-oriented activities of satisfying their needs for membership and belonging. But the development of their behavior patterns beyond this point became unbalanced: although their activities satisfied some of their higher-level needs for association, these activities were separate from rather than integrated with the purposes of the company. Their interactions with one another had the appearance of being surreptitious, of taking time away from work.

When activities that lead to the satisfaction of individuals' needs become separated from activities that contribute to the company's purposes at one level of the need hierarchy, the separation carries over to higher levels. In workshop A, for example, the workers tended to seek recognition and standing through activities that had little to do with their tasks in ways sometimes described as "goofing off." They did not pursue any of a whole repertoire of activities, such as looking for new ways of doing their work, that could simultaneously satisfy their needs for recognition and contribute to the purposes of the company. In this sense they gave the appearance of being apathetic about their work. To express their standing with each other, they turned to such nontask-oriented activities as the discussion of outside interests.

When the leaders and regular members of a group look to nontask activities for the satisfaction of their needs for recognition, the deviants and isolates are the ones likely to initiate activities that improve output. In the context of the group's social organization, these activities become an expression of their separation from the regulars, who continue their production at the group's norm. That the isolates Edgar, Léon, and Carlos were the high producers in workshop A was thus no accident but rather behavior that was grounded in the processes that maintained the structure and integrity of the group. In Santuario, the potters could follow the lead of Ramiro, the moderate in the group, when he took the action that initiated the junta; his relationship with them did not block their doing so, but no such initiatives that all the garment workers in workshop A could follow were likely to occur at El Dandy so long as the regulars' needs for association were carried out surreptitiously.

The garment workers' incapacity to develop new ways of behaving that contributed to the purposes of the company and satisfied their needs had a further consequence. It also meant that they did not develop ways to solve the problems their work environment presented to them. At Santuario and La Blanca the workers developed behavior patterns that solved some of their problems, such as questions about the standing of preeminent persons in their groups whose status was threatened by change, the just distribution of rewards among the members of the group, and the selection, training, and promotion of new and younger workers. At El Dandy, the garment workers' behavior, including their friendships and antagonisms, was based on how they had learned to behave outside the factory rather than on patterns they developed at work.

When values and behavior that have been learned in one situation come to dominate behavior in another, learning new ways to behave in the second situation becomes difficult. For when this happens, the behavior in the second situation easily falls into the pattern of a vicious circle in which the values appropriate to the other situation become dominant and block attention to problems of the present. No new learning takes place, and the incapacity to learn leads to the continuance of unresolved problems. Changes *of* the system do not occur, and neither do changes *within* it. Instead, the participants tend to resist changes. Their behavior becomes repetitive, even though they might benefit from change and satisfy some of their unfulfilled needs. The situation becomes what sociologists call stasis, a socially determined incapacity to learn and solve new problems, characterized by unchanging and unchangeable behavior.

Something like this seems to have happened in workshop A; the behavior patterns of the garment workers contrasted sharply with the patterns that developed at Santuario and La Blanca. The behavior patterns at the last two sites supported the work groups in learning new ways of behaving. Changes occurred rapidly and spread throughout the community. At El Dandy no such changes occurred.

I had gone to Medellín from Santuario and La Blanca to study a situation in which the processes of change had lasted longer and progressed further than they had at Santuario and La Blanca.[7] What I discovered at El Dandy was a frozen group in which the social forces among the members and in their relations with their managers constrained the members from developing new ways of behaving. The results were the all too familiar problems of industrial societies, attitudes of apathy and alienation toward work and divisions among the workers and between the workers and the managers that made cooperation difficult.

As a student of organizational behavior, I wondered what further consequences these limitations might have in respect to issues of productivity, satisfaction, growth, and learning among the garment makers. I was not able to answer these questions as clearly as I would have liked because confrontations between the company and the unions dominated subsequent events. Nevertheless, I could not fail to record and take account of the dramatic and significant events that ensued.

One has to wonder if the events that I am about to describe could have been avoided, to the advantage of the productive purposes of the company as well as of the social and personal needs of the workers, if management's arrangements for the garment makers had permitted their social organization to develop in a balanced and integrated way that permitted their growth and development as individuals as well as the resolution of problems they encountered at work.

11

The Failure of Dr. Medina's Dream

Several contests between El Dandy's management and its unions occurred before a dispute over the company store led to a confrontation between Dr. Medina and Hugo Soto. Indeed, for some time the garment makers' union seemed to contest every move that Dr. Medina made to forward his dream of industrial peace and collaboration.

The standards program had long been a point of friction between the company and the union. Hugo Soto told me, "With minor changes, this could be a model plant, a pilot company for others in the industry. What we should have here are basic wages, not standards. The fact that we do not have basic wages is the reason why the union has to play the role of demagogue—I am in agreement with the management that we do that—to obtain benefits for the workers. Many of the benefits represent a heavy load for the company without bringing much to the workers. Previously there was camaraderie and harmony here. It is difficult now, because the company is not after equality among the workers but rivalry and competition.

"I am not against standards as such. I am sure that they work well in the United States, where they have trained technicians to apply them. Before I became president of the union, I took out a passport to go there to study them. I was even offered a fellowship, but the federation refused to give me permission to accept it. They wanted to send me behind the Iron Curtain for training; but when things got that far, I drew the line. I believe in unionism, but I am also a Catholic.

"Standards are out of tune with what is going on in Colombia at the moment. Management uses standards to break up worker solidarity by pitting one worker against another, by destroying class consciousness. The union has urged its affiliates to have their members keep their output at the required minimum in order not to compete with their class brothers, but we can't force people, and we've had little success."

The *Union Bulletin* referred to the standards program as, "[t]his new slavery, this melancholic dance that lacks any trace of sensitivity to the differences that exist between individuals, that clashes violently with their distinctive human nature and degenerates into physical damage, bitter sweat, and abundant tears to the point of ending up in nervous breakdowns, which the company attempts to disguise."

As a means of countering such claims, of increasing the workers' understanding of the program, and of advising them of their rights under it, Dr. Medina offered to allow one member of the garment makers' union to join the standards department. From a list of three candidates that Hugo Soto submitted, management selected a member of the union's board who had been one of its vice presidents. He went to work at a desk in the standards office but continued at factory wages and as a member of the union's board.

The arrangement survived only briefly. After the man had been in the position a few months, he refused to sign a union statement that attacked the standards program because his work in the department had convinced him the program was run fairly. Hugo Soto ordered him to return to factory work, but Don Antonio urged him to stay in the standards office on the grounds that his appointment to it had been for an indefinite period. He decided to stay and wrote an open letter to the workers to explain his decision. Hugo Soto responded with an attack in the *Union Bulletin*: "Only a clouded mind, a selfish spirit that could be bought for a trinket would bring you, a former defender of the working class, to so betray your comrades, now your ex-comrades." Hugo accused him of having become a "defender of management interests" and called a general assembly to expel him from the union. The expulsion notice was sent to local newspapers and to union affiliates throughout the country.

Earlier, when Dr. Medina had proposed a stock purchase plan, whereby workers might buy company stock on exceptionally favorable terms, the *Union Bulletin* had designated the proposal a "tactic of popular capitalism, a plan invented in Washington, D.C., to salvage the free enterprise system that Karl Marx predicted would destroy itself by making the rich richer and the poor poorer. With every worker converted into an entrepreneur, the hopes are that the labor movement will be so divided that each member will become an *exploiter* of his own class. The only true course for the proletariat is to transform society and to *destroy once and for all* the historic arena where the inhuman exploitation of man by man takes place."

Dr. Medina commented on these matters: "One of two things happens. The individual comes to accept the company's proposals and programs and attempts to negotiate them. Then he gets tagged as a tool of management, as in the case of this fellow in the standards controversy. Or else he becomes irreconcilable, as in the case of Hugo Soto. A union president must become a communist or he loses the support of his board and falls into disgrace with those who run it.

"I'm not against unionism as such. I'm sure that it works well in the United States. It's just that we don't have authentic unionism in Colombia. What we have is personal exploitation for political purposes."

Disagreements over the Company Stores

Before the consolidation of El Dandy's operations at the new location, the workers in the cloth division could buy food and pharmaceuticals at reduced prices at their own store and pay for them through payroll deductions. The store was organized as a workers' cooperative and, though supported by a subsidy from the company, was managed by the officers of the cloth makers' union, who took considerable pride in its success.

The garment makers' store was established in 1949. It was also organized as a cooperative, but management held two-thirds of the shares, and workers subscribed the balance. Three members of the board—the superintendents of the manufacturing divisions and Don Fernando, the personnel manager—were management's representatives; two, usually the president and secretary of the union, that is, Hugo Soto and Silvio, represented the workers. Dr. Medina remembered the establishment of the store as a conciliatory, goodwill gesture on management's part to heal wounds caused by a three-week strike, the only one in the company's history. The union leaders held a different view. They spoke of the store as "our store," an example of the kind of concession that could be wrested from an unwilling management when members of the working class acted together in a successful strike.

The board that administered the store's affairs met regularly. Union leaders came to regard these meetings as important, for there were no formal provisions under the bargaining contract for settling grievances or negotiating differences that arose between the management and the union. The meetings provided occasions when the two parties could discuss topics of concern in addition to the regularly scheduled ones.

When the cloth-making and the garment-making divisions of the company were combined, management decided that the two stores should also be merged. Because the arrangements for the garment makers' store were part of the labor agreement between the management and the union, management thought the cloth makers' store, which lacked any formal legal status, was the obvious candidate for elimination, and the company entered into negotiations to purchase its assets. In the course of these discussions, it became apparent that the garment makers did not want the cloth makers as members of their cooperative. Under pressure from management, however, they finally accepted them as nonvoting, nonstockholding members. Hence the cloth makers had no representatives on the board that governed the store. The leaders of the cloth makers' union protested against being "forsaken" and "dispossessed" of their status. They tried to open a separate cooperative in the center of the city. Many of the cloth makers, however, continued to make their purchases at what had been the garment makers' store, and the new one failed.

After a few years, the garment makers relented and offered the cloth makers full membership in the store. At that time the presidents of both unions were elected to serve as worker representatives on the board, but hard feelings between members of the two unions continued. The following year the cloth makers offered their own slate of candidates for the board. It easily defeated the several slates advanced by the garment makers. That was the last year that the cloth makers had direct representation on the board, for the garment makers subsequently put forward a single slate, which they easily elected. Thus this channel of access to management returned to the garment makers' union.

This was the forum in which Hugo Soto mounted his argument with management. The issue that he chose concerned the size of the reserves to be set aside for depreciation of the store's property. When the question of closing the store's accounts arose at the end of 1966, the union members of the board maintained that management was insisting on a higher allowance for depreciation than necessary. The result, they pointed out, reduced the store's profit for the year and therefore the amount available for the end-of-the-year dividend to members. Although the amount an individual worker received was in any case not large, many of them counted on receiving it as a way of financing their purchases of gifts for Christmas. Hugo Soto took this fact into account when he attempted to pressure management into agreeing that a small depreciation allowance was adequate, but the company representatives on the board, on instructions from Dr. Medina, held firm to their position on the grounds of a need to maintain accepted accounting principles.

Several weeks went by, and Christmas Eve arrived without the board of the cooperative having made any announcement about dividends. The rainy season had ended by the time the workers and managers left the factory for the holidays. A full moon hung behind luminous clouds and outlined the mountain walls on either side of the valley. As they headed home through the orchid gardens, managers and workers alike picked up copies of the year-end editions of the union's and the company's bulletins. Both sounded notes that boded ill for the year ahead.

The *Union Bulletin* argued: "What a contrast, comrades! The industrialists, the directors and codirectors, take their ease at their large country estates and lordly residences. They raise their glasses in happy toasts, while others of their number travel as tourists to Mexico, Europe, or the United States. Our general manager presents his stockholders a financial balance far higher than last year. But the balance that he presents to us, his workers, is one of *misery, hunger, pawn tickets,* and *debts.* This is what remains for those of us who have spent our efforts for the benefit of the few.

"Comrades, either we close ranks under the standard of *working unity* or next year will be worse than this year. The forecast of the general manager, that *'Whoever wants to make money cannot hold his heart in his hand,'* will come true."

The *Company Bulletin* argued: "How curious that some would wish to impose upon our search for harmony elements of conflict, confrontation, and antagonism! Management seeks social peace. It will continue to seek social peace within the spirit of the law, which is our only defense against arbitrary action. As the company seeks to perfect its human relations, truth can help answer many questions. For instance, is it worthwhile for management to maintain a company that has been attacked by the cancer of communism? Does such a cancer exist? If it exists, should it be cut out in order to save the rest of the organization? Will the company find those who will cooperate in this essential salvaging operation? If force, coercion, and the 'class struggle' prevail, the blame cannot be placed on management. The blame must be placed on those who promote these ends in the full knowledge of what they entail."

A few months later, when there had been no further news about the dividend, Hugo Soto decided to speak to Dr. Medina about it. He called on him during the hours that Dr. Medina kept open for unscheduled discussions with any employee who wanted to see him. What passed between the two men that morning was not recorded. According to the reports that circulated throughout the factory, Hugo Soto opened the conversation with "Look, you like to be regarded as a philanthropist, Dr. Medina. The workers need the money that is tied up in this depreciation dispute. Why don't you advance it out of your own pocket?"

When Dr. Medina pointed out that accounting principles had their own integrity and did not lend themselves to casual manipulation, Hugo Soto lost his temper. He shouted, "This company is ours! We built it with our work and our sweat. One day it will belong to us. If you can't meet a legitimate request, then we will be forced to strike."

According to the reports, Dr. Medina became furious. He was reported to have said, "This company exists to make profits. It is not a home for the aged, a branch of the Soviet Union, or a plaything of Mr. Castro. Those who want to earn their keep here have to work." Whereupon he was said to have ordered Hugo Soto out of his office.

The next day each worker received a letter from the management that gave its view of the dispute and offered the workers their choice among three solutions: (1) the workers could buy out the company's part in the store; (2) the company could buy out the workers' part; or (3) the workers' representatives on the board could be replaced with others, as management could not work with the current ones. As a result of the letter, Hugo Soto and Silvio, the workers' representatives, resigned from the board for "the good of the workers." Dividends were paid in an amount that accorded with management's view of proper accounting for depreciation. Two weeks later Hugo Soto and Silvio were reelected to the board.

Ideological Disputes

During this period, as earlier, the *Union Bulletin* adopted an implicit Marxist line. It featured such concepts as the class struggle, class consciousness, world peace, and national and international class affiliation. It urged workers toward "unity in a war of the classes" for the protection of their "birthright" and argued that all members of "the exploited classes" should unite in a common defense against their "exploiters."

The *Company Bulletin* pleaded for the rights and responsibilities of individuals, Christianity, and, above all, a concept of social peace drawn from papal encyclicals and the literature of free enterprise. The *Company Bulletin* took the position that the subordination of a small minority of union leaders to "outside interests" blocked the resolution of employee problems and the achievement of social peace.

The *Union Bulletin* resisted these charges. It urged, "Ours is the only federation that bends its knee to no patrón, no church, no political party, but only to the workers it serves." Affiliation with other workers through unionism, it argued, was essential in a world locked in class struggle. If the company wished its workers to surrender the benefits of national affiliation, let management sever its connections with the industrial associations to which it belonged.

A further break between management and the union came when the *Union Bulletin* republished without attribution "a course for the working man" that was taken from a pamphlet whose author was a well-known local communist. The material was used as a part of the *Union Bulletin*'s campaign to rebut management's charges against the union's affiliation with its national federation, to show the need for national and international affiliation, and to put the blame for the lack of social peace on management. The article argued that man-made laws represented a departure from the principles that ordered the universe, a device used by members of the dominant class to defend their interests. Civil law assumed equal status between parties in conflict. Since equal status was nowhere to be found, man-made laws favored the rich and the exploiters. The workers' only recourse was to promote equalizing national labor laws by class action or to offset by other means the consequences of civil laws that were at the service of the dominant class.

The article's lack of attribution made it appear to express the views of El Dandy's workers. Dr. Medina immediately arranged for a refutation to be published in the *Company Bulletin*. Under the title, "The Harvest of Hate," it said: "We cannot contribute by our silence to the harvest of hate that is being sown by the *Union Bulletin* in its textual reproduction of a known communist pamphlet that promulgates philosophical theories in open conflict with the Christian concept of life and the religious beliefs of the vast majority of our workers. These are lessons of hate, belligerency, subversion, immorality, slander, and atheism that have as their object nothing less than the servicing of the communist principle of the 'class struggle,' upon which the entire structure of Marxian strategy is constructed.

"We set out to sow the Christian seed of understanding; we had embarked on the extraordinary adventure of creating a climate of peace, wherein we would be able to fashion a perfect company, the kind that we all aspire to be associated with one day, a company cut to the exact measure of our dreams. But our union bulletin responds with international communism, infiltrated into the nation's labor movement, to confound whatever attempts at affection and mutual comprehension have been attempted by those of us who together constitute the company.

"Let this commentary serve as protest and a clarification, a protest against those who are responsible for the *Union Bulletin* and a clarification for those workers who unfortunately are subjected to the communist poison disguised as class solidarity."

The *Union Bulletin*, in a response that was surprisingly mild, suggested simply that whoever clamored for social justice should be labeled a communist, and it concluded with the slogan "Freedom Yes! But Not Freedom to Massacre. Democracy Yes! But Not to Exploit and Oppress."

The next issue of the *Company Bulletin* included a statement signed by Dr. Medina, the first time that his name appeared in connection with a formal statement about unionism. In the statement

Dr. Medina pleaded for reestablishment of the common identity in which both management and the union had earlier invested. It was titled "The Problems That Don't Get Resolved." In the article Dr. Medina wrote, "Everybody in the company has his worries. Unfortunately, not everybody is aware of all of the problems that the company faces at a given moment.

"Recently, it has been especially difficult for management to convey to its personnel the difficulties that the company is going through. It is especially delicate to speak only of difficulties, but the truth is that it has also been difficult to speak of achievements, because in one way or another, the personnel of the company have adopted such passive positions at all times.

"This is management's complaint, but it is not the most serious issue. The greatest difficulty is that an important number of workers are supporting communist policy, unaware perhaps that with their union fees they help pay for the expenses of the Communist Party.

"Let this statement scandalize no one! It is better that we tell each other the truth in order to know where we stand.

"The company embarked on a 'Compass of Confidence,' a period of trust, on the occasion of the change in the representatives on the board of the store. Within this 'Compass of Confidence,' the company continues its permanent concern of resolving each and every one of the problems the company faces. These are: labor-management relations, the sales of goods, efficiency, obtaining enough money to meet obligations, social security for the workers' families (housing and medical insurance), wages set by the law, the competition of other manufacturers of cloth goods and suits, new taxes set by government on industries and on the consumption of cloth goods and clothes, distribution to stores that are closed in the main cities, import licenses that cannot be obtained for linings and buttons, etc.

"The company is aware that it is not managing an amount of wealth that is large enough to be divided among all its personnel so that each of its employees and workers would be fully satisfied. The company would like to have enough resources so that none of its operators lacked for anything. Unfortunately, what the company has available for sharing is not enough to permit itself this satisfaction. Therefore, it has to limit its action to finding a balance between what it gives its workers, the price at which it sells its products to consumers, the taxes it pays the state, and the dividends it pays to its owners and stockholders. This is the old story of the four pillars that support a business organization, among which balance has to be maintained for the benefit of the company's future, made up by the four human groups that represent these pillars.

"But artificial problems arise, unconsciously promoted by some and intentionally by others, to maintain the spirit of discord between workers and managers. Suspicions are spread out of pure gossip, because no one is sure of anything. For example, on the reorganization of the workers' cafeteria, everyone believes he himself knows to what the reorganization is due and how it was contracted. There are those who think they will die of hunger with the increase of waste and, moreover, that the world is coming to an end because of a small reorganization.

"Working men, why do you not open a period of trust in the company's management?

"Why do not the oldest among you take up the cudgels to explain to the newer employees what the policy of the company has been throughout its existence? Why do you not contribute with your prestige and experience to create an environment of normal relations in a minor tone and at a normal pace, without unacceptable pressures, within a climate of understanding and not of shouts and threats, without causing the dismissal of those that proceed in this way, and without becoming the immovable owners of positions that have union power? Why do we not all collaborate? Then perhaps the problems that fall within the possibilities of the country and the industry can be resolved without destroying the company of which we were a part."

The article was signed by Dr. Medina and concluded with the slogans "UNIONISM, YES!" and "COMMUNISM, NO!"

Hugo Soto's Resignation

A few weeks after Dr. Medina's plea was published, Hugo Soto requested a meeting with him at his home in the evening. On that occasion he informed Dr. Medina of his decision to retire from the union and the company. He accepted Dr. Medina's commendation on his decision and his offer to help him locate a position elsewhere.

The next morning Hugo Soto mounted a crate at the gates of the factory, where the workers were awaiting the bell that signaled the start of the day. In a few words he announced his decision and urged those present to "keep aloft the banner" of the struggle he had led. Both the *Union Bulletin* and the *Company Bulletin* published tributes to him. The *Union Bulletin* wrote: "Last Friday, his fellow workers heard the eloquent words of our comrade, Hugo Soto, for the last time. His voice did not resound as it had on other occasions. On that day the marvelous and resonant echo of the words that in other times had harangued the masses gave evidence of the weariness and fatigue of more than ten years of struggle on behalf of the proletariat and its cause.

"Thus on a single day, as sometimes happens, a voice has been silenced, perhaps forever; a voice that without fear of persecution, unemployment, and the power of wealth raised itself impetuously; now to unmask the traitor, now to point out and combat injustice, now to show the luminous light of the UNITY that will give the proletariat its final triumph. One cause alone, the one that creates discontent, the one that destroys people by hunger, the one that on many occasions vanquishes persistent and brave spirits in the struggle determined the end of Comrade Soto's leadership: POVERTY!!!

"The ridiculous starvation wages that not only he but all the working class earn did not allow him to continue the struggle that he as a man, head of a family, and a union leader undertook responsibly and reliably. But it was impossible for him to continue in such a situation.

"As a tribute to his memory and his struggle, which is also ours, the workers of El Dandy must close ranks to achieve the unity he so greatly desired and to be watchful, as he was, to keep our organization FIRM, PURE, VIGOROUS, BELLIGERENT, and FREE of all MANAGERIAL, POLITICAL, and RELIGIOUS influences!!! MARCH ON!!!"

The *Company Bulletin* offered the following: "At times a man finds himself in circumstances of apparent contradiction; on the one hand his innermost thought, on the other his external behavior.

"A man's innermost thoughts are related to the formation of his family, to his fundamental beliefs, to the sacred duties of husband, father, and Christian. External behavior, on the other hand, is determined by the strong pressures of social life, the commitments imposed upon him by the community at any given moment. But when there are intimate moral reservations still latent in a man, an enormous struggle surges within him and ends in his triumph or defeat.

"Hugo Soto devoted a good part of his life to the union without regret, he says. His manner of being, his obstinacy in defending what he considers just, and the ideas that have inspired his union behavior have led him to impose on the union in recent times a dynamic of intransigence and opposition that we, in all honesty, consider mistaken and damaging to the workers and to the union itself.

"As a realist, Hugo Soto now decides that his next phase in life cannot be played out on the stage of union activities. He is therefore withdrawing from El Dandy.

"It is now his family's turn—a wife and seven children. He wants to dedicate himself to them—this is his decision. A little peace to meditate and to put his private economy in order and to face the ever heavier responsibilities of the home.

"Actually the family has rights that need defending and Hugo Soto's family recovers a good defender. That he will defend them in all Christianity as he has resolved, we have no doubt."

Hugo Soto told me, "You might think that I hate Dr. Medina, but I love him. I think of him as a father, but as a father who must be straightened out. He is a good man, but when it becomes a personal matter between the two of us, the time has arrived for me to get out." He said that he resigned from the company and the union to have more time to spend with his family. His oldest son, about to graduate from high school with high academic honors, intended to enter a seminary to prepare for the priesthood. Hugo Soto himself soon announced his employment as a lecturer and conference leader at a local Catholic action center.

The Escalation of Tensions

Events moved rapidly after Hugo Soto's resignation, Ignacio Porras succeeded him as president of the garment makers' union. The same issue of the Company Bulletin that paid tribute to him also featured an interview with Victor Valdez, a worker from another part of El Dandy, who had preceded Hugo Soto as the union president. The interview resulted from Dr. Medina's plea that older workers "take up the cudgels in support of management's 'Compass of Confidence.'"

In the interview Valdez endorsed Dr. Medina's appeal for improved relations, urged a break with the militant national federation and its "hard line," and proposed the establishment of a "free and independent" union that would collaborate in the creation of the social peace that Dr. Medina envisioned. Later, Valdez and several older workers established a Unity Committee of Free and Independent Workers to promote these purposes, but the committee failed to generate support. Its principal accomplishment was to add another bulletin, The Truth, to the workers' reading. The bulletin of the garment makers' union countered the stories that appeared in The Truth and denounced Valdez as a traitor to the working class. The article recalled that during his term as president he had been labeled by management a communist whose purpose was to convert the company into an "agency of Moscow." Valdez was soon expelled from the union.

The Strike and Its Aftermath

Some months later, the company was faced with high inventories and a drop in sales. To solve these problems, which Dr. Medina judged were temporary, he proposed a reduced work week for both the cloth-making and the garment-making divisions. To soften the economic impact of the move, he also proposed a ten percent increase in wages, and the company offered to buy the outstanding shares that the workers held in the company store without curtailing its services.

The officers of the cloth makers' union accepted the proposal, and it went into effect in the cloth-making division. Officers of the union picked up the workers' shares of stock in the store for redemption, not only the shares of their own members but also the shares of garment makers who wished to accept the cash settlement that the company offered.

The officers of the garment makers' union reacted differently. They charged that the shortened work week was a management scheme to reduce inventories at the workers' expense. They claimed that the raise was inadequate, and they attacked the company's plan to redeem the shares in the store as an attempt to deprive the workers of their patrimony. The Company Bulletin asked in astonishment, "How can it be that for the first time in history a group of workers rejects an increase in wages that management offers?" Despite the cloth makers' active role in the campaign to redeem the workers' shares, garment makers refused to surrender their certificates. This number was more than enough to ensure the store's continuation as a cooperative.

At about this time the officers of the cloth makers' union changed their position. For the first time they dropped their competition with the garment makers' union and endorsed a collection that was being taken up for an injured garment maker. Concurrently the tenor of their comments against the company stiffened. In fact, their bulletin was the first to broach the idea of plant-wide, general strike. When the *Company Bulletin* chided the cloth makers' union for this drastic suggestion, their bulletin replied: "Why does militancy directed against you by the cloth makers bother you so much, Mr. Boss? Is it that one union is seen as more dangerous than the other? Or is this another scheme to divide the two? This will not happen! Previously, propaganda was directed only at unionism. Now, with a wasted capitalism about to expire, even the Church supports legal unionism. Both unions have come to realize that what matters now are the needs of the workers and both share the responsibility for meeting these needs."

When the workers began to feel increased financial pressure from the shortened work week, rumors of a plant-wide strike mounted. The strike came in July 1968. The cloth makers led the way, but Ignacio Porras and the garment workers endorsed and joined it. It lasted for 100 days, the longest work stoppage in Colombian history.

The strike leaders were forced to accept what was generally considered an unfavorable settlement. On the grounds that two unions could not legally represent a single work force, the National Labor Ministry insisted on a plebiscite in which the workers were to choose one union as the sole negotiating agency for the whole company. The outnumbered and now discredited cloth makers' union lost at the polls, and exclusive representation of El Dandy's workers passed to the garment makers' union, which was affiliated with the more militant of the country's two national federations.

After the strike, I managed only brief visits to El Dandy. A garment maker from workshop B, regarded as lacking Hugo Soto's charisma but as better educated and more of an intellectual leader, replaced Ignacio Porras as president of the union. One of the factory supervisors said of him, "He is more authentic in his Marxism than Hugo Soto."

Don Antonio was transferred from the garment-making division, and the football team that represented the company in competition with other teams in the city ceased to exist. Instead, after reading an early draft of the report of my research, the managers organized a new league within the company itself. Teams represented different sections of the factory and offices, including both the standards department and the union. And Flavio received support for the chorus that he had long wanted.

After work one day, I went with Diego to visit a disabled worker who was in the hospital. Afterward we had a beer in a tavern at the main plaza. He asked me, "What do I do now, Don Carlos? I'm under pressure to join the union board, and I can no longer say that the football team takes up my free time." A few months later, he left El Dandy to seek a job elsewhere.

Some months after the strike I had a chance to talk with Silvio. The opportunity came late one afternoon after a visit with Dr. Medina, who had asked me, "What's happened to that guy Silvio? When I was driving through the patio yesterday, I waved at him, and he turned his back on me." I walked outside the plant from Dr. Medina's office to the union office. Evening had fallen; both the company store and the football field were empty. Silvio rose to greet me and to see that the door to the office remained open. A woman from the factory came in to serve us coffee and to type the notes for the *Union Bulletin*, on which Silvio had been working.

I could not fail to notice the contrast between the way Silvio talked with me on this occasion and the conversation we had had when I visited his home. On that occasion we talked about *compañerismo* and good fellowship. On this occasion he remained standing throughout the hour-long conversation, as was his habit in union meetings with management representatives. His eyes never met mine; instead, while he spoke, he faced the empty playing fields outside the open door. He, who had previously coached his associates in practical rather than political conversations with management, laboriously contrived for me a halting diatribe pieced together from odd bits of militant union ideology. I found no way to develop a normal conversation with him.

The Nonstructural Character of the Changes at El Dandy

I concluded that at El Dandy, under conditions of industrialization more advanced than those at Santuario or at La Blanca, the changes that occurred did not affect the structure of the social system in workshop A. At Santuario and La Blanca the changes that were significant for the workers and their managers were the ones that took place in the structures of the workers' social organizations regarded as systems. At El Dandy, despite all the other kinds of changes that occurred, it was not clear that comparable changes took place. Certainly many changes occurred among management, the unions, and the workers. These changes included workers moving from full-time to part-time work and changes in pay scales. Hugo Soto resigned, and Don Antonio was transferred. El Dandy's football team was dropped, and a chorus was started. The union that represented the garment makers changed, and so did Silvio's behavior. Despite these and other changes, it did not seem that the structure of the workers' social organization and their views about how they should behave changed at all. These were changes in the system, not changes of it.

Many circumstances led to these results. Prominent among them was the incapacity of the persons in the situation to develop the behavior appropriate for resolving the problems that they encountered in working with one another. In the absence of such values and ways of behaving, values that had been learned in other situations, even though they were not relevant to the problems of the collaboration, controlled the workers' behavior. These egocentric and stereotypical evaluations were typical of the patterns of evaluation in the community outside the factory. The result was that the divisions that existed among the people outside work persisted inside the factory. With one possible exception, new patterns of behavior did not develop.

The possible exception pertained to what the country-born workers may have learned from the strike about working in the city. Before the strike, the city-born workers assisted each other in resolving the problems that they encountered at work. Their cooperation did not extend to the point where they worked easily and congenially with those from the country. The difference was as though those who had been brought up in the country perceived cooperation as a way of life, an end in itself. In contrast, those from the city perceived cooperation as a means, not an end—a means to handle the competitions and confrontations that characterized the city environment. For the country-born workers, cooperating in the strike with the city-born was perhaps their first effective lesson in becoming urban.

The Egocentric Character of the Leaders' Behavior

These egocentric and stereotypical aspects of the behavior patterns among the managers and workers in the company and in the unions had particularly unfortunate consequences in the behavior of the leaders. These patterns allowed the leaders to express, sometimes eloquently, the values important to them but did not encourage them to understand others' values or points of view. Thus communications from the leaders was limited to presentations of their own views and arguments about and denunciations of the views of others. Discussion of social structures that could have been created to bridge the gaps between the divisions was thus restricted. The structures did not develop, and the bridging did not occur. No one among the leaders consistently took account of the situation as a whole or reached out, as Don José did at Santuario and Arturo at La Blanca, to accommodate the values of those with whom they worked. Silvio showed some capacity to work with people who held values different from his, but even before the strike he was clearly uncomfortable when his role was to represent the needs and values of workers to management. The differences among his roles as an employee of El Dandy, an officer of the union, a member of the social organization of workshop A, and the father of a family immobilized him; and he was ill at ease, tense, uncomfortable, silent, and often ineffective. His behavior gave no evidence of the social competence and skill that Arturo showed. Lamberto operated under Silvio's guidance without the capacity for independent leadership.

Hugo Soto's energies and commitment were directed to the organizational needs and purposes of his union rather than directly to the personal and social needs of the workers. To point this out is not a criticism of him or of his union but a confirmation that there was no one in workshop A who had Arturo's talents for promoting cooperation among the members of a group.

The top managers of the company, the supervisors, and the inspectors did nothing to provide support and recognition for the development of the garment makers' social organization. They did not consult with the garment makers before reorganizing the layout of the production lines, for example. They went ahead and did it. Dr. Medina's good intentions toward the employees were not a substitute. Instead of supporting the garment makers' social organization, the managers' actions prevented its development. At least during the period of the research, they exercised their leadership by what Burns called heroic methods, that is, "as leaders because of their personage alone,"[1] as though they were the sole source of change for the factory.

In the absence of persons with more competence in leadership and communications, any issue that arose, whether it was a question of the depreciation rates to be charged at the store or a temporary drop in the demand for the company's products, became a contest between two parties, in which the expectation was that one party was going to win and the other was going to lose. The possibility that a compromise could develop or that both could gain was thereby excluded.

The frustration and dissatisfaction that Hugo Soto and the officers and members of his union felt over the company store reinforced the existing attitudes of apathy and malaise. The next occasion to express their dissatisfaction occurred when the cloth makers refused to accept reduced work schedules. When the cloth makers decided to strike in protest, the garment makers supported them for the first time.

This represented a substantial escalation of the conflict. The garment makers' dissatisfaction, previously expressed primarily through their social organization, became allied with a formal organization in the unions' strike action. With the strike the managers of the company, the officers of the unions, and the workers found themselves in a confrontation in which one of the issues concerned the relative standing of the company and the unions: Which organization could do more for its members? Which was the more powerful?

Once these political and institutional issues entered the negotiation, it became necessary that they be included in its settlement. In the process the personal and social concerns of the workers that formed the background of the dispute became lost. The process of settling the confrontation thus repeated the failure in which it began, namely, the neglect of the personal and social values of the workers.

In negotiations of this kind the financial needs of workers often lead them to trade their social concerns for a financial settlement. If the frustrations are not too intense and if the settlement is good enough, the workers may accept their financial gains as substitutes for their unremedied frustrations and feel that overall they are better off.

A process of this kind seems to have happened at El Dandy, although the outcomes were confused because neither side gained a clear victory. The workers and the union accepted a wage settlement that was not generally regarded as favorable. On that issue management won. The garment makers gained, if gain it eventually proved to be, a militant union. They lost in Don Antonio the one person in management to whom some of them felt that they could speak freely, if only in connection with matters related to football. They also lost Hugo Soto, a dedicated union leader, and Cheese Face, the worker who with Lamberto helped the most to connect Silvio's leadership of their social organization with its members. Though Silvio remained, it was not clear that he could function effectively to help the workers without either Hugo Soto or Cheese Face.

In addition, neither side could take credit for the settlement, which was reached at the insistence of the labor ministry of the national government. For its role the government generally stood to gain in the eyes of the people as much as or more than the company or the unions. Although I did not study the gains because they were outside the scope of my research, I have no doubt that the arrangements made between the company, the unions, and the labor ministry activated a wide range of reciprocities and obligations that had not previously existed. These considerations, however extraneous they may have been to the origins of the dispute, continued into the future as additional constraints on the capacity of the workers, the company, and the unions to settle in ways of their own choosing any new disputes that arose among them.

It is of course not unusual for disputes to be settled in ways that do not make it clear who won and who lost. There is often much to be gained from such settlements, for the stability that a situation derives from them may be important to the participants, as it was at El Dandy. The settlement there allowed the company to resume operating with ensuing benefits to the workers and to the unions as well as to the company. But the settlement confirmed the positions of the persons who were already at the top of those organizations, just as it confirmed the positions of those at the bottom. Thus the settlement contributed no change to the participants' behavior or to the tensions within and between their organizations. The attainment of Dr. Medina's dream of peace, efficiency, and social justice for all was thus postponed.

My observations about what happened at El Dandy raise important questions about leadership in industrial situations. Most current discussions focus on the acts of the leader as the critical factor in changing workers' behavior. The discussions focus on the charisma of the leader's personality or on the level of his or her position in the hierarchy of a bureaucracy, and they stress the importance of the leader's persuasiveness. At El Dandy it did not work that way. The eloquence of Dr. Medina and of Hugo Soto in articulating their respective ideologies did not lead to changes in the workers' behavior or in the structure of their social organization. Instead the leaders became part of a confrontation that overwhelmed both the managers and the workers. The missing element was the leaders' failure to present their initiatives in ways that allowed the workers' responses to the changes to develop in their own social organization.

Communications from the managers to the workers thus lacked authority in the sense that Barnard defined it. He wrote, "Authority is the character of a communication . . . by virtue of which it is accepted by a contributor or 'member' of an organization as governing the action he contributes."[2] At Santuario and La Blanca, even though the leaders were not aware in any explicit or conceptual sense of the workers' social organization, their behavior allowed the workers the time and opportunity to accept their—the leaders'— initiatives through development of their social organization. The workers thus improved their productivity and satisfactions and changed their behavior in ways that gave them additional choices about how they would live.

In this connection the sense of accomplishment that the workers at Santuario and at La Blanca derived from their activities at work contrasted with the unsettlement that remained at El Dandy. The contrast is the more important, because many of the affairs of the world are conducted in the belief that the advocacy of ideologies and debates about them are the way to get individuals to change their behavior and improve their relations with each other and the organizations in which they work. My studies showed no such simple connection between advocacy on the part of one person and changes in the behavior of others. Rather, when changes occurred, they did so as the result of complex patterns of interactions that included challenges and responses and the invention and development of accommodations. Chapters 12 and 13 summarize the patterns I observed.

Silvio, El Dandy tailor.

Lamberto, El Dandy tailor.

Hugo Soto, leader of the garment makers' union at
El Dandy.

IV

**Structural Change and Its Significance for
Participants and Managers**

12

The Process of Structural Change

The principal finding of Savage's research is that the behavior of industrial men and women transcend the machinelike aspects of the tasks that bring them together. "The men and women in the groups I observed," Savage wrote, "were not socially inert, as workers have frequently been portrayed. On the contrary, they were highly organized and socially active. They functioned in their groups as principal agents of social change. Except at El Dandy, their workplaces were the arenas where new structural models, including new concepts of association and authority and new identities were forged, tested, and transmitted to the adjacent communities."

Savage's field work produced two additional findings. The first concerns the pace of structural change in work groups. The changes that he observed occurred episodically, in bursts, not continuously at a steady rate and were preceded and followed by relatively long periods of stability. Furthermore, the changes were not followed by fallback from the new patterns that emerged in the behavior of the workers. On the contrary, the new patterns became stabilized outside the factory in the community.

Since Darwin's time the conventional wisdom about the pace of social change has been that it occurs gradually and continuously over extended periods of time at a more of less steady rate. In addition, it has generally been assumed that changes are followed by reactions that result in the outcome's becoming stabilized at some point short of the advances reached earlier in the process.[1] Savage's studies call both these aspects of the conventional wisdom into question.

Finally, Savage found that leadership of structural change was a multifaceted process that was not restricted to the acts of one person at the top of the organization. He noted instead that leadership was embedded in and emerged from a complex of interactions in which persons at all levels of the organization, including workers, were engaged.[2] This is not to deny that for some purposes it is useful to think of the person at the top of a business or other formal organization as its leader, especially when that person is also its owner.[3] It does suggest that ideas about leadership based solely or even primarily on the problems and behavior of that person are inadequate as a basis for thinking about the patterns of leadership needed throughout an organization.[4]

Like his findings about the pace of change, Savage's findings about leadership are contrary to the conventional wisdom, in which it is assumed that leadership is unitary and personal and that its effectiveness is determined by the charisma, persuasiveness, and power of the highest-level person in the bureaucratic hierarchy. Savage's studies suggest, instead, that leadership is a social process, in which persons—at least persons who understand the process, who are lucky, or who are both—make a difference.[5]

In connection with his findings about leadership, Savage noted that a leader's understanding of his workers' situation was as important as his persuasiveness in determining their acceptance of his leadership.[6] If he showed that he understood their situation, as Don José and Arturo did, then his efforts at persuasion were likely to be effective; otherwise they were not, as at El Dandy.

Savage's first finding is documented throughout this book and commented on at the ends of chapters 5 and 8. The present chapter reviews the perspectives from which Savage carried out his research, describes the process of structural change that he observed, summarizes the factors that influence social change, and discusses the significance of social change for the members of the work groups who participated in it. In chapter 13 the role of managers in connection with structural changes in work groups is discussed.

Social Organization of Work Groups

Savage went to Latin America to study why workers and managers behaved as they did. While he was there, his attention became fastened on the processes through which changes occurred in their behavior, both at the workplace and in the surrounding communities. He approached his research with the assumption that he was studying systems of happenings, that the events he witnessed at each site were not separate and discrete but connected with each other in some orderly fashion that could be identified and described. He regarded a group of people who have frequent contact with one another on a continuing basis as a natural social system, not as a formal or strategic one.[7] Natural systems emerge as a matter of course from the ongoing behavior of groups of people at work, without forethought on their part, and in such a way that the members may not be conscious of the existence of the systemic aspects of their behavior. Shown a carefully researched map or other description of the group to which they belong, however, the members will recognize and confirm it. Each system has its own structure, which is determined by its tasks—both economic and social—and the sentiments, needs, and personal histories of its members.

As in the case of a biological system or cell, a social system has an outer boundary, composed of both physical and psychic partitions, that helps provide the members with a sense of cohesiveness and identity. The boundary helps protect the system's well-being by delineating the establishment, revision, communication, enforcement, and existence of the codes and protocols that hold it together. Social systems are vulnerable, and they are mortal. Yet many outlive the constituencies of which they are composed at any one time.

In observing the systems that Savage selected for study, we see that he chose to deal at the level of deep structure.[8] He posited a change module composed of psychological, sociological, economic, and technological elements; he could trace the fate of this module as it moved up to and over the threshold of change. Thus he conceived of the patterns of behavior that he observed at Santuario and at La Blanca as the journey of a cluster of elements in contact with an equivalent set of forces in the environment. The process could be traced at several levels—in the workroom, the factory, or the village. Savage's vantage points—the potting room at Santuario, the plate room at La Blanca, and workshop A at El Dandy—afforded him the opportunity to make observations at the equivalent of the level of events seen through a microscope, the level of interactions between persons.

The need for intimate acquaintance with each situation that this approach required meant that Savage had to concentrate his attention on single work groups. He counted on collecting data through observation of and interviews with the group members.[9] Savage then used this information to seek an understanding of the groups' transactions with their environments.

Savage assumed that each group had a set of characteristics that transcended the histories and fates of its individual members and the technological schemes of its managers, a distinctive structure that could be described, and a momentum that could be traced as it responded to changes in the environment. He further assumed that changes in the social order and its evolution and development took place in terms of these structures.

The Pace of Structural Change

Debates over the pace of change have been long and arduous for many years. At one extreme, members of the catastrophe school of thought hold that change occurs in abrupt, explosivelike episodes.[10] Uniformitarians argue, on the other hand, that change occurs gradually and continuously at a steady rate. The arguments have been carried over from the fields in which they started, including the origins of the planets, to changes in the geology of the earth and in the species of life on it. Social scientists, at least in small-group studies, generally follow the uniformitarians' view. In recent years studies in several fields have led to revisions in arguments about these classic views. Paleobiology—study of the origins of species as shown in the records of fossils—continues to provide some of the most specific and convincing of the newer studies. Even though the field is far removed from the study of changes in work groups in South America, it is informative to examine some of them.

Writing in 1972 about the fossil record of mollusks, Eldredge and Gould concluded that in the development of a new species "the alternative picture [to gradual and continuous change is] of stasis punctuated by episodic events,"[11] in the course of which the development of a new species occurs in rapid and concentrated fashion, thus interrupting a system that is otherwise in homeostatic equilibrium.[12] They go on to say that the periods of stability in the life of a species are not characterized at microscopic levels by passive immobility. Rather, during these periods the species' homeostatic mechanisms and processes actively maintain its stability and thereby inhibit change.

In the fossil record that Eldredge and Gould studied, a new species originated in relative isolation from its parent species.[13] A geologic event—an earthquake, a volcanic eruption, a glacier, even a flood or a major storm—created an island, peninsula, basin, or other area separated from its surroundings. The altered location favored the development of a new species. The separation permitted the new species to develop its own processes of self-regulation to the point where it could maintain its new identity. The new developments penetrated to and affected the structure of the species, so that the processes and mechanisms that contributed to the species' stability during its period of stasis became involved in the change. Savage's descriptions of the process of change in the structure of work groups suggest analogous patterns.[14]

Factors Underlying the Process of Structural Change

The following paragraphs and table 12.1 summarize those patterns and describe the factors underlying them as Savage observed them. Although these factors do not always occur in the order in which they are presented here, indeed sometimes they overlap, they can be described separately without distorting the totality of which each is a part. The statements should not be read in a causative mode, for Savage's research was not intended or designed to test such propositions. Rather the statements were written first as descriptive of the uniformities—the differences and similarities—in the processes of change that he observed and second as oriented to the needs of practitioners and researchers, including among the latter those who work at analytic levels. To avoid repetition, the summaries, organized under the following headings, are intentionally brief:[15]

1. The general cultural setting and the local environment
2. The challenge from the environment
3. Patterns of communication and leadership
4. The work group's readiness for change
5. Initiation of change in the work group
6. Consolidation of structural change in the work group
7. Transmission to and consolidation of change in the community
8. Outcomes

Table 12.1
Factors Underlying Structural Change at Santuario, La Blanca, and El Dandy

Studied group	General cultural setting and the local environment	Challenge from the environment	Patterns of communication and leadership	Work group readiness for change	Initiation of structural change in the work group	Consolidation of structural change in the work group	Transmission to and consolidation of change in the community	Outcomes
Potters at Santuario	Small village; Destiny concept; Plaza phenomenon; Patronal system	Economic; Technological	Transformational leadership; Accessible, frequent, and face-to-face communication	Small size; Travelers from the outside returned; Age groups ready for change	From within the group after a pause; Protected trial sites available	Regular members of the group support the change; New leaders within the group; External rewards congruent with changes in the group	Rapid and pervasive; Football games; Emergence of alternative gathering sites	New levels of productivity; Work groups with members of more diverse backgrounds; New patterns of individual choice and responsibility
Plate makers at La Blanca	Large town; In transition	Economic; Technological	Expert plus transactional leadership; Accessible, two-way through Arturo, plus Zambariffi and La Montaña	Small size	Not observed; Introduction of doctores; Protected trial sites available	One-year pause in activation of football team for consolidation of developments in the group	Rapid and pervasive; Patrones move away; Doctores move in; Football games	Same as Santuario; New mechanisms for indoctrinating, promoting, and rewarding members of the work group
Workshop A at El Dandy	Metropolitan city; Modern transportation, communication, and entertainment; Delinquency and crime; Unions; Paternalism	Economic; Ideological	Charismatic and heroic leadership; Attenuated communication; Better among city-born than among village-born	Lack of cohesiveness; Large size; Group patterns inhibit change	By management without consultation; No protected sites available for trials	No observed structural or behavioral change	No new values to transmit	A frozen group; Disruptions caused by confrontations and strike finally settled by national labor ministry

The General Cultural Setting and the Local Environment

The general cultural setting provides the background for social change in specific settings and exerts a strong influence on the attitudes of individuals toward change. The general cultural settings of all three of Savage's research sites in Antioquia were characterized by respect for both tradition and change. The culture emphasized hard work, tolerated innovation and differences, lacked ostentation, and expressed pride in the region's history of accomplishment and autonomy.

Within this heritage, Santuario and Medellín presented extremes. Santuario was the smallest of the three communities, the most somnolent, and the least touched by modernization. For Santuarians, continuity with the past was paramount and the individuality of persons restricted. The members of the community shared a set of beliefs about fixed destinies, which gave every person and family a place, and a set of reciprocities, which established what individuals and families owed each other.

The cultural settings also exposed Santuarians and Blanqueros to alternative lifestyles with different material standards and different values. Modern means of travel, education, entertainment, and communication were at their doorsteps. The question could not be put aside, particularly among Santuarians, one of the least modernized communities left in the region: If for others, why not for us? The local environment provided centers apart from the mainstream of village life for experimenting with these new ways of life. At La Blance there were three such centers: Primavera, the factory, and the football field.

At Medellín, by far the largest of Savage's sites, urbanization had made its greatest inroads, although the older traditions had not disappeared. The city retained a distinctly Colombian and Antioquian character.

The Challenge from the Environment

A challenge from the environment often results in the initiation of change. All three communities faced such challenges, which in the first instance were economic. Santuario and La Blanca faced the severe curtailment and possible loss of the livelihood for their families. To meet the challenges, investments had to be made in new buildings and equipment. New skills had to be cultivated. Would the behavior of the workers also change to meet the new conditions, or would the villages have to find new ways of surviving?

At El Dandy the challenge came before Savage's visits. All that remained to be carried out was an additional rearrangement of the production lines to give management flexibility to schedule production to meet fluctuations in the demand for its products. In this setting, Hugo Soto, in his capacity as an officer of the garment makers' union, challenged management on an ideological basis about its method of accounting for depreciation of the company's store. After a prolonged controversy, Hugo Soto resigned. When another economic challenge arose in the environment, in the form of what management held to be a temporary decline in the demand for men's garments, it did so in the context of this ideological debate, which fell into the pattern that a win for one side was a loss for the other. A prolonged and costly strike resulted.

Patterns of Communication and Leadership

Patterns of communication and leadership that are accessible to the members of a work group, especially if the leaders convey a sense of direction for the development of the group without preempting the members' participation in determining it, favor the process of change. The patterns of communication and leadership at the three sites differed substantially. At Santuario and La Blanca, the patterns, although different from each other, were accessible and worked relatively well both among the workers and between the workers and their managers. Information was transmitted effectively through them. This was not so at El Dandy.

Although La Nueva had doubled in size, it was still small enough that Don José could easily and frequently keep in touch with the workers. He had ideas about what his factory and community could become[16] and allowed the potters the opportunity to participate in the development by asking for their suggestions about piece rates. Communication among the potters, the polishers, and their assistants took place around the table at which the men worked. At the time of Savage's studies, these factors outweighed the inconsistencies and overlaps that were beginning to develop in the supervisory structure of the company.

At La Blanca Arturo acted as a skillful mediator and facilitated the development of accommodations between the value systems of the workers, the doctores, and the patrones. As a transactional leader who exchanged with the workers his support for and goodwill toward their social organization for their efforts in making plates, he was effective in fostering communication between the workers and the doctores, who were experts in and advocates of efficiency. Zambariffi served under La Montaña's leadership as the principal means of communication among the workers.

Don José's and Arturo's methods of supervision brought the potters and plate makers into the decision-making process concerning output, payment systems, production orders, work locations, and the like and thus gave them opportunities to satisfy their needs for recognition and standing in their own eyes and in those of their associates.

The heroic style of leadership practiced by Dr. Medina, Hugo Soto, and the other officers and managers of the company and the unions and the paternal relationships that they developed at El Dandy contained no such mechanisms. Instead, their behavior was self-centered and egocentric, focused on statements about and arguments for the values important to them. The managers recognized and took account of the workers' values only in terms of what they thought these values should be, not in terms of what they actually were. Like the doctores at La Blanca, the managers at El Dandy acted as though they were the sole source of change in behavior in the factory, but they had to operate without someone who had skills like Arturo's to mediate the conflicts between their values and the workers'.

Complaints came to management in the context of formalized negotiations between management and the unions. Although Silvio and Lamberto helped the workers with personal problems they encountered at work, they were in touch primarily with the men who were born and brought up in the city. Their services did not effectively reach men from the country or women in the department. Communication between the garment workers and people outside the workshop was limited to the football players who saw Don Antonio and to topics that could be communicated in the formal bargaining sessions between management and the unions.

These channels were not adequate to communicate to management the garment makers' personal and social needs for growth and development or to communicate to the workers management's problems in running the company. Instead, the company's problem of reducing its inventory, when faced with a temporary drop in sales, became entangled in the ideological disputes between the management and the unions.

The Work Group's Readiness for Change

Readiness for change within a work group facilitates the acceptance and accommodation of change. At Santuario the readiness of the potters for changes in their lives facilitated the introduction of the technological changes that were appropriate for the company's productive process. If a similar readiness existed among the workers at El Dandy, its expression was inhibited by the gap that existed between the city-born and the village-born workers. At La Blanca the process of change had already passed from initiation to consolidation. Hence Savage had no opportunity to assess the community's readiness for change before it happened. There is no reason to doubt that its circumstances differed greatly from Santuario's.

Specifically, at Santuario it was appropriate for the sons of the workers who tended the kilns to move away from their fathers' supervision and scrutiny, because both fathers and sons were at the point in their lives when doing so was both timely and meaningful to them. Don Noah, at 44, after protesting to Don José and being rebuffed, could accept the changes without actively promoting them and, together with the other fathers, move away from the responsibilities of direct leadership toward the "burdens and satisfactions of senior leadership and authority."[17] Thus younger men— Ramiro, Héctor, and Atilio—whose interests represented the values toward which the group was moving, had the opportunity to become more active in its leadership. The compensation issue associated with the introduction of the new technology could be settled because the social issues associated with it could be. In addition, many of the men had lived and worked outside the village and thus had direct experience with a different way of life that some of them, particularly Atilio, preferred.

At El Dandy the patronal premises present at both Santuario and La Blanca had disappeared and had been replaced by Dr. Medina's well-articulated paternal interest in the welfare of his employees. This interest was based on his beliefs about how workers should behave and what they should want rather than on observation of how in fact they did behave and of what in fact they wanted.

The social organization of the garment workers in workshop A did not provide either a sense of participation in the productive purposes of the company or an opportunity for their own growth beyond the level of satisfying their needs for the safety and security of their jobs. Their organization became frozen at this level because the beliefs of management about how workers should behave inhibited them from interacting and developing behavior patterns that would have brought them satisfaction at higher levels of the need hierarchy. As a result, the garment makers' interactions occurred surreptitiously and primarily in connection with activities not directly related to their tasks. New values and new behavior patterns did not emerge from their interactions, and their social organization did not solve the new problems they encountered at work.

Initiation of Structural Change in the Work Group

An opportunity for the members of a group to develop their own response to an external change, rather than having it imposed on them, favors the initiation of structural change in the group. This is especially likely to be true if the external change is accompanied by a change in leadership within the group. Such a change, if it is to be accomplished gracefully without affront to the displaced leaders, takes time. The pause that followed Don José's request to the potters to form a junta gave the potters the chance to discuss differences in their views and to consider the consequences of the change, so that when Ramiro, Héctor, and Atilio went to Don José, they did so with the tolerance, indeed the relief, of the group as a whole. The interlude permitted the potters to work out their response at their own pace and to make the changes genuinely theirs. Their commitment to the changes went beyond an involvement in changes requested by someone else. They themselves created the changes and, in a sense, "owned" them, for the changes were meaningful in terms of their lives.

At El Dandy there was no pause between the managers' announcement of the planned changes in the layout of the production line in workshop A and their implementation of them. The managers did not seek the garment makers' views of the changes; they simply went ahead and carried them out. The arrangements for work, engineered for efficiency, provided no niches in which the workers could try out changes in their behavior privately. Instead, attempts at change—whether those of adolescent sons whose escapes from restrictive family life were announced over the radio by parents seeking their return or those of workers striking against a paternalistic management that stifled their initiatives—were accompanied from the beginning with the publicity of modern media coverage.

Consolidation of Structural Change in the Work Group
The participation of the regular members of a work group in the process of change, especially if the change is confirmed from outside the group, favors the consolidation of the changes. If, as happened at Santuario, the regulars support the change, it will rapidly affect all the members of the group, and new leaders may emerge. Perhaps the deviants and isolates will express their separation by rivaling and even exceeding the efforts of the regulars, as Carmelo did for a while at Santuario. If, on the other hand, only the deviants and the isolates in the group become interested in the change, then it will be minimal and will progress slowly, if at all. In these circumstances, it is likely that the interests of the regular members of the group to maintain their customary ways of behaving will prevail; there will be no change in the leadership or in the structure of the group. Changes that the deviants and isolates make in their behavior will not be structural in character and will not affect the members of the group as a whole.

At La Blanca under La Montaña's leadership and with Zambariffi's assistance, the regulars among the plate makers participated fully in the development of the mechanisms in the structure of the social organization that controlled the indoctrination of new members and the promotion of others. The development of these mechanisms benefited from a period of freedom from external intervention. The post-patronal decay provided an opportunity for Arturo and the others who shared his inclinations to nurture a new pattern of behavior that, as it were, budded from the old traditions. The doctores effectively screened themselves out of the process of change at the workers' level by their ideological preoccupation with surface structure. This buffer helped the plate makers adopt the changes in their behavior during the year when there were no football games.

At El Dandy the social organization of the workers did not develop to the point where it supported changes in behavior. Values that the workers had learned in other settings—in the city and in the villages—controlled their behavior.

Transmission to and Consolidation of Change in the Community

When structural change has been effectively consolidated within the work group, new patterns of behavior will spread to the adjacent community, particularly if an effective vehicle exists to demonstrate them. A shift in the structural forces that maintain the stability of behavior in a work group will affect related behavior in the community as a whole.

At both Santuario and La Blanca, once the changes in behavior had penetrated and modified the structure of the workers' social organization, football games provided a vehicle for the transmission of change to the larger community. When the workers and managers demonstrated new kinds and qualities of relationships before large turnouts of spectators, more than a game was being played. All parties were participating in highly visible ceremonies that proclaimed a new era that permitted new relationships.

At El Dandy the workers did not develop new patterns of behavior to solve the problems they encountered at work. They were, however, able to protect the ways of behavior they had learned in their communities and brought with them to work. Their social organization thus secured a measure of safety for their ways of life, but it did not contribute anything new to them.

Outcomes

When a challenge arises in a culture that is generally favorable to change, when the patterns of communication are accessible, when the leader conveys a sense of direction for development without monopolizing its determination, when the group has an opportunity to initiate a response and the regular members have a chance to support it, change in the group will be rapid and pervasive. The changes will affect the community as a whole and the relationships of authority in it. The changes will also affect the workers' productivity, their roles, and their sense of identity and self-worth.

The changes that occurred at Santuario and La Blanca reinforced the Antioquian cultural values of innovation, hard work, and independence. In addition, they produced tangible manifestations—increased wages, profits, and output. These outcomes were achieved not on the basis of a belief in fixed destinies but as a result of the social organization and values the workers developed from their experiences with each other and the challenges they encountered in their environment. The new structures were oriented toward members acting on their own inclinations and potentials for the future as contrasted with traditions and fixed destinies. These structures replaced the destiny concept, the plaza phenomenon, and the patronal system as determinants of their members' behavior.

At Santuario the workers achieved new levels of productivity and new forms of association with one another both inside and outside the factory. It became accepted that younger people could do things differently from older people.

At La Blanca developments in the structure of the social organization of the plate makers solved the problems introduced by the doctores' innovations. These developments defused the threat that the polishers posed to the standing of the potters. The developments also found places for new workers, both women and young men from the mountain villages, and trained them in the ways in which they were expected to behave. The workers' social organization thus incorporated in its membership the additional workers the company needed for increased production.

At El Dandy cooperation and collaboration among the different organizations and individuals who worked together to make men's clothing broke down. The changes in the structures of the social organizations at Santuario and at La Blanca maintained and enhanced the integrity of those systems, whereas the events at El Dandy signaled the failure of that system to maintain itself from its own resources. The public aspects of the contest among management, the unions, and the workers signified not the emergence of a new sense of unity or integrity in the community but differences and divisions. Rather than providing new values and energies for the community, together they allowed the central government to settle their disputes. These happenings thus represented a lack of capacity among the institutions to settle their own affairs.

The Meaning of Social Change to Participants

Savage wrote that as essential as he found the concept of social structure to the understanding of behavior in the workplace, he also found it inadequate to characterize the significance of the events to those who participated in them. The potters at Santuario and the plate makers at La Blanca experienced something other than a structural advance during the events, and the garment makers at El Dandy suffered something in addition to a structural breakdown of their social organizations. The potters and plate makers found new opportunities in their work and environment, opportunities that had existed before without being acted on. When the fragile network that the garment makers put together cracked and collapsed under the succession of blows it received during the confrontations between management and the unions, meaning drained from their workplace associations.

Persons who find themselves caught up in rapid changes in their lives experience them as crises. Savage found Erikson's ideas[18] about the identity crises of individuals useful in understanding the meaning of the events at Santuario, La Blanca, and El Dandy to those who participated in them. Throughout his work Erikson focused on the pressures that mark the passage from one stage of an individual's life to the next. Especially tender, he wrote, are the circumstances that attend the crisis of the late adolescent boy, who must, as a condition of his normal development, differentiate himself from his father and the recent past, which both have shared, as a means of finding a place in the present and future from which his own father will be largely excluded. In reaching for his own identity, the youngster uses his father as a benchmark, sometimes imposing on him the status of adversary, by which the son's differentiation may be stimulated and modified and the identity that emerges measured. Although this is a normal process by which life is renewed and personal history carried forward, it can be painful for the parties concerned.

Erikson suggested that what is being settled in these processes is a sense of personal integrity toward which individuals strive in relating their specific experiences and histories to a tentative social accommodation. The peace and sense of well-being that achievement of this accommodation brings is never permanent. It requires renegotiation at later stages of life, with the result that an individual's life takes on the character of a series of continuities and discontinuities through time. The passage from one life stage to the next, the negotiation of the discontinuity that links two continuities, may be difficult and trying. People need others to help define and establish the revised identities on which they are entering.

Savage thought that there were equivalent happenings in the factories and that work groups obtained new identities from their origins in a patronal system. At first, conflict was contained, and the mood was one of separation or withdrawal. Productivity remained constant, which camouflaged new stirrings from management scrutiny. The results at both Santuario and La Blanca were that plant authorities were unaware that anything was afoot. When management was uninvolved, as in the case of La Blanca's doctores, or preoccupied, as in the case of Don José, passage to the new structure was accomplished with a minimum of stress. Only a need for confirmation of the new structure remained before rapprochement between "parent" and "child" became possible.

The plate makers at La Blanca were caught up in one of these discontinuities. They had watched their village evolve from a condition of plaza-centered unity to one of polarization. This uneasy state affected all parts of their lives. The community processes that the patrones cultivated no longer provided a sufficient social basis for the plate makers' sense of integrity as individuals. The basis offered by the doctores was not acceptable. With their integrity as individuals at stake, issues that for them arose at work did not remain exclusively work issues. The identity reforms toward which their malaise pushed them had aspects they could not work out solely among themselves, for their relations with the polishers were central to their problems. Neither could the reforms be left in unresolved conflict.

The alternative for the plate makers was to seek ways to renew their sense of peace in the drama that was unfolding on the factory floor. They found this in the structure of the social organization that developed among them. This structure protected their status by making it inappropriate for polishers to earn more than potters and by arranging things so that other workers did not become polishers until they understood that polishers did not earn more than potters. At times of social change and discontinuity, juxtapositions and opportunities such as these give the factory, in terms of its significance to the members of its community, a role as agent of change in its community that takes precedence over its role with respect to its products and formal purposes.

At Santuario the social issues of leadership and membership were resolved in addressing the question of incentive compensation. The issues were complex and intertwined, for transitions among three age groups, adolescents, young adults, and middle-aged adults, were at stake. At El Dandy events did not progress this far. Management chose to turn back the clock, to try to recapture the peace and affection of an earlier age. The effect was to frustrate the garment makers' efforts to realize new identities for themselves and to repress and postpone what could have been a vital developmental breakthrough.

The El Dandy story is shot through with references to the classic struggle between a parent, who seeks to recapture the precrisis quiet, and an adolescent child, who knows that only in its rupture will he or she find the means of coming to terms with an unsettled present and the prospects of an even more disquieting future. Throughout the events the workers' struggle was for standing in human terms that was at least roughly equivalent to management's. But the parent gained an empty victory, and the future was postponed.

The situation at El Dandy was, however, not simply an inter-personal struggle between Dr. Medina and Hugo Soto. Hugo Soto symbolized the identity issues in which Silvio and the other workers were also caught up. His contest with Dr. Medina constituted, like the football games at Santuario, a kind of morality play onto which his coworkers could project their concerns about their individual integrity. In the absence of new ways of behaving at work, the garment makers chose to maintain and protect the way of life they had learned outside of work. Unlike the football games at Santuario and La Blanca, in the contest at El Dandy the garment makers' role was that of audience for, not participants in, a game that Hugo Soto played for them.

The garment makers understood that Hugo Soto was putting on a show, one that they appreciated because it deflected powerful changes that their group's structure could not have sustained. But when his activities were eliminated, their social organization was left exposed and vulnerable. In the circumstances of their unfulfilled and poorly understood strivings, the recourse for maintaining a sense of integrity in their own identities was to support the damaging strike that none of them wanted. In this way their identities re-mained free from Dr. Medina's all-encompassing and paternalistic embrace, just as Arturo's rejection of the doctores' suggestion of a company-sponsored football league maintained the independence and integrity of the workers' activities at La Blanca.

Perhaps because it was not a success story, El Dandy highlighted for Savage the human and personal dimensions of processes of change. Caught in a period of intense urbanization and social dis-location, the garment makers turned to their workplace as the instrument with which to get a handle on a world out of orbit and to struggle through to new personal identities that would sustain them not only at work but also in their communities. When access to this instrument was denied them, they were left exposed and vulnerable. Unresolved work, personal, and social issues backed up until the pressures became intolerable. They sought release in a strike that had results other than those that the parties who began it anticipated.

At work perhaps more than elsewhere, Savage concluded, individuals need to relate the experiences of their lives to what has gone before and to share in the processes by which the present is carried forward. Such continuity, when it exists, makes it possible for men and women to establish their identities through interactions with others against the backdrop of appropriate historical and cultural values. Under modern conditions of urbanized living, industry may be the primary or even the only site that men and women have in which to achieve this integration. Social structure provides the circuitry through which these interactions occur. Yet by itself structure is little more than a tracing of the energy flow through a social organization at any given moment. Thus while Savage grieved for the garment workers' loss of their interactional circuitry in workshop A, he grieved even more for the loss of the energy that flowed through it; this energy provided them with a measure of effective engagement with others and had the potential to bring new meaning into their lives. Thus the processes of structural change function to help individuals negotiate the series of passages through which they adapt to and accommodate activities that require increasing complexity and diversity.

Workplace structures manifest successive episodes of stability and change, rest and unsettlement, quiescence and upheaval, continuity and discontinuity. During periods of continuity or stability, these structures reinforce existing social apparatuses both inside and outside the factory. Relationships are quiescent and manifest a sense of peace and arrival. The structures are overtly at rest, although alive with the microevents contained within them. Individual identities are expressed through established work routines. Work issues dominate. Established protocols ensure continuity and stability that can be measured in terms such as the number of cups, plates, saucers, and garments that are made.

During periods of discontinuity or change, the role of the work-place as matrix maker for its community takes precedence. Structures knot in tension in a prelude to release and reformation around a new structural design. The carving out and defense of revised identities adequate to the new circumstances become the key issues. These may include issues of authority and leadership. Workplace structures respond to whichever of their twin mandates—production or reform—is paramount at the time. Sometimes, as at Santuario and La Blanca, the responses achieve their magic. At other times, as at El Dandy, the response is overwhelmed by offsetting forces. In any instance, the episodes feature division into subidentities and drastic separation of once joined elements. The episodes are attended by pain for both parties, because what emerges has to do so on its own terms and at the expense of the past if it is to withstand what the future holds.

In Erikson's schema, natural processing that has been temporarily aborted gets a second crack at resolution. The possibility that events at El Dandy might move toward resolution remains. Who knows what new cluster may have been created as a result of the post-strike activities.

Some Methodological and Other Issues

Savage came away from Antioquia convinced that he had witnessed significant events. Yet he was also aware that students of society come to identify with the portions of their work that are the focus of their attention and interest and that they are subject to the human claims made on them by those they study.

"I remember one gracious lady," Savage wrote, "who served me a demitasse of coffee at her home on La Blanca's plaza and worried that I would portray her villagers as primitives. She need not have been concerned. The people whom I studied were well within the framework of contemporary Western experience. In a world of space capsules, it was sometimes difficult for me to remember that Santuario and La Blanca still provide the typical work environment for mankind. Especially on-site and subject to the pull of the local perspective, it was far-off New England's advanced industrialization, approached at El Dandy at only a technological level, that seemed the esoteric work setting.

"More seriously, I attempted to avoid a partisanship that might cause me to identify with some rather than others of the forces at work in the factories where I studied—with Atilio, for example, the plate maker who challenged Santuarian tradition; with Arturo, who put together La Blanca's sentimental mafia; or with Silvio, who in his despair at El Dandy turned finally to Marxism. My imperfect reciprocity, in return for their considerable efforts for me, was to offer them a wider audience for my understanding of their situation by making it available in print. I know of no evidence that my first publications about their stories increased their problems. When I left La Blanca at the end of my intensive visits, the workers honored me by baptizing me into their tribe—with aguardiente instead of water. They invited me back to serve as a bearer of the Virgin's statue at their annual fiestas. I returned whenever I could to enjoy their company, godfather their children, and listen to their concerns."

Specifically, at Santuario and La Blanca Savage noted the following modifications in social protocols.

1. Before the events there was only one site of social assembly other than the factories; afterward, there were many, including new subplazas and outlying taverns and playing fields.

2. Before the events social encounters occurred primarily on a multigenerational basis; afterward, single-generational encounters became possible, notably in athletic activities but also in others, including the authentic union activity that followed the period of change.

3. Before the events the norms of the community acted as a barrier that maintained the community's separation from the surrounding area; afterward, the barrier was permeated by increased traffic and intercourse with neighboring communities and the weakening of the plaza phenomenon generally.

4. At Santuario before the events, patrones felt obligated to reside in the village; afterward, they felt free to move their residences from the village to the city, where they could attend more adequately to their families' needs. Don José was the first of several who believed that he could make this move without jeopardizing his commercial activities. At La Blanca after the events, the doctores, believing that their identities were sufficiently distinguished from the patrones, moved their residences to the town.

One test of the validity of a report of social events is its credibility to those who took part in them. Does it describe events as they experienced them? On this point Claude Lévi-Strauss[19] quoted

Mauss[20]: "What counts is the Melanesian of such-and-such an island." Lévi-Strauss went on to say, "*Contra* the theoretician, the observer should always have the last word; and against the observer, the native."

Most of the "natives" of Don José's potting room became familiar with the account of their activities that Savage prepared. Some read a Spanish translation of an early version. Whenever he returned to the village, they discussed this report, and, as described in chapter 1, their reactions helped shape the account in this book.

Although the principals to these studies thus accepted the social facts as Savage reported them, others did not. Members of a group of industrial managers in Medellín challenged his report. They argued that events of such interest and drama could not have happened in the region where they were born and raised and "knew" the daily life. Savage brought Don José to a subsequent meeting of the group to help set the record straight.

At La Blanca the plate makers hired a translator to read them an early version of Savage's report. They felt comfortable with the way he told their story. The doctores' reaction to an early reading may have resulted in their offer of a football league. This event may have accelerated the final stages of the change process, but did not, Savage thought, materially alter it. He remained convinced that the plate makers' support of Arturio's rejection of the doctores' first offer to support the league was structurally derived. There were more important factors at play in the factory during this period than the presence of an outsider reporting its story.

Savage's research should not be interpreted as suggesting that structural changes in work groups and in communities are not influenced by stirrings that originate in institutions other than the factory—families, schools, and religious and government institutions. Certainly they are, and Savage documented how changes in family relationships between fathers and sons affected work in the factory.

Savage did not study whether the changes he observed in the factories affected behavior in other hierarchically organized institutions, such as the government and the Church. In some of them— for example, in Santuario's town council—positions of responsibility went to senior citizens who were not likely to espouse the new behavior patterns, even though they may have utilized the technological changes that initiated them. Furthermore, in both the government and the Church conservative attitudes were strongly reinforced by controls handed down through impressive layers of supervision, leading in the one case to Bogotá and in the other to Rome. Rather than rapid change in these institutions, it seems likely that the new behavior patterns will result in an increase in tensions and disputes between those who support them and those who follow tradition.

The changes at Santuario and La Blanca did not affect everyone in the same way. At all three sites men dominated the work activities. Savage observed no instance of a woman in a position of prestige—potter, plate maker, or tailor. He did record one instance of a woman having been a polisher at La Blanca, but she did not last long in that position.

In one of his working papers[21] Savage commented that some people in contemporary societies, especially senior ones, regard at least the early stage of social change as tragedies. Those who feel strong ties to the old values are uncertain that the new ones merit their loyalties. When Savage first went to La Blanca, some of the neighboring towns were experiencing the first tremors from these changes. In them some families were breaking up, and there was delinquency, violence, drug traffic, child exploitation, prostitution, and perversion, all problems that Santuarians and Blanqueros had yet to confront.

Savage wished that persons who held such views would visit communities like Santuario and La Blanca, where traditional patterns still held sway, before they condemned social change. He thought that such visits would help them understand the costs of maintaining traditionalism. These costs were borne, he pointed out, by the lives of a few individuals—lives that came and went and never came again: young Marco Antonio Sanchez, whose destiny was to be the village drunk; Alcibiades, who would live and die the unreconstructed outcast; and ambitious little Pablo Mejía, whose destiny would not let him rise above his father's occupation of village bootblack. The costs borne by their lives, Savage thought, should be offset by the costs of change.

At El Dandy Savage found that apathy, boredom, and alienation characterized the attitudes of the workers toward their work. Conflicts and divisions marked their attitudes toward each other and toward management. Structures to support the new freedoms of choice that industrialization had won them were not available. To settle their disputes the company, the unions, and the workers accepted terms arranged with the help of an outside agency, the National Labor Ministry. It seemed as though they were losing the capacity to make their own choices that their counterparts at Santuario and La Blanca had won with such effort.

Clearly, at the end of Savage's research there was unfinished business in the communities he studied. It would be easy to argue that the path from a traditional to a modern industrial society leads over time from low to high productivity and from conformity, cooperation, happiness, and integration to individual choice, conflict, apathy, alienation, and division. This conclusion, though, ignores the significance of the social structures of work groups to their members, as discussed in this chapter, and of the role of managers in relation to those structures, the topic that provides the subject matter for chapter 13, the concluding chapter of this book.

13

Managers' Roles in Structural Change

Readers may wonder about the utility of discussing such questions as the pace of change and its meaning for the individual members of work groups. The answer is that views on such topics, whether they are explicit or implicit, determine the events that those who manage and are responsible for change in organizations select for their attention, decision, and action. Surely managers who view their own and their workers' behavior as subject to bursts of rapid change that the participants experience as crises in their lives give their attention to different questions than managers who view these patterns as characterized by gradual but continuous change. The differences are especially great if managers realize that the self-regulating aspects of behavior in work groups in periods of stability are not inert and quiescent with respect to change but actively resistant, whereas in periods of rapid change, the members of work groups may welcome change and change their behavior willingly. Managers' assumptions about such phenomena as the pace of change thus have far-reaching consequences for those with whom they work.

Savage's studies of the structure of the workers' social organizations provide an unusual perspective on the role of managers. He focused on managers' roles with respect to the structural changes that work groups in a traditional society go through in becoming modern. The approach differs from that of most modern management research in that he did not study the decisions that executives make about the strategic purposes of their firms, for example, about whether they should expand production.[1] Rather, by focusing on interactions at the level of the workplace, Savage learned about managers and their styles of leadership by observing how workers respond to their initiatives. In discussing his observations it is helpful to consider first the historical context of the roles of managers in Latin America under Taylorist and other ideas about the organization and management of work.

Traditional Roles of Managers

In Colombia and elsewhere in Latin America, as described in chapter 2, at the start of industrialization patrones and workers replicated in their factories managerial and organizational arrangements that were familiar to them. As a result the patrón-turned-manager had a fairly complete understanding, at least at intuitive levels, of the total social context—the deep structure of the situation—within which they operated. The patrón, however, was unable to convey his knowledge to his Taylorist successor, who attempted to accomplish his purposes largely through formal programs designed to order work activities and stimulate the efforts of workers by means of monetary incentives.

Savage saw at La Blanca that Taylorist principles became more than a scheme for organizing production and setting standards for workers. The principles served also to make their practitioners, the doctores, into a new management elite whose members were differentiated from the fading patronal premises. The new doctrines became invested with a specific elitist ethic and a set of egocentric myths. Thus Savage noted the religious coloring that attached to the doctores' dialogue and byplay among themselves, the myth about workers' irresponsibility, and the pretense that the new managers represented the primary order-imposing agency in the factory. However necessary these fictions were to the installation of new production methods and the survival of the new priesthood in the factory, they also reduced the doctores' exposure to the territory of workers' behavior to a much narrower slice than that to which the patrones had had access.

The doctores protested the apparent indifference of workers to their concerns in the only language at their command, the need for productivity. Savage's inquiry suggested that these protests were based on false grounds. His observations showed that workplace associations, even when they were in social ferment, did not exclude productive goals. He observed social mechanisms that served concurrently the personal and social needs of the workers and the organizational goals of the companies.

In adopting Taylorist views of their roles, the doctores were caught in a classic subject-object dilemma. The professional manager directed his attention to the appropriate object, the workplace, instead of to the traditional romantic vision, but he did so in ways that underscored his own centrality as the organizing principle.

The approach was not without early advantage, as the achievements of Taylorism attest. The practice provided a simplistic, although incomplete, basis for a first calibration of its methods of observation. The limitation of Taylorism was that its premises suppressed distinctive features of experience with the result that much of the scene that managers could have observed eluded them.

Because workers' social organizations and their values of autonomy, spontaneity, and friendship do not exist in Taylorist perspectives or MacGregor's Theory X, managers who take the orientation of their roles from these views hold that there is nothing to attend to or discuss with respect to them. Doing so is perceived as dysfunctional and a waste of time and as behavior inappropriate for managers. Managers thus find themselves becoming advocates of formal organizational values, as the doctores at La Blanca did. And as Savage pointed out in his study of El Dandy, advocacy roles on the part of some reinforce or create adversary roles on the part of others who have different interests in the questions at issue.

This tendency is especially volatile in organizational settings in which advocacy and adversary roles are superimposed on the roles of superiors and subordinates. Advocacy on the part of superiors of values that subordinates do not hold threatens the subordinates' positions in the organization, if not their personal integrity. At El Dandy the subordinates' responses were either acquiescent and apathetic or adversarial. And to the extent that subordinates advocate values that their superiors view as unwanted or unnecessary, the subordinates are viewed as undermining the values that their superiors hold.

If the parties continue in association with each other—as they will, if the organization persists—they are forced into fixed roles vis-à-vis each other, either acquiescing in or acting as adversaries to values that they do not hold while at the same time advocating values that the other does not espouse. The fixed and egocentric character of their evaluations of the situation then makes it difficult for change to emerge in their relationship.

Thus managers are seldom in the position of being able to make nonnegotiable demands for the values of the formal organization that they represent. If they do, they lose opportunities to support changes in the structure and roles of their workers' social organization. Indeed, in their single-minded search for efficiency they may unknowingly prevent the development of these changes, as the managers did at El Dandy. A manager's lack of attention to his workers' social organization thus defeats his purposes and leads to stalemate and stasis.

Savage's observations highlight the dilemmas of managers' roles in modern societies. On the one hand, Taylorist and Theory X views of management call for managers to act as advocates of efficiency. For this purpose notions about the unity of command and about the importance of persuasion have much to be said for them. On the other hand, giving support to the processes of change in the workers' social organization calls for managers to engage their workers in leadership activities and to understand workers' needs. Securing a balance between these two stances is never easy. The dilemmas and paradoxes include conflicts between objectives as well as doubts and uncertainties about one's own competence to choose among and deal with them. Zaleznik's The Human Dilemmas of Leadership[2] is a useful source in which to pursue these questions. The discussion here is limited to the suggestions that follow from Savage's work for resolving these paradoxes.

Savage's Views on Managerial Roles

Savage's studies call for the managers of industrial organizations to have a conception of their roles that goes beyond their economic and technological aspects to include support for the development of the social structures of the groups they supervise.[3] His studies do not suggest new techniques for manipulating followers for the leaders' purposes or for promoting the leaders as a new managerial elite, as the techniques of participative management and related ideas are sometimes presented in the journals and textbooks on contemporary management.[4] Rather, Savage's goal is to unlock the potentials for productivity, growth, learning, and satisfaction in the structure of work groups, including the members' relations with one another as well as with their supervisors.

The point is not an easy one to appreciate; so firmly is it established in the conventional wisdom of management that the productivity and development of workers is a property of the relations between managers and workers.[5] The assumption, relatively unexamined in our culture, underlies most of the studies about managers' intervening in their relations with their workers. These interventions seek to improve the workers' productivity and satisfaction.[6] The problem is to describe ways for managers to behave that do not result in workers becoming dependent on managers for changes in their—the workers'—activities.

One way to do this is for managers to engage the workers in activities that the managers—following ideas about the division of labor, the specialization of roles, and other Theory X–oriented views of management—customarily do for the workers. Thus managers open opportunities for workers to restore their sense of integrity, to govern their own affairs, to suggest innovations in their work, and through these activities to satisfy their higher level needs for standing and esteem in their own eyes and in those of their fellows. These were the opportunities that were available to the potters at Santuario but withheld from the garment workers at El Dandy.

Helpful as research-based findings on these questions would be, managers are not without recourse in their absence.[7] In these respects systematic knowledge cannot do more than give guidance to what a manager should do in specific situations. These are clinical decisions that depend on managers' observations of and intuitions about the situations they face and on their estimates of the consequences of their actions.

Managers have occasions to take such steps during periods of stability preceding change, during periods of change, and during periods of stability following change. The suggestions in the following paragraphs, being normative in character, are necessarily broad; to help make them specific, I have illustrated them with examples from Savage's studies. In addition to suggesting actions for managers to take during these periods, Savage's studies raise questions for further research. These questions concern whether and to what extent managers can affect the times at which periods of change and stability begin and end. I discuss these questions subsequently.

In Periods of Stability Preceding Periods of Change

In periods of stability and continuity preceding periods of change, managers need to support and show respect for their workers' social organizations. They also need to establish a climate within their organization that will facilitate the changes that will come during the period of change that will inevitably follow.

The managers at Santuario and La Blanca supported and showed their respect—on the whole inadvertently but not thereby ineffectively—for their workers' social organizations in the way they designed and administered the spatial aspects, the task arrangements, and the work assignments of the potting room and the plate room and by not interfering with their workers' social organization.[8] Although they made these plans and designs with the technical aspects of machine locations and work flows in mind, their designs provided space for private conversations, which the large open rooms at El Dandy did not. The managers also drew up rules of conduct to guide the behavior of their workers. At Santuario and La Blanca these rules did not forbid the workers from interacting; at both sites the workers were able to communicate easily with each other. At El Dandy the rules forbade talking among the garment makers, and communication was either surreptitious or ineffective and sometimes both.

Arturo showed that he understood and respected the plate makers' values in the way he assigned work locations and production orders. He made it evident that he did not regard their organization and its values as opposing the productive purposes of the company. On the contrary, he made it clear that he recognized their values as important aspects of production in the department. He also expressed these views to management. In these ways he arranged exchanges that accommodated the different value systems of the workers and the doctores. His style of leadership added an element of stability to the situation in the plate room and reinforced the stability that was developing in the plate makers' relations with each other. His behavior was thus congruent with their needs at the stage in the processes of change and stability during which Savage made his observations.

Arturo's accommodative, transactional style of leadership, however, was not without its costs. For example, by allowing the senior plate makers the advantages of working at their fixed work stations on long production runs, the workers did not receive the recognition or satisfaction from exercising the full range of their skills on the more difficult short runs. As mentioned in chapter 8, the company also lost the benefits of the greater productivity that would have been available to it if the most skilled plate makers had worked on the most difficult products.

Savage came to believe that managers should use group production quotas, output measures, and payment plans because they support workers' social organizations better than ones based on individual performance. He thought that workers themselves should participate in determining what share of their group's total compensation each member should receive. Don José and the potters were fortunate that the new piece rates established by the junta confirmed so precisely the changes in the potters' social structure as described in chapter 5.

Savage thought that managers should also consider workers' views in the selection and employment of new workers. His observations showed that a work group may reject a new worker who is not acceptable to its members and that the group's acceptance of a new worker plays an important part in the conditions of membership and of the role that the new worker is to have in the group's affairs.

During periods of stability managers also need to find ways of expressing the values of the enterprise as a whole through ceremonies and symbols that are meaningful in the particular situation. These occasions help clarify that the organization appreciates the contributions of its members. In this sense the revival of the ceremonies at La Blanca was important and so too was the Christmas party in the plate room that the men and women prepared and celebrated together. Don José's meeting with all the workers in the potting room—the potters, polishers, and their assistants—functioned in an integrative fashion. Although Dr. Medina also espoused meetings, his managers did not welcome them, and the topic proposed for them, like his orchid gardens, were determined by his, not his workers', interests. This left only football and the collection of funds to buy flowers for a colleague who was ill or who had died as the principal integrative activities among the workers in workshop A. Although these activities socially integrated the workers, they divided the workers and the managers because they had to be carried out surreptitiously, since management was against them.

During periods of stability, managers also have opportunities to affect the climate of relationships[9] in their organizations in ways that will facilitate future changes. The word "planning," even when it refers to sophisticated and computerized planning processes, is an inappropriate and superficial term for the activities that managers need to undertake. What is needed is the establishment of relationships in the present that permit open communication and trust[10] between the parties, so that divergent opinions and points of view can be discussed. In this connection, it is important for managers to be acquainted with what is happening in the lives of their employees. Don José, some of the other patrones, and Arturo were acquainted with their workers in this way. The value of this knowledge for their actions was apparent on many occasions. The doctores at La Blanca and the managers at El Dandy did not have it, and the consequences of that lack were fully apparent.

In Periods of Change and Discontinuity

When a structural change is underway in a work group, its managers need to realize that, although they establish some of the conditions that allow such a change to take place, they do not themselves create it; workers do that—with or without their managers' assistance. Whether managers like it, this aspect of the creation and management of a workers' social organization is inescapably their prerogative. They build and sustain their social organizations with their sweat and tears. They have to do so if the organizations are to have meaning for them.

In these respects, a manager's role is to guide and encourage the development of the workers' social oganization by clarifying its relationship with the purposes of the company. Managers should see that their communications—about, for example, a challenge from the environment—reach the leaders and regular members of a work group, as Don José's did. The changes can then move rapidly and pervasively to affect the behavior of the members of the group as a whole. Don Alfredo behaved appropriately in this connection in discussing with his workers the results of his trip to Brazil, and Don José did so when he told the potters about the opportunity for increased sales during the Christmas season. Dr. Medina and the managers at El Dandy, however, ignored the workers' values when they changed the production lines in workshop A without discussing the change with the workers.

Managers need to give their workers time to generate responses to changes. They should be tolerant of unusual behavior and make it evident that they are aware that something of significance is going on in the workers' social organization, for the events concern its structure and the roles and identities of its members. If the managers act too quickly, too frequently, or too forcefully, they interrupt the pause that the workers need to work out their solutions to the problems. Don José acted appropriately in this sense, for he suggested that the potters take three or four days to think about how they would respond to his request that they form a junta to discuss the piece rates. And although it was ten days before they came back to him, he did not hurry them. If he had acted sooner to settle the question of their pay, the resolution would have been his, not theirs, and it is unlikely that their values would have become involved in the change. Without that involvement there would not have been a systemic change of the workers' social organization.

A manager should not align himself with any faction that will inevitably develop. Don José behaved appropriately in this connection too, for he did not let himself be used for partisan purposes, either when Atilio and Rodrigo spoke to him about their need to earn more money or when Don Noah called on him at his house on the plaza to protest the introduction of incentive rates. In situations like this a manager needs to support the disputing factions without identifying himself with any. Doing so takes effort, because those who support tradition have in their favor the momentum of established procedures and protocols, and the reform parties do not.

Hesitation and inaction on the part of a manager are sometimes evaluated as weakness and vacillation, and sometimes no doubt they are. Savage's studies show, however, that delay and lack of action on the part of a manager can be essential to allow workers to integrate their manager's changes into their social organization. Different points of view, such as those among managers and workers, provide opportunities for discussion and clarification of the assumptions and values about actions in organizations that underlie them.

A manager's neglect of his workers' social organization does not prevent it from developing, for some of the factors that affect its development are outside his control. Changes in the lives of the workers that occur because of maturing and aging are examples.

Without the guidance of a manager, as Savage observed at El Dandy, the structure may then develop in ways that fail to integrate the technical and economic values of the firm with the social and personal values of the workers. Gaps in communication and understanding between managers and workers may then grow rapidly and provide fertile ground for the proliferation of misunderstandings and miscommunications.

The structural reform of a subordinate group may threaten the authoritarian and paternalistic elements that are present in a manager's relations with his workers. Values once shared are withdrawn as the evolving group seeks a separation, moratorium, or niche within which to develop new identities for its members. This isolation from traditional styles of interaction with authorities is necessary if the passage is to be accomplished and the new structure experienced as the group's own achievement. Surrender of control to superiors, no matter how cherished the past that was shared with them, would invite dilution of the new identities at the stage in their development when integrity is most at issue. Thus, in the process of working through an episode of crisis, managers become for a time the challenged, not the challengers, a role which in Taylorist perspectives they are ill-prepared to accept.

Managers need to understand that structural reform does not occur without crisis, which may be either mild or intense. During the period when a reform is being worked out, tensions and anxieties increase, as they did at Santuario. A manager's intervention cannot eliminate the need for reform, but it may hasten or block it. Usually neither is desirable, for the group's members need to feel that the conclusion is their own achievement, reached on their own terms at their own pace. The episode will be important and valuable to the group, and its successful resolution will add strength to the productive processes of the firm.

Once a social organization has a new structure, its members seek to create an identity for it that is different from the ones that surround it, especially from any that managers may want to impose on it. A manager needs to be alert for signals that the group has reached a conclusion, for that will free him to make more active interventions. The signal may be given in a small event, such as the awarding of a nickname for a new worker, as was customary among the plate makers at La Blanca. Or the signal may be given in an unexpected event, as, for example, Arturo's acceptance of the proposal for the football league at La Blanca a year after the doctores first suggested it.

In a Period of Stability Following a Period of Change

When a work group has successfully negotiated the passage to a new period of stability and continuity, managers need to be alert so that the themes of the preceding period of change and discontinuity do not become problems in the following period of stability. For example, during a traditional society's period of change to a modern one, an emphasis on higher levels of productivity is entirely appropriate and, as at Santuario and La Blanca, may be accepted by all parties. But if this emphasis is continued and the feelings and attitudes of workers are neglected in the succeeding period of stability, as may well happen under Taylorist and Theory X assumptions about management, the workers may come to feel, as the garment makers in workshop A did, that their managers and their company are using them as the means to achieve the managers' ends.

Unless attended to, the workers' feelings of being overlooked, left out, and used for others' purposes and their attitudes of alienation and apathy will increase. The workers will lose any initial willingness they may have had to tolerate in their group people with backgrounds different from theirs. Differences of age, sex, religion, education, experience, geographical origin, and ethnicity will make cooperation difficult. Although these divisions exist in a traditional society, it is not expected that persons from different sectors will work together. Rather it is understood that, for example, women's work is different from men's and young people's different from older people's. In the initial burst of energy that accompanies the transition to a new form of organization, these divisions may be overlooked and new workers tolerated and perhaps welcomed into the work group. But if its members do not find an appropriate structure for the new group—a structure that preserves respect for the senior members at the same time that it allows the new values to be expressed, as happened among the potters at Santuario—the divisions may reappear, and managers will be faced with the problems of discrimination and apathy that are familiar in modern industrial societies.

Thus, in a period of renewed stability after a period of change, there is a clear increase in the complexity of managers' tasks. Managers cannot turn away from the need for the higher levels of productivity to which the change in their society has committed them. At the same time they cannot neglect the new problems that arise from this commitment. They must treat the feelings and attitudes of workers with compassion, understanding, and respect, lest the workers feel that their needs are neglected.

Initiating Periods of Change and Stability: Questions for Further Research

Like all good research, Savage's provides answers for some questions of practice and application at the same time that it raises questions for further study.[11] Some of these questions are how-to-do-it ones that derive from suggestions in the preceding paragraphs, but broader questions are also at issue.

The preceding discussion places managers in the position of responding to the technological, economic, social, and personal forces that affect the situations they supervise. It is not fair to say that this position makes managers' actions entirely reactive to these forces, for as Savage's studies show, managers' actions, when they do not neglect these forces, go beyond ameliorating the conditions of work to create positive opportunities for workers' growth, development, and learning and for satisfaction of workers' higher level needs.

At the same time, the suggestions in the preceding paragraphs leave open questions about whether managers' actions are limited to responding to occasions that the forces permit for the growth and development of the workers' social organizations. Or are managers sufficiently free of these forces that they can act proactively to affect the times at which structural changes begin and end?[12] For example, Don José surely affected the timing of the changes among the potters at La Nueva when he turned his attention to expanding his factory's output after the other patrones rebuffed his suggestion for a consortium. After his decision to expand, the changes in the potters' behavior rapidly developed, and the value system in Santuario was transformed. Yet it is not accurate to say that Don José's behavior caused the changes, for the circumstances of the potters' families, in which the potters who were fathers and their sons who were their assistants were ready to take on new levels of responsibility, existed independently of his actions and were important among the conditions that allowed his actions to be effective. The juxtaposition of Don José's actions and of these circumstances was fortuitous, not arranged. Indeed, it may be nearer the truth to say that the circumstances in the families led to his actions rather than that his actions led to the circumstances.

Savage's studies delineate how these forces were interconnected in the situations in which he carried out his research. The studies suggest that the failure of a leader to act when the conditions for change are present may postpone and perhaps even prevent change from occurring. When the other conditions for structural change are present, a leader's acts are critical in initiating the change. Had Don José not acted to expand La Nueva when he did, the changes there and at Santuario would not have occurred. Whether the delay would have been long or short and what the process of change would have been, we cannot say.

Savage's studies do not tell us what a leader can do to create the conditions for change when they are not already present. The forces that influence the timing of periods of change and stability are deeply embedded in the history and structure of society. Even with respect to specific work groups, they are not the creation of any one person or group of persons and are not subject entirely to their management and control. We cannot expect the behavior of managers and leaders to replace these forces and, so to speak, substitute for them.

The managers of a company may support technological research and development and thereby ensure that technological innovations for change are present. They may be ready to take advantage of the economic conditions that favor change. Within limits they may staff work groups with a mix of persons whose backgrounds and attitudes toward each other and toward change are likely to lead them to work well together and to have positive attitudes toward change. But answers to questions about how effective managers can be in recognizing that these conditions exist in a specific situation or how effective they can be in arranging that all these conditions occur approximately at the same time—a much more difficult question—await further research.[13]

Judgments about whether the forces that affect a group's work call for structural change in its social organization are among the most difficult and important that managers make. Some innovations—for example, as Savage mentioned, the possible replacement of Don Noah by Don Pablo as the leader of the potters—can be accommodated without structural change.

On other occasions the technological and economic changes that affect a group's work may match the individual and social changes for which its members are ready. Then structural change in the group may move rapidly and almost without the managers' attention. Don José and the potters at Santuario were fortunate that at the time when new markets were available for La Nueva's chinaware, it made sense in terms of the life cycles of the individual potters for Don Noah to accept a senior role in the group, for Ramiro, Héctor, and Atilio to move toward positions of active leadership, and for the sons of the potters to move into positions of increased responsibility either in the factory or away from it.

Sometimes, though, when technological and social changes to express what is meaningful to workers are not available, changes in the roles and identities of individual workers are appropriate to the cycles of the lives. At such times, the workers' needs to change their behavior do not diminish but remain either frustrated or expressed in ways not connected to the productive purposes of the firm.

On still other occasions technological changes occur when workers are not ready for them. Some observers argue that at least in advanced industrial and postindustrial societies, the pace of technological change is so rapid that it surpasses the capacity of the members of the society to keep up with it. These observers adopt one of two views: either they blame culture as a barrier to technological change or they blame technology for alienating individuals and groups from each other and from their work. In the first instance, the observers fail to understand how culture functions to maintain a sense of integrity and continuity in the lives of individuals and groups. In the second, they fail to see the opportunities for growth and development that technological change holds for the lives and welfare of individuals. Blaming either culture or technology accomplishes little, for the need is for understanding of the interface between the two.

Savage's studies provide no easy answers for managers with respect to how they should behave. They suggest no simple solutions or techniques, no rhetoric or dogma, that used in all situations will lead to success. Rather they call on managers to assess the specifics of the situations that they encounter and to diagnose and act with respect to them in a broad framework of thought about a business organization as a social system that encompasses both its productive purposes and the personal and social needs of its members.[14] They suggest that a manager's role is like that of a catalyst who is himself willing to enter into the processes he seeks to guide rather than like that of a Taylorist or Theory X leader who behaves as though he is the source of change for the organization as a whole. In contrast to being experts in and advocates of efficiency, the role for managers that emerges from Savage's studies emphasizes the integrative, innovative, entrepreneurial, communicative, information-processing, and educational aspects of their tasks. The role calls for them to bring together information about the technological, economic, social, and personal forces affecting a work situation; to initiate action with respect to these forces; and to inform and educate the participants about them in order to secure their actions. Don Alfredo did this when he talked with the workers following his trip to Brazil, and Don José did it when he talked with the potters about the opportunities for increased production that were available to La Neuva.

The Implementation of Savage's Findings: Some Problems and Opportunities

Managers' acceptance of responsibility for assisting workers with structural developments in their social organizations would be a major change in managers' understanding of their roles and in societies' expectations of them. Paraphrasing Ortega y Gasset,[15] Savage wrote in an early draft of the conclusions for his book, "It is not our institutions as institutions that are doing badly. It is the functions for which we employ them that are at fault. This tendency is especially marked in industry, where typically managers regard factories as existing solely for the purpose of producing goods. Santuario, La Blanca, and El Dandy taught me that a factory is more than that and that there is more to a tribe than its chieftains. In describing the events that I observed in Don José's factory, I could not omit the deeper ferments—emanating from Don Noah, for instance, and from Atilio—that factored in, sometimes critically, when processes hovered at the threshold of change. To acknowledge such influences is in no sense to discount Don José's contributions in bringing events to the threshold of change. On the contrary, it highlights them. But to derive the lessons of Santuario it was necessary for me to move from surface to deep structure and to take account of events as seen from the potting room's window on the world. What I saw was that, unbeknownst to their leaders, workers weave delicate social and human structures, without which management's strategic architecture would collapse overnight.

"The patrón-turned-manager possessed social as well as technical information about the situations he managed. Indeed, he probably had more social than technical knowledge, since in early times technical information was in short supply. In any case, he was familiar with the territory of his workers' behavior. He understood it and them. Can this capability be found, revived, and put to work again? Can our crippled, half-paralyzed institutions be led to function in all their dimensions, the human and social as well as the economic and technological, and do so knowledgeably and with a sense of élan?"

In the conventional wisdom of our times the skills of management are thought to lie in how managers determine and deal with a company's purposes. This evaluation occurs because the conventional wisdom overconceptualizes the complexity of these formal organizational problems, and underconceptualizes the potentials for change that are available in the concrete social structures of groups at work. Of course the logical problems associated with an organization's purposes must be dealt with. Beyond that, Savage's studies suggest a preventive approach to the nonlogical problems, an approach that seeks to resolve the problems as they arise in the workplace[16] before they escalate and become intractable in formal confrontational settings at high levels of an organization or a society.[17] He suggests the development of managers' skills in their face-to-face interactions with the members of the groups they supervise. Discernment of opportunities in these situations for acts of leadership that transform the structure of a work group is a task that among other characteristics has conceptual, political, and moral aspects that require an inquiring mind and a vision of how things in the future may differ from those in the present as well as a capacity for understanding and persuading others and for understanding one's self.

The central conceptual and intellectual questions concern whether managers can be trained to perceive the pattern of a work group's structure in the acts of its individual members, the form in which they frequently encounter it.[18] Managers are usually chosen for their skills of action rather than for their capacities for reflection and imagination, the abilities that they need to conceptualize a group's structure. Difficult though this process may be for some managers, others deal with it successfully every day—as, for example, when they resolve a problem of an age or seniority difference between workers—even though what they do is neither clearly recognized nor rewarded.

The political questions concern the locus of power and control as it is distributed among managers at the top, middle, and lower levels of organizations considered as hierarchies. When managers at top levels decide that decisions about the work and its organization should be transferred to lower levels, the positions and roles of those in the middle become highly ambiguous and uncertain.[19] Persons at those levels are likely to form coalitions to resist the transfer with colleagues who are similarly affected. These reactions thus activate a political process within the organization that is not likely to be congruent with the efficient accomplishment of its purposes.

To correct the process, managers need to realize that they do not give up the authority of their positions when they allow workers to take part in decisions about their activities at work. Rather, they show that they recognize that their decisions affect workers and that workers have the knowledge and capacity to contribute to the decisions.

The moral questions concern whether managers can be trusted to evaluate and act on interests different from their own. The development of skill in this sense—the capacity to diagnose and act in terms of what in fact is important in a situation in contrast to acting in terms of one's self-interest and preconceptions—is never easy. Some say that everyone's evaluations are inescapably limited by their personal positions and interests. In a sense this is true. There is much experience—and not just in times that have passed—to support these views. Yet everyone knows of individuals whose evaluations of the happenings in which they are involved are better—in the sense that their suggestions are accepted as more trustworthy as a basis for action—than those that others make. Hence I assume that there are processes of education or experience that lead to these results, that these processes can be specified, and that others can be trained in them.

The important questions of implementation are thus as much educational as conceptual, political, and moral. The ideas about which I have been speaking have been available in schools of administration and management for many years, but even when they have had strong support, they have not been best-sellers. Take, for example, the concept of social structure. As the literature cited in note 5 to this chapter indicates, attention to the idea has not increased. There is more interest on the part of professors, students, and practitioners—and more rewards—in addressing matters of policy and strategy at formal organizational levels at what Savage referred to as surface structure. Even in the foremost schools, these other ideas do not get more than one hour out of eight or ten in the curriculum—and they may not get that. Instead, the emphasis is on formal and rational systems of strategy and control, on new techniques and devices, including computers, for implementing managers' roles as the source of order and structure in the workplace.

Even if the educational problems about which I have been speaking can be resolved and the leaders of organizations trained to act with respect to the technical and economic problems that they face in the context of their meaning for the social structure of workers' organizations, questions remain about whether there is time to accomplish the results that are needed. The needs are not for hundreds but for thousands of supervisors and higher-level managers trained to manage social change at the level of specific work groups in organizations everywhere.

Savage ended his manuscript, "If I am not optimistic—and one cannot be in the face of the complexity, size, and immediacy of the problem—neither am I pessimistic. Leaders of industry do not want to impede developments of the spirit. There are many who look for ways to shake off the obsolete concepts of managers' roles that result in these outcomes. They are searching for ways out and up and beyond, for a workable formula, a demanding idea toward which to aspire, a sense of possibility. If such an idea for managers' roles could be found, tested, and refined, the axis of their perceptions and actions would shift, and a drama of significance would unfold where society is least likely to look for it, in its factories and business organizations."

Appendixes

A

Selecting the Research Site and Collecting the Data

Selecting the Site

Before he set out for South America in January 1960, Savage developed the following criteria to aid him in the selection of a research site.

1. *Nationality of management* Savage preferred a plant owned and operated by nationals rather than expatriates. Although a binational management offered interesting questions for research, he wanted to study how a Latin American work group functioned under national supervision.

2. *Plant layout* Savage wanted a setting that would permit him to make observations easily. This meant one in which the work force was not dispersed over a large area and in which conditions would make it possible to hold conversations during working hours.

3. *Stable employment* Savage hoped to find a work group in which the membership would remain stable during the period of his study.

4. *Measurable individual output* Savage considered the availability of records of individual output important.

5. *A modern but not complex production process* Savage wanted to find a technology that called for job specialization and other behavior that departed from the traditional.

6. *A work group mixed as to age, sex, ethnicity, and the like* Savage thought that the stresses of the workplace would be more apparent in work groups with a mixed rather than a homogeneous membership.

7. *A receptive management and work force* Finally, Savage was looking for a management and work force that would be receptive

to the idea of an outsider making observations in their plant for a matter of months.

Savage did not regard these criteria as rigid. He thought they should yield to actual conditions when circumstances warranted. His experiences on his first trip quickly indicated the following modifications: (1) Because of the complexity of their background and the inadequacies of company records, it proved impossible in the time available to make useful observations about the ethnicity of members of work groups. (2) Output records were available in almost all areas of the plants that Savage visited. He did not have time, nor did it seem proper in his role as guest, to pursue in detail the usefulness of these records for his study. (3) Savage's preference to study a plant owned and operated by nationals was reinforced but for different reasons. He found that the sentiments in plants with binational managements were such that scrutiny of the kind he wanted to make would not be welcomed. (4) The importance of the community where the factory was located came into sharp focus. After all, modern technology was challenging the standards of the community. Therefore to have a community that was small enough that its standards could be easily assessed was important.

The plants that Savage visited on this three-week trip ranged from a one-room broom factory to a large textile complex that employed 7000 people. They fell into two groups: factories owned and operated by nationals and those owned and managed by expatriates. In the first group, the products were brooms, tobacco, garments, pottery, beer, cement, and textiles, all with modern plants but not highly capitalized in their operations. In the second group were footwear, petroleum, tires, and extractive industries, all with highly specialized and highly capitalized operations.

On the second day before Savage's departure, the young economist assigned as his guide by his hosts, a national association of manufacturers, escorted him to the head offices of a chinaware company in Medellín. The company manager, a young man, met them at the door and took them without delay to the office of the president, Don Adolfo. After dark Colombian coffee served in small china cups, the conversation turned to the purpose of Savage's visit and the special appropriateness of Antioquia for his studies. At the conclusion of the discussion, Don Adolfo said, "We hope you will find the research opportunity that you are seeking here at our plant, or at least in Medellín. We Medellienos thrive on innovation. We may get some new ideas from your study. If you decide to do it here, we will see that you get full cooperation."

That afternoon the company manager drove Savage to the plant some 20 miles from the city and high up in the surrounding hills. After passing through an industrial area of the city and open country with small scattered villages, they turned up a winding asphalt road into a narrow valley with alternating patches of corn and grazing land. La Blanca, where the plant was located, seemed typical of other Andean towns but had no sign of the extreme poverty found in some of them. Just beyond the plaza was the plant, long, low, and grey. It was old, and Savage was told a new one was planned. Dr. Gomez, the plant general manager, was waiting for them.

This was the twelfth time Savage had presented the plan for his research. The terms came readily to him: *sentimientos, interacciones, actividades, los miembres regulares, aislados, y los desviadores.* The company representatives discussed work groups that met the research requirements, the existence of individual output records, and work teams with readily observable tasks. They took Savage on a tour of the plant, then returned to the conference room for a review of the discussion and final cups of coffee. Three hours after he arrived, Savage realized that he had seen the plant with the combination of factors that would allow him to pursue his research. In addition, it was located in a town small enough and far enough away from other centers to constitute a distinct community that could be easily studied.

Collecting the Data

When Savage began his research in the field, his methods were typical of other factory and community studies at the time.[1] He began his work at the La Blanca factory by studying the organization of its production. His initial efforts caused the workers to identify him as another Taylorist, interested in production alone. He next sought information about what people did in both their job and personal activities, what they believed and felt, and how they interacted with one another. What resulted was a mass of floor plans, job descriptions, output statistics, interview notes, interaction maps, and diaries of both daily routines and special occurrences that he witnessed from his station on the factory floor. Later he combined these data into a loose social system scheme, as described in Homans' *The Human Group*,[2] in order to analyze the forces that guided the collective as well as the individual events and especially to answer the question: Was some sense of community, clan, or tribe at work in each group?

With the passage of time, the workers found Savage responsive to secondary levels of experience beyond Taylorist limits, and they accepted his explanation that he was an independent observer who had come to write a book about their experiences. It was then possible for him to move out of the factory into village life and to undertake the community aspects of his survey.

He began documenting the interchanges that took place during home visits, baptisms, wakes, fiestas, tavern discussions over dominoes and glasses of aguardiente, and Sunday excursions to city markets and upland settlements. These data were easy to record when he resided in the villages. With slightly greater effort, it proved possible to collect similar data in the city after he moved to Medellín. Next, he combined these data into a rough community profile for each site, which he related to the profiles he had already developed for the factories; he attempted to plot the interplay between the factory and its community as parts of a single totality.

B

Tables

Table B.1
Age, Marital Status, and Pay Grade of Santuario Workers

Position	Number	Average age	Married	Pay grade High	Middle	Low
Potters	9	37	7	6	2	1
Polishers	8	26	4	2	5	1
Assistants	17	16	0	0	0	17

Table B.2
Type of Headgear Worn by Santuario Workers

Postion	Caps	Straw hats	Berets	Other
Potters	5	0	2	2
Polishers	0	4	0	4
Assistants	2	4	7	4

Table B.3
Individual Potters' Attitudes toward Change in Santuario

Potter	Age	Exposure to city life	Union member	Not a don	Speaks up	Simpatico	Accepts transfer	Change orientation index
Don Noah	44	–	–	–	–	–	–	0
Don Pablo	40	–	x	–	–	–	–	1
Rodrigo	39	–	x	x	x	x	x	5
Héctor	39	–	x	x	x	x	( )	4
Ramiro	38	x	x	x	x	( )[a]	( )	4
Samuel	37	–	–	x	–	–	–	1
Fernando	34	–	x	x	–	x	–	3
Atilio	34	x	x	x	x	x	x	6
Carmelo	26	–	–	–	–	x	–	1

a. ( ) indicates ambiguous response.

Table B.4
Differentiation Factors among Individual Santuario Potters

Potter	Corner position	Makes plates	High producer	Nonstandard headgear	Resists reassignment	Differentiation index
Don Noah	x	x	x	x	x	5
Don Pablo	–	–	x	–	x	2
Rodrigo	x	x	x	–	–	3
Héctor	–	–	–	x	–	1
Ramiro	–	–	–	x	–	1
Samuel	–	–	–	–	–	0
Fernando	–	–	–	–	–	0
Atilio	x	x	x	x	–	4
Carmelo	–	–	–	–	–	0

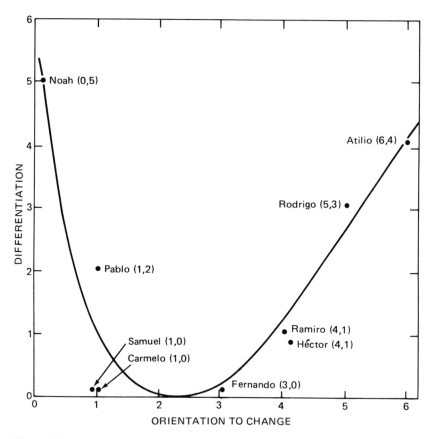

Figure B.1
Change orientation and differentiation indexes of the potters at
Santuario.

Table B.5
Santuario Potters' Actual Weekly Earnings Compared with Projected Piece Rate Earnings (Pesos)

Potter	Actual earnings: day rates	Projected earnings with incentive (piece) rates: 6-week average	Overpayment (Underpayment)	
			Actual minus projected	% Change from actual earnings
Don Pablo	79.20	89.00	−9.80	−12.4
Don Noah	79.20	88.00	−8.80	−11.1
Ramiro	79.20	80.00	−0.80	−1.0
Héctor	79.20	77.00	2.20	2.8
Atilio	79.20	72.00	7.20	9.8
Rodrigo	79.20	NA	NA	NA
Fernando	76.80	67.00	9.80	12.8
Samuel	76.80	60.00	16.80	21.9
Carmelo	67.20	87.00	−19.80	−29.5
Total	696.00	NA	NA	NA
Average	77.33	NA	NA	NA
Total without Rodrigo	616.90	620.00	−3.20	−0.5
Average without Rodrigo	77.10	77.50	−0.40	−0.5

NA = Not available.

Table B.6
Nominations to Serve on the Junta at Santuario

Recalled by	Recalled as nominees						
	Atilio	Rodrigo	Ramiro	Héctor	Carmelo	Pablo	Noah
Don Noah	x			x		x	
Don Pablo							
Carmelo					x	x	x
Héctor	x[a]			x[a]		x	x
Ramiro	x					x[a]	x
Rodrigo	x			x			x
Atilio	x			x			x
Total	4	0	0	3	1	3	5

a. Name mentioned first; later changed as indicated by totals.

Table B.7
Santuario Potters' Potential Earnings before Change versus Actual
Earnings after Change (Pesos)

Potter	Potential earnings with piece rates before change: 6-week average	Actual earnings after change: 6-week average	Difference	
			Actual minus potential	% Change from potential earnings
Don Pablo	89.00	119.00	30.00	33.7
Don Noah	88.0	112.00	24.00	27.3
Ramiro	80.00	97.00	17.00	21.3
Héctor	77.00	105.00	28.00	36.4
Atilio	72.00	108.00	36.00	50.0
Rodrigo	NA	103.00	NA	NA
Fernando	67.00	NA	NA	NA
Samuel	60.00	84.00	24.00	40.0
Carmelo	87.00	125.00	38.00	43.6
Total	620.00[a]	853.00[b]	233.00	37.6
Average	77.50 (8[c])	106.63 (8[c])	29.13	37.6
Total without Rodrigo and Fernando	553.00	750.00	197.00	35.6
Average	79.00 (7[c])	107.14 (7[c])	28.14 (7[c])	35.6

NA = not available.
a. Without Rodrigo.
b. Without Fernando.
c. Number of potters used to compute the average.

Table B.8
Santuario Potters' Actual Earnings Before and After the Change (Pesos)

Potter	Earnings under day rates before change	Earnings under incentive rates after change: 6-week average	Increase after change Earnings after minus earnings before	% Change from day rates
Don Pablo	79.20	119.00	39.80	50.3
Don Noah	79.20	112.00	32.80	41.4
Ramiro	79.20	97.00	17.80	22.5
Héctor	79.20	105.00	25.80	32.6
Atilio	79.20	108.00	28.80	36.4
Rodrigo	79.20	103.00	23.80	30.1
Fernando	76.80	NA	NA	NA
Samuel	76.80	84.00	7.20	9.0
Carmelo	67.20	125.00	57.80	86.0
Total	696.00	853.00[a]	157.00	22.6
Average	77.33 (9[b])	106.63 (8[b])	29.30	36.6
Total without Rodrigo and Fernando	540.00	750.00	210.00	38.9
Average	77.14 (7[b])	107.14 (7[b])	30.00 (7[b])	38.9

NA = not available
a. Without Fernando.
b. Number of potters used to compute the average.

Table B.9
Ranking of Santuario Potters' Actual Earnings after the Change
Compared with Increases in Their Actual Earnings (Pesos)

Potter	Rank	Actual earnings on piece rates after change: 6-week average	Increases in actual earnings
Carmelo	1	125.00	57.80
Don Pablo	2	119.00	39.80
Don Noah	3	112.00	32.80
Atilio	4	108.00	28.80
Héctor	5	105.00	25.80
Rodrigo	6	103.00	23.80
Ramiro	7	97.00	17.80
Samuel	8	84.00	7.20

Table B.10
Selected Information about Employees in Workshop A at El Dandy

Worker	City-born (C) or Village-born (V)	Age	Years of schooling	Number of children	Seniority in years	Union membership	Production in standard hours[a]
Cutters (Job rating 3)							
Roberto	V	45	2	6	13	No	62
Favián	C	41	2	9	14	Yes	66
Hugo Soto	C	40	4	7	12	President	43
Ignacio	V	44	5	7	15	Board	64
Basters (Job rating 7)							
Flavio	C	31	9	4	10	Yes	66
Carmelo	V	47	5	6	11	Yes	56
Arcesio	C	42	5	2	2	Yes	51
Héctor	C	37	5	5	15	Yes	69
Assemblers (Job rating 7)							
Gonzalo	V	31	3	6	3	No	60
Simón	V	47	4	6	17	Yes	57
Lamberto	C	46	5	4	9	Board	40
Don	V	44	7	9	1	Yes	54
Alberto							
Ricardo	V	37	5	5	7	Yes	46
Silvio	C	40	5	9	15	Secretary	52
Alonso	V	30	4	5	2	Yes	54
Mario	C	26	5	2	5	Yes	57
Pressers (Job rating 4)							
Alvaro	V	43	3	6	17	Yes	62
Diego	C	37	4	5	8	Yes	67
Eliseo	C	45	5	6	7	No	63
Jairo	V	20	5	1	4	Yes	52
Edgar	V	31	5	7	7	Yes	74
Léon	V	32	3	0 (not married)	3	Yes	78
Carlos	V	42	4	5	9	No	77

a. The average weekly production of each operator for a six-week period expressed in terms of a sixty-minute standard hour.

Notes

Chapter 1

1. Taylor, Frederick W., *The Principles of Scientific Management* (New York: Harper and Brothers, 1911).

2. For a more detailed account and evaluation of Taylor's ideology, see Simmons, John, and William Mares, *Working Together* (New York: Alfred A. Knopf, 1983).

3. Paz, Octavio, *The Labyrinth of Solitude: Life and Thought in Mexico*, translated by Lysander Kemp (New York: Grove, 1961).

4. McGregor, Douglas, *The Human Side of Enterprise* (New York: McGraw-Hill, 1960).

5. Roethlisberger, F. J., and W. J. Dickson, *Management and the Worker* (Cambridge: Harvard University Press, 1939).

6. Weber, Max, *The Protestant Ethic and the Spirit of Capitalism*, translated by Talcott Parsons (New York: Charles Scribner's Sons, 1958).

7. Weber, *Protestant Ethic*, 109.

8. Weber, *Protestant Ethic*, 112.

9. Malinowski, Bronislaw, *Argonauts of the Western Pacific* (New York: E. F. Dutton, 1932).

10. Nash, Manning, *Machine Age Maya* (Glencoe: The Free Press, 1958).

11. June Nash in her later study of a tin mining community in Bolivia, provocatively entitled *We Eat the Mines and the Mines Eat Us: Dependency and Exploitation in Bolivian Tin Mines* (New York: Columbia University Press, 1979), spent only five shifts in the mine during her sixteen-month study in 1969 and 1970.

12. Abegglen, James C., *The Japanese Factory: Aspects of Its Social Organization* (Glencoe: The Free Press, 1958).

13. Hagen, Everett E., *On the Theory of Social Change: How Economic Growth Begins* (Homewood: The Dorsey Press, 1962), 353–354.

14. For historical accounts of the development of Antioquia, see among others, Manuel, Antonio, *Historical elemental del departmento de Antioquia*

(Medellín: Editorial Bedout, 1952); López de Messa, Luis, *Escrutinio sociológica de la historia Colombiana* (Bogota: Academia Colombiana de Historia, 1956); and Fluharty, Vernon L., *Dance of the Millions* (Pittsburgh: University of Pittsburgh Press, 1957).

15. Rostow, Walt W., *The Process of Economic Growth* (New York: W. W. Norton and Company, 1952), and *The Stages of Economic Growth* (Cambridge: Cambridge University Press, 1960).

16. See, for example, Hagen, Everett E., *The Economics of Development*, third edition (Homewood: Richard D. Irwin, 1980), 81–82.

17. Rostow defined takeoff in strictly economic terms "as an increase in the volume and productivity of investment in a society, such that an increase in per capita real income results" (*Process of Economic Growth*, 102). Rostow spoke of the duration of a takeoff as a period of 20 years or so.

18. See, for example, Blanksten, George I., "Transference of Social and Political Loyalties," in *Industrialization and Society*, Bert F. Hoselitz and Wilbert E. Moore, eds. (The Hague: UNESCO-Mouton, 1963), 175–196.

19. Hagen, *Theory of Social Change*, chap. 3. Later he went further and wrote that the acceptance of new roles—that is, a social phenomenon—"is a necessary part of economic growth" (Hagen, Everett E. "Wealth and the Economy," in *Comparative Theories of Social Change*, Hollis W. Peter, ed. (Ann Arbor: Foundation for Research on Human Behavior, 1966), 54). See also Nash, June, Juan Corradi, and Hobart Spalding, Jr., eds., *Ideology and Social Change in Latin America* (New York: Gordon and Breach, 1977).

20. Hagen, "Wealth and the Economy," 84.

21. Arroyave, Julio, *El pueblo Antioqueno*, second edition (Medellín: Imprenta de Universidad, 1960).

22. Hagen, *Theory of Social Change*, 280 ff. See also Levy, Kurt L., *Vidas y obras de Tomás Carrasquilla*, translated by C. López Narvaez (Medellín: Editorial Bedout, 1958), 173, where he quotes Tomás Carrasquilla, Antioquia's leading literary figure, to the same effect ("Reconquista," *El Corree Liberal obras completas*, 27 (Medellín, 1913), 2031–2035).

23. Hagen, *Theory of Social Change*, chap. 14.

24. Savage disguised the names of two of the three sites, as well as the names of all the factories and the persons he studied. Medellín, the third site, is so distinctive as the only large city in Antioquia that no effective disguise is possible for it. To help preserve their anonymity, Savage also disguised or left vague some aspects of the environmental background of the work groups that he studied. His accounts of events within these groups and of their members' encounters with persons in their immediate environment are described as he observed them.

25. Rojas, Alfonso, and Charles H. Savage, *Social Organization in an Urban Factory in Colombia*, Alfred P. Sloan School of Management, Working Paper 201-66 (Cambridge: Massachusetts Institute of Technology, 1966). Charles H. Savage, *Management Behavior in a Developing Economy* (Cambridge:

Inter-American Program in Civil Engineering, School of Engineering, Massachusetts Institute of Technology, 1962); *Social Reorganization in a Factory in the Andes*, SAA Monograph 7 (Ithaca, New York: Society for Applied Anthropology, 1964); *Village Ways and Factory Ways: A Study of the Interplay between Technology and Social Structure in a Traditional Andean Village*, Alfred P. Sloan School of Management, Working Paper 236-67 (Cambridge: Massachusetts Institute of Technology, 1967).

26. Compare Wolff, Kurt A., "Surrender and Community Study: The Study of Land," in *Reflections on Community Studies*, Arthur J. Vidich, Joseph Bensman, and Maurice R. Stein, eds. (New York: John Wiley and Sons, 1964).

27. In connection with the title of the book, I would like to point out that the word "sons" is used in a biblical sense to refer to both sons and daughters. At the same time, this emphasis on maleness is descriptive of the conditions of male and female workers in the culture that Savage studied. It should not be taken as an indication of a chauvinistic attitude on Savage's part or for that matter on mine. I have used the pronouns "he" and "his" rather than "he or she" and "his or her" for simplicity of style.

28. Roethlisberger, F. J., *The Elusive Phenomenon*, George F. F. Lombard, ed. (Boston: Harvard University, Graduate School of Business Administration, 1977).

29. Burns, James MacGregor, *Leadership* (New York: Harper and Row, 1978).

30. Brinton, Crane, *The Anatomy of Revolution*, revised edition (New York: Prentice-Hall, 1958).

31. Homans, George C., *The Human Group* (New York: Harcourt, Brace, 1950).

32. Maslow, Abraham H., *Motivation and Personality* (New York: Harper and Brothers, 1954).

33. McGregor, *Human Side of Enterprise*.

34. Zaleznik, Abraham, C. Roland Christensen, and F. J. Roethlisberger, *The Motivation, Productivity, and Satisfaction of Workers: A Prediction Study* (Boston: Harvard University, Graduate School of Business Administration, 1958).

35. Erikson, Erik H., *Childhood and Society* (New York: W. W. Norton and Co., 1950); and *Young Man Luther: A Study in Psychoanalysis and History* (New York: W. W. Norton, 1958).

Chapter 2

1. See Hirschman, Albert O., *Journeys toward Progress: Studies of Economic Policy Making in Latin America* (New York: The Twentieth Century Fund, 1963), chap. 20.

2. Compare Parsons, Talcott, *The Social System* (Glencoe: The Free Press, 1951), esp. chap. 7.

3. Inkeles and Smith envisioned such lines of influence running from the factory to the community in *Becoming Modern* (Cambridge: Harvard University Press), published in 1974, the year after Savage's death. They have chapters entitled "The Factory as a School in Modernity" (chap. 11) and "Factory Modernity" (chap. 12). The results of their studies, which used survey research methods, clearly demonstrate the importance of this influence. Pages 154–164 provide an excellent summary of the arguments about these connections.

Chapter 4

1. Tables B.1 and B.2 in appendix B summarize some of the information presented in the text that follows.

2. Since Colombians like other Latin Americans use both their father's and their mother's last names, a total of nearly 70 names was possible among the workers in the plate room if one's father and mother had a name different from everyone else's. The fact that there were only 33 indicated that almost everyone had at least one relative working nearby.

3. During the period Rodrigo was out sick a good deal of the time. Therefore the figures do not include data for his output. In addition, during this period the output records for the individual potters were kept rather loosely. For instance, if Don Ignacio sent a worker on an errand or transferred him temporarily, he added an amount to the man's actual output that was his estimate of what the man would have produced if he had stayed at his position. Events like this did not happen frequently, and the differences between the figures before and after the change are clear enough to be a useful way of clarifying the forces circulating in the potters' life at work.

Chapter 5

1. Compare Migdal's description of who the innovators are in peasant societies that are undergoing change (Migdal, Joel S., *Peasants, Politics, and Revolution: Pressure toward Political and Social Change in the Third World* (Princeton: Princeton University Press, 1974), 142–148).

2. When I continued the analysis of the potters' output and earnings that Savage had begun, the original output data were not available. However, Savage had multiplied the units of each potter's output during the six-week period before the change by the appropriate piece rate—as established by Don José and the junta—for each of the products on which the potters had worked. Although it would have been preferable to have worked with the original data, I considered Savage's figures a satisfactory alternative. There were no variations in the clay and other materials that affected the potters' output, so that differences in what they would have earned on piece rates reflected differences in their output.

3. See table B.7 in appendix B. The calculations are based on the value of the potters' output as established under the piece rates agreed to between Don José and the junta. There were no important changes in the mix of products that the potters made in the weeks before and after the change.

Hence the figures, though expressed in pesos, accurately reflect the changes in the number of units that they produced.

The figures are based on the output of the seven potters who worked both before and after the change. That is, they exclude Rodrigo, because he was ill before the change, and Fernando, because he was transferred after it. The comparison is statistically more valid than a comparison based on the available figures for all the potters. In any case, the difference between the two sets of figures for average production, two percentage points, is not large; both are shown in table B.7.

4. Before the change, in a week when Rodrigo was at work, the total wage bill for the potters would have been 696 pesos (appendix B, table B.8), so that the increase in the wage bill after the change would have been 7.8%, from 696 pesos to 853 pesos. However, because without Fernando there was one less potter after the change, the increase in an average share would have been from 77.33 pesos to 106.63 pesos or 36.6%.

5. Conversely, after the change the share of the value of the potters' output that was available to management for all purposes other than the potters' wages—including the wages of workers in other departments, the costs of materials, the salaries of managers, overhead expenses, and the profits of the owners—decreased. As a profitable enterprise, however, the company was already meeting these operating and overhead costs. From its share of the receipts of the potters' increased output, the company therefore had only to meet the costs of the materials needed for the additional output, of extra supervision, and of extra maintenance for the equipment. Thus a substantial proportion of the company's share was available for profits. This condition would hold so long as the company sold the increased output. But if sales volume did not hold up, the company would be faced with higher labor costs in a declining market. In these circumstance the change in the payment system would not have been to the company's advantage.

6. Kuhn, Thomas S., The Structure of Scientific Revolutions (Chicago: University of Chicago Press, 1962), especially chap. 12.

7. Kahl, Joseph A., The Measurement of Modernism: A Study of Values in Brazil and Mexico (Austin: University of Texas Press, 1968), 6.

8. Hagen, Theory of Social Change, 55–56.

9. June Nash (We Eat the Mines) makes an important point in this connection about the mining community that she studied in Bolivia. She writes that sports activities there are "another way in which male leadership is sponsored and consolidated" (p. 107).

10. June Nash's observations about the athletic events that she witnessed provide an interesting perspective on Savage's discussion. She points out, "Soccer teams are an expression of the segmentation of social groups in the mining community as well as an exhibition of the overall solidarity of the work force. Each major level of the mines forms a team which plays competitive matches. . . . The best of these players make up the first-string

team that plays against other mines and in national competitions. . . . During the play, workers have an opportunity to vent their hostility not only against the visiting team but also against certain of the less liked administrative staff, who might get hit in the cross-fire of refuse thrown, supposedly, at the field to express disgust at the visitors" (*We Eat the Mines*, 107). Nash's observations apply equally well to the football games in Santuario, even though the community she studied was not undergoing a period of rapid change.

11. Anderson, Ross Alan, and Omar Khayyam Moore. "Autotelic Folk Models," *The Sociological Quarterly* 1, no. 4 (October 1960). Piaget has also documented the role of games in a society by describing the part that they play in the socialization of children (Piaget, Jean, *The Child's Conception of the World* (New York: Harcourt, Brace, 1929)). See also Burns, *Leadership*, 83, and Erikson, E. H., *Insight and Responsibility: Lectures on the Ethical Implications of Psychoanalytic Insight* (New York: W. W. Norton, 1964), 120 (quoted by Burns).

12. Compare Stinchcombe, Arthur L., "Social Structure and Organization," in *Handbook of Organization*, James G. March, ed. (Chicago: Rand McNally, 1965), 145–153.

13. Rostow, *Stages of Economic Growth*, 36.

14. Kahl, *Measurement of Modernism*, 149.

15. Mead, Margaret, *New Lives for Old: Cultural Transformation—Manus 1928-1953* (New York: William Morrow, 1956). See also Brintnall, Douglas E., *Revolt Against the Dead: The Modernization of a Mayan Community in the Highlands of Guatemala* (New York: Gordon and Breach, 1979), esp. 105–148.

16. Compare Burns, *Leadership*, chap. 1.

17. Burns, *Leadership*, 4 and 20.

Chapter 6
1. Paz, *Labyrinth of Solitude*.

Chapter 7
1. See also the discussions of output and social standing in Roethlisberger and Dickson, *Management and the Worker*, esp. chap. 22, 511–524; and Whyte, William F., *Street Corner Society: The Social Structure of an Italian Slum*, third edition (Chicago: University of Chicago Press, 1981), 14–25 and 318–320.

Chapter 8
1. For a discussion of several meanings of the term "communism" in Colombia, see Hobsbawm, E. J., "Ideology and Social Change in Colombia," in *Ideology and Social Change*, Nash et al., eds., 195–196.

2. In Parsonian terms, it would be said that Arturo's strength as a leader derived from both his achievement orientation and his ascriptive char-

acteristics as a member of his father's family (Parsons, *The Social System*, 64).

3. Burns, *Leadership*, esp. 19 and 20.

4. Compare Hagen, "Wealth and the Economy," 107ff, and Brintnall, *Revolt Against the Dead: The Modernization of a Mayan Community in the Highlands of Guatemala* (New York: Gordon and Breach, 1979), 176–179.

5. See Parsons, *The Social System*, 481–483. See also Radcliffe-Brown, A. R., *A Natural Science of Society* (Glencoe: The Free Press, 1957), in which he makes the distinction between a change in a system that allows the system to maintain itself without a change in its structure and a change of the system in which it passes from one type of structure to another (p. 87). Burns (*Leadership*) comments on Radcliffe-Brown's point, "The vast proportion of the decisions of decision makers . . . is readjustment that maintains the equilibrium of the social structure" (p. 416).

6. In 1951 Parsons (*The Social System*, 58–67, 180 ff) developed a theoretical schema for describing and classifying social systems. A decade later Bert F. Hoselitz (*Sociological Aspects of Economic Growth* (Glencoe: The Free Press, 1960), 29–42; and "Main Concepts in the Analysis of the Social Implications of Technical Change," in Hoselitz and Moore, *Industrialization and Society* (The Hague: UNESCO-Mouton, 1963), 16–19) pointed out that three of the five dimensions of Parsons's schema directly related to the differences between a traditional and a modern industrial society. The differences were apparent in Savage's data (see also note 4, chapter 10).

Parsons's first dimension concerned the characteristics that qualified people in the society for occupational roles, including leadership. Though both Parsons and Hoselitz were careful to say that in an actual society the people in occupational roles would have both achievement-oriented and ascriptive-oriented (kinship) characteristics, Hoselitz pointed out that relative to a traditional society occupational roles in a modern one were open to persons who were successful in performing the functions of the roles. Thus in Santuario and La Blanca, leadership roles among the managers and among the potters were becoming open to persons who were successful in them—or in being trained for them—whether or not they were related through their families to those whom they were succeeding.

Hoselitz said that Parsons's second dimension, which related to the differences between a traditional and a modern society, had to do with whether occupational roles were open to members of the society universally or only to persons with particular backgrounds, for example, the members of certain families or castes. Clearly Santuario and especially La Blanca moved in this sense in the direction of universally—rather than particularistically—open roles, for persons with diverse backgrounds were moving into the roles of potters as well as into those of managers.

Third, as happens generally under the impetus of the division of labor and Taylorism, the activities required in these roles were becoming functionally specific rather than diffuse with relation to the purpose of the role. Thus a potter's activities were more circumscribed if all he did was pot—

particularly if all he did was to make only one product, such as a plate—when previously he had also polished the products he made. Similarly, the range of activities that the doctores performed as managers was more circumscribed than the patrones' had been.

7. Brinton, *Anatomy of Revolution*, 271.

8. Homans, *The Human Group*, 316–321.

Chapter 9

1. See Hirschman, *Journeys toward Progress*.

2. Monahan, Cynthia, "Bogotá's Gamins—They Defy Adult Society," *Christian Science Monitor*, August 15, 1974.

3. Dickens, Charles, *Oliver Twist*, Kathleen Tillotson, ed. (Oxford: Clarendon Press, 1966).

4. June Nash's account of the personnel programs at the tin mines in Bolivia makes an interesting comparison (*We Eat the Mines*, 87–120).

Chapter 10

1. Maslow, *Motivation and Personality*, chap. 5.

2. McGregor, *The Human Side of Enterprise*, chaps. 3 and 4.

3. Zaleznik et al. *Motivation, Productivity and Satisfaction*, 391 and 401. See also Clark, James V., "Motivation in Work Groups: A Tentative View," *Human Organization*, 19(4) (Winter 1960).

4. Zaleznik et al., *Motivation, Productivity and Satisfaction*, 401.

5. Zaleznik et al., *Motivation, Productivity and Satisfaction*, 401.

6. Zaleznik et al., *Motivation, Productivity and Satisfaction*, 391.

7. Movement at El Dandy along the dimensions of Parsons's schema, which Hoselitz said characterized the transition of a traditional society to a modern one, was well advanced. The importance of success- and achievement-oriented motivations in filling occupational roles among both managers and workers in the company and in the unions was clear, although ascriptive qualifications for a position—such as friendship among the football players—still had their influence. Manager and worker roles were clearly available to persons, irrespective of their backgrounds, on a universal rather than on a particularistic basis, just as activities in the roles of managers and workers had become specific rather than diffuse in character. Advances in the division of labor had especially affected the work of the tailors. (See note 6, chapter 8.)

Chapter 11

1. Burns, *Leadership*, 244.

2. Barnard, Chester I., *The Functions of the Executive* (Cambridge: Harvard University Press, 1938), 163.

Chapter 12

1. See, for example, Brinton, *Anatomy of Revolution*, 262–263.

2. Compare Burns, *Leadership*, chap. 1. Lawrence, Paul R., and Davis Dyer, *Renewing American Industry* (New York: The Free Press, 1983) envision an ideal organization as one in which "every employee at every level define[s] himself or herself as a manager" (p. 264). Jeffrey Pfeffer ("The Ambiguity of Leadership," in *Leadership: Where Else Can We Go?* Morgan W. McCall, Jr., and Michael M. Lombardo, eds. (Durham: Duke University Press, 1978)) and Michael Maccoby (*The Leader* (New York: Ballantine Books, 1981)) both recognize that leadership is needed at different levels of organizations. Neither goes so far as Savage, however, for they limit their discussions to levels within management and do not consider leadership among workers.

3. See Selznick, Philip, *Leadership in Administration: A Sociological Interpretation* (New York: Harper and Row, 1957).

4. Compare Burns (*Leadership*): "Traditional conceptions of leadership tend to be so dominated by images of presidents and prime ministers speaking to the masses from on high that we may forget that the vast preponderance of personal influence is exerted quietly and subtly in everyday relationships" (p. 442). Later Burns writes, "*Leadership is collective.* 'One-man leadership' is a contradiction in terms" (p. 452; emphasis in the original). See also Hirschman, Albert O., *A Bias for Hope* (New Haven: Yale University Press, 1971), 337ff.

5. See John Junkerman's report of Professor Zaleznik's conference on leadership ("Leadership: The Search for the 'Heroic Man,' " *Harvard Business School Bulletin*, June 1984, 66–77).

6. See Roethlisberger, F. J., "Understanding: A Prerequisite of Leadership," in his *Management and Morale* (Cambridge: Harvard University Press, 1941).

7. Compare the ideas about social change in Feldman, Arnold S., "Evolutionary Theory and Social Change," in *Social Change in Developing Areas: A Reinterpretation of Evolutionary Theory*, Herbert R. Barringer, George I. Blanksten, and Raymond W. Mack, eds. (Cambridge: Schenkman Publishing Co., 1965). See also Radcliffe-Brown, *Natural Science of Society*, esp. 86f.

8. Chomsky, Noam, *Aspects of the Theory of Syntax* (Cambridge: MIT Press, 1965).

9. In this sense Savage's research methodology presents an interesting contrast with that of both Manning Nash (*Machine Age Maya*) and June Nash (*The Mines Eat Us*), who in their respective studies of industrialization in a Mayan village in Guatemala and of tin mines in Bolivia gave the major part of their attention to the communities and went only briefly into their workplaces.

10. See Gould, Stephen Jay, *Hen's Teeth and Horse's Toes* (New York: W. W. Norton, 1983), 104–105. John McPhee (*In Suspect Terrain* (New York: Farrar, Strauss & Giroux, 1983)) quotes Anita Harris, a geologist, in this connection: "We were taught all wrong . . . that changes on the face of the

earth come in a slow steady march. But that isn't what happens. The slow steady march of geologic times is punctuated with catastrophes. . . . The evolution of the world does not happen a grain at a time. It happens in the hundred-year storm, the hundred-year flood" (p. 87).

For a discussion of the modifications that Darwin himself made in his views about the pace of change, see Darwin, Charles, *The Essential Darwin*, Robert Jastrow, ed. (Boston: Little, Brown, 1984), esp. 238–239 and 301–304.

In the literature of management, as recently as 1981, William Ouchi wrote (*Theory Z: How American Business Can Meet the Japanese Challenge* (Reading: Addison-Wesley, 1981)), "A culture changes slowly because its values reach deeply and integrate into a consistent network of beliefs that tends to maintain the status quo" (pp. 88–89). A. K. Rice (*The Enterprise and Its Environment: A System Theory of Management Organization* (London: Tavistock Publications, 1963)) speaks of change as being continuous with a long time scale: "Changes in structure that require personal adjustment can seldom be hurried, and the building of the change into the structure is invariably even slower" (p. 268). He considered the major issue in the management of change to be "the development of more sophisticated techniques for the controlled assimilation of continuous change" (p. 264).

Mead, however, documented an instance of rapid and pervasive structural change in *New Lives for Old*. She argued that structural change should be rapid and gave an interesting example (pp. 447–448). She concluded, "Partial change . . . can be seen not as a bridge between old and new, something that permits men . . . some respite from the unbearable burden of change, but rather as the condition within which discordant and discrepant institutions develop and proliferate—with corresponding discrepancies and discordancies in the lives of those who live within them. The alternative . . . is the culture in which . . . the whole pattern is transformed at once" (pp. 446 and 447). See also Brintnall, *Revolt Against the Dead*.

Studies in a number of other fields also document patterns of change that are rapid. Psychologists and others who study the behavior of individuals, for example, describe the bursts of insight called *croyances déclenchée*, that characterize some of the changes in their behavior that their subjects make (see Mayo, G. Elton, *Some Notes on the Psychology of Pierre Janet* (Cambridge: Harvard University Press, 1948), 17).

In experimental groups arranged to test the interventions of those who study behavior, the initial bursts of change that sometimes occur are referred to as the "Hawthorne effect," in reference to the responses of workers to experiments at the Hawthorne plant of the Western Electric Company (Roethlisberger and Dickson, *Management and the Worker*).

Kuhn (*Structure of Scientific Revolutions*, chap. 3) speaks of episodes of rapid change in the development of scientific thinking, when he contrasts the changes in paradigms that bring revolutions in a science with the "mop-up" operations of normal science. And Lewin's description of successful change in the behavior of the members of groups as including "three aspects": *Unfreezing* . . . the present level, *moving* to the new level, and *freezing* group life at the new level" (emphasis in the original) is often referred to (Lewin, Kurt, "Frontiers in Group Dynamics: Concept, Methods, and Reality in Social Science; Social Equilibria and Social Change," *Human Relations* (1) (1947), 35).

In an interesting article John Platt ("Hierarchical Growth," *Bulletin of the Atomic Scientists* 26(9), November 1970) wrote, "Sudden changes of structure are among the more startling features of living systems" (p. 2) and gave examples.

In all these discussions the view of structural change as occurring rapidly and in bursts is curiously limited to the specific instance. The concept is not generalized to apply to the process of change as a whole. The dominant view is that change occurs gradually and continuously at a steady rate.

Alvin Toffler, however, writes that in advanced industrial societies, continuous change at a rapid rate is the norm (*Future Shock* (New York: Random House, 1970), especially pt. 1), and Warren G. Bennis (*Changing Organizations: Essays on the Development and Evolution of Human Organizations* (New York: McGraw-Hill, 1966)) says "Stability has vanished" (p. 9). Change at this pace was not typical of Antioquia or even of Medellín at the time of Savage's studies. Also, Toffler neglects the distinction between changes within a system and changes of a system, that is, of its structure. Many of his examples are consequently no more than surface changes in Savage's perspective.

11. Eldredge, Niles, and Stephen J. Gould. "Punctuated Equilibria: An Alternative to Phyletic Gradualism," in *Models in Paleobiology*, Thomas J. M. Schopf, ed. (San Francisco: Freeman, Cooper, 1972), 98.

12. Eldredge and Gould, "Punctuated Equilibria," 115.

13. Eldredge and Gould, "Punctuated Equilibria," 92–97.

14. Lawrence and Dyer (*Renewing American Industry*) are clear that the process of change that they call readaptation at the level of an entire organization is unevenly paced and not continuous (see especially the section "Dynamics of Organizational Adaptation," 310–311).

15. The interested reader may wish to compare these headings with the "guidelines for the diffusion of new ideas into communities of other cultures" found in Arensberg, Conrad M., and Arthur H. Niehoff, *Introducing Social Change*, second edition (Chicago: Aldine-Atherton, 1971), chaps. 4–8, esp. pp. 174 and 175.

16. Burns, *Leadership*, 414.

17. Levinson, Daniel J., et al., *The Seasons of a Man's Life* (New York: Ballantine Books, 1978), 29.

18. Erikson, *Childhood and Society* and *Young Man Luther*.

19. Lévi-Strauss, Claude, *The Scope of Anthropology*, translated by Sherry C. Paul and Robert A. Paul (London: Jonathan Cape, 1967), 12.

20. Mauss, Marcel, "Essai sur la don: Forme et raison de l'echange dans les societés archaiques," in *Sociologie et Anthropologie* (Paris, 1950), 274.

21. Savage, Charles H., Jr., *Particulars of Early Change*.

Chapter 13

1. In this way Savage restricted his research to the first two of what Barnard (*Functions of the Executive*, 217) described as the three functions of executives—namely, communicating with workers and securing their motivation and cooperation for work. Savage omitted the third, what Barnard called the determination of an organization's purpose or strategy.

2. New York: Harper and Row, 1966.

3. Compare Ralph M. Stogdill, who wrote that leadership "can best be defined in terms of *the initiation and maintenance of structure in expectation and interaction*" ("Intragroup-Intergroup Theory and Research," in *Intergroup Relations and Leadership: Approaches and Research in Industrial, Ethnic, Cultural, and Political Areas*, Muzafer Sherif, ed. (New York: John Wiley and Sons, Inc., 1962), 56; emphasis in the original).

4. See, for example, the comprehensive and authoritative accounts in Zager, Robert, and Michael P. Rosow, eds., *The Innovative Organization: Productivity Programs in Action* (New York: Pergamon Press Inc., 1982).

5. Warren G. Bennis and Herbert A. Shepard ("A Theory of Group Development," *Human Relations* 9 (4), November 1956) wrote of this problem: "Two major areas . . . can be identified . . . The first of these is the area of group members' orientation toward authority, or more generally toward the handling and distribution of power in the group. The second is the area of members' orientation toward one another. These areas are not independent of each other: a particular set of inter-member orientations will be associated with a particular authority structure. But the two sets of orientations are as distinct from each other as are the concepts of power and love" (p. 416).

A study by Nancy B. Graves and Theodore D. Graves ("The Impact of Modernization on the Personality of a Polynesian People," *Human Relations* 37 (2), Summer 1978, 115–135), even though it is far removed in other respects from the work of factory groups in Colombia, further clarifies the point. This study was made with twelve-year-old children in the Cook Islands in Polynesia. For the study, the children were formed into 38 groups of four and instructed to carry out a standardized task by manipulating a pen to which strings were attached. A point was awarded each time a child succeeded in getting the line made by the pen to go through a circle marked on the corner of the paper nearest the child. The task involved both co-operation and competition, for no one child could by him- or herself get the pen to go through his or her circle. Observers classified the groups according to whether they were successful or unsuccessful in reaching their goals. They also classified the acts of individual children according to whether they were oriented to achieving group or individual goals and whether they were leadership or membership acts. Directing and reproving, for example, were classified as leadership acts; and listening, looking at, watching others, conferring, and agreeing with others as membership acts. Thus the study allowed the proportion of membership and leadership acts in the successful and unsuccessful groups to be compared. A total of 662 acts were observed in the 17 successful groups and 815 in the 21 unsuccessful groups.

The authors wrote, "The most striking result . . . was that leadership behavior was far less important for the success or failure of these groups than membership behavior. Successful groups did exhibit more leadership directed toward group goals than did unsuccessful groups (18% to 8% of all acts recorded), [but] in successful groups the proportion of membership behavior which was oriented toward group goals was very high: 38% to only 10% among unsuccessful groups. [The members of successful groups] more often listened to each other, conferred, watched each other for cues and directions, and mutually agreed upon a course of action. . . . It would seem that while a certain degree of positive leadership is helpful, the major factor involved in cooperation is for members to be willing to entertain each other's suggestions and keep in touch with one another" (pp. 131–132).

6. In the literature on management there is a large number of books on specific aspects of the process of change, such as the administration of change and the dynamics of planned change. The topics just mentioned are discussed in two well-known books (Ronken, Harriet O., and Paul R. Lawrence, *Administering Changes: A Case Study of Human Relations in a Factory* (Boston: Harvard University, Graduate School of Business Administration, 1952); and Lippitt, Ronald, Jeanne Watson, and Bruce Westley, *The Dynamics of Planned Change* (New York: Harcourt, Brace, 1958)).

Most of this literature has been written from the point of view of a consultant from outside an organization who has been asked to advise its upper and middle levels of management (for example, Lippitt et al. *Dynamics of Planned Change*; Bennis, Warren G., Kenneth D. Benne, and Robert Chin, *The Planning of Change* (New York: Holt, Rinehart and Winston, 1961); Blake, Robert R., and Jane S. Moulton, *The Managerial Grid: Key Orientations for Achieving Production through People* (Houston: Gulf Publishing Co., 1964); and Blake, Robert R., *Consultation: A Handbook for Individual and Organization Development* (Reading: Addison-Wesley, 1983); Bennis, *Changing Organizations*; Hornstein, Harvey A., Barbara B. Bunker, W. Warner Burke, Marion Gindes, and Roy J. Lewicki, eds., *Social Intervention: A Behavioral Science Approach* (New York: The Free Press, 1971); and Argyris, Chris, and Donald A. Schon, *Organizational Learning: A Theory of Action Perspective* (Reading: Addison-Wesley, 1978)). Furthermore, much of the literature is concerned with the importance of democratic values in the relations between leaders and followers and does not deal with questions about the structure of and the relations among the members of work groups (see, for example, Gordon, Thomas, *Group-Centered Leadership: A Way of Releasing the Creative Power of Groups* (Boston: Houghton Mifflin Co., 1955); and Davis, Louis E., and Albert B. Cherns and Associates, *The Quality of Working Life*, 2 vols. (New York: The Free Press, 1975). In this literature, Whyte, William Foote (*Leadership and Group Participation*, New York State School of Industrial and Labor Relations Bulletin 24 (Ithaca: Cornell University, 1953)) is an often overlooked exception.

Even in the most recent literature on such participative management topics as quality control circles, the quality of life at work, and high commitment work groups (for example, Kimberley, John R., Robert H. Miles, and associates, eds., *The Organizational Life Cycle: Issues in Creation, Transformation and Decline of Organizations* (San Francisco: Jossey-Bass Publishers, 1980); and Zager and Rosow, *The Innovative Organization*), the authors tend to present their ideas as techniques for managers and to neglect the topic of structure in the social organizations of workers. The literature on Japanese management methods necessarily refers to the cultural values of social organizations but usually in only general terms (see, Ouchi, *Theory Z*, and Pascale, Richard T., and Anthony G. Athos, *The Art of Japanese Management: Applications for American Executives* (New York: Simon and Schuster, 1981)). Thomas P. Rohlen (*For Harmony and Strength* (Berkeley: University of California Press, 1974)), however, is more specific. (See also Beckhard, Richard, and Dale G. Lake, "Short- and Long-Range Effects of a Team Development Effort," in Hornstein et al., *Social Intervention*; Soler, E., *The World of the Industrial Worker: Peru*, Alfred P. Sloan School of Management Working Paper 185-66 (Cambridge: Massachusetts Institute of Technology, 1966); and Soler, E., and Charles H. Savage, Jr., *Technological Impact on a Community in Transitiion—Peru*, Alfred P. Sloan School of Management, Working Paper 202-66 (Cambridge: Massachusetts Institute of Technology, 1966).

In contrast to management-oriented studies, research on the subject of community change seldom neglects questions of social structure (Holmberg, Allan R., "The Changing Values and Institutions of Vicos in the Context of National Development," *The American Behavioral Scientist* 8(7) (March 1965); Doughty, Paul L., "The Interrelationship of Power, Respect, Affection and Rectitude in Vicos," *The American Behavioral Scientist* 8(7) (March 1965); Adams, D. W., and A. E. Havens, "The Use of Socio-Economic Research in Developing a Strategy of Change for Rural Communities: A Colombian Example," in Hornstein et al., *Social Intervention*; Arensberg and Niehoff, *Introducing Social Change*; Migdal, *Peasants, Politics and Revolution*; Reck, Gregory G., *In the Shadow of Tlaloc* (New York: Penguin Books, 1978); and Brintnall, *Revolt Against the Dead*. Because these studies are usually of rural and agricultural societies, in which factories are not to be found, this research has little to say about the role of managers in industry.

For research based on different approaches to questions of authority, power, and dependence in groups versus love, friendship, and independence, see George Homans and David M. Schneider, *Marriage, Authority and Final Causes* (New York: The Free Press, 1955); Warren G. Bennis and Herbert A. Shepard, "A Theory of Group Development," *Human Relations* 9 (4) (November 1956), 415–437; and Bales, Robert F., and Stephen P. Cohen with the assistance of Stephen A. Williamson, SYMLOG: *A System for the Multiple Level Observation of Groups* (New York: The Free Press, 1979).

7. Trist et al. wrote that "the most commonly adopted approach to the practical management of change situations [is] to proceed one step at a

time and to try again what has previously succeeded" (*Organizational Choice: Capabilities of Groups at the Coal Face Under Changing Conditions* (London: Tavistock Publications, 1963), 163).

8. See Walton, Richard E., "From Control to Commitment in the Workplace," *Harvard Business Review* 2 (March–April 1985), 77. Also see Poza, Ernesto J., and M. Lynne Markus, "Success Story: The Team Approach to Work Restructuring," *Organizational Dynamics* (Winter 1980), 3–25. For a primarily analytical study of a group supervised by these methods, see Herbst, P.G., *Autonomous Group Functioning* (London: Tavistock Publications, 1962).

9. For a discussion of the concept of organizational climate, see Tagiuri, Renato, and George H. Litwin, eds., *Organizational Climate: Exploration of a Concept* (Boston: Harvard University, Graduate School of Business Administration, 1968).

10. For a discussion of trust in organizational relationships, see Gabarro, John J., "The Development of Trust, Influence and Expectations," *Interpersonal Behavior: Communication and Understanding in Relationships*, Anthony C. Athos, et al., eds. (Englewood Cliffs: Prentice-Hall, Inc., 1978), 290–303; and "The Development of Working Relationships," in *Handbook of Organizational Behavior*, Lorsch, Jay W. (Englewood Cliffs: Prentice-Hall, Inc., to be published).

11. See Kuhn, *Structure of Scientific Revolutions*, especially chap. 9.

12. See Zaleznik, Abraham, "Managers and Leaders: Are They Different?" *Harvard Business Review* 55(3), May–June 1977, 67–78. See also Junkerman, "Leadership."

13. Compare Burns, *Leadership*, "Planning for structural change . . . is the ultimate moral test of decision-making leadership. . . ." (p. 419)

14. Early writers, including Henderson, Mayo, Roethlisberger, Malinowski, Radcliffe-Brown, and others, used the term "social system" broadly to refer to aspects of relationships among persons, including those governed by technological factors. More recently, writers in the field of organizational development, following Trist (1963), have used the term sociotechnical system as though it referred to something different. Because in a phenomenological sense no system with relationships among persons exists without technological aspects and no technological system exists without relationships among persons, I prefer the use of the term social system in its earlier sense. (For a discussion of these and related terminological problems, see Roethlisberger, *The Elusive Phenomenon*, especially chap. 23.)

15. Ortega y Gasset, José, *The Revolt of the Masses* (New York: W. W. Norton, 1932).

16. Mayo pointed out in *The Human Problems of an Industrial Civilization* (New York: Macmillan, 1933), chap. 7, that changes in political systems are not a substitute for understanding persons who encounter each other at work or elsewhere in life. Peter Winn's discussion ("Workers into Managers: Worker Participation in the Chilean Textile Industry," in *Popular*

Participation in Social Change: Cooperatives, Collectives, and Nationalized Industry, June Nash, Jorge Dandler, and Nicholas S. Hopkins, eds. (The Hague: Mouton Publishers, 1976)) provides an excellent negative example of Mayo's thesis.

17. See Kerr, Clark, et al. *Industrialism and Industrial Man* (Cambridge: Harvard University Press, 1960).

18. Radcliffe-Brown (*A Natural Science of Society*, 147) refers to this problem as the psychological illusion, "the notion that since . . . social life consists of the actions of individual human beings, therefore an explanation of the actions of individual human beings is an explanation of social behavior." The notion that human behavior as presented in the acts of individuals represents solely the behavior of individuals is an instance of what A. N. Whitehead called the fallacy of misplaced concreteness.

19. See Walton, "From Control to Commitment"; also see Schlesinger, Leonard A., and Barry Oshry, "Quality of Work Life and the Manager: Muddle in the Middle," *Organizational Dynamics* (Summer 1984); and Klein, Janice A., "Why Supervisors Resist Employee Involvement," *Harvard Business Review* no. 5 (1984).

Appendix A

1. Many of the reports of field studies listed in the references contain detailed discussions of research methods; see especially Malinowski, *Argonauts of the Western Pacific*; Roethlisberger and Dickson, *Management and the Worker*; Arensberg and Niehoff, *Introducing Social Change*; Vidich, Arthur J., Joseph Bensman, and Maurice R. Stein, *Reflections on Community Studies* (New York: John Wiley and Sons, 1964); and Rohlen, *For Harmony and Strength*.

2. Homans, *The Human Group*, esp. chaps. 4–6.

References

Abegglen, James C. *The Japanese Factory: Aspects of Its Social Organization.* Glencoe: The Free Press, 1958.

Adams, D. W., and A. E. Havens. "The Use of Socio-Economic Research in Developing a Strategy of Change for Rural Communities: A Colombian Example," in *Social Intervention: A Behavioral Science Approach,* Harvey A. Hornstein, Barbara B. Bunker, W. Warner Burke, Marion Gindes, and Roy J. Lewicki, eds. New York: The Free Press, 1971.

Anderson, Ross Alan, and Omar Khayyam Moore. "Autotelic Folk Models." *The Sociological Quarterly* 1 (4) (October 1960).

Arensberg, Conrad M., and Arthur H. Niehoff. *Introducing Social Change.* Second edition. Chicago: Aldine-Atherton, 1971.

Argyris, Chris, and Donald A. Schon. *Organizational Learning: A Theory of Action Perspective.* Reading: Addison-Wesley, 1978.

Arroyave, Julio. *El pueblo Antioqueno.* Second edition. Medellín, Colombia: Imprenta de Universidad, 1960.

Athos, Anthony C., and John J. Gabarro with the assistance of Jane L. Holtz. *Interpersonal Behavior: Communication and Understanding in Relationships.* Englewood Cliffs: Prentice-Hall, Inc., 1978.

Bales, Robert F., and Stephen P. Cohen with the assistance of Stephen A. Williamson. SYMLOG: *A System for the Multiple Level Observation of Groups.* New York: The Free Press, 1979.

Barnard, Chester I. *The Functions of the Executive.* Cambridge: Harvard University Press, 1938.

Barringer, Herbert R., George I. Blanksten, and Raymond W. Mack, eds. *Social Change in Developing Areas: A Reinterpretation of Evolutionary Theory.* Cambridge: Schenkman Publishing Company, 1965.

Beckhard, Richard, and Dale G. Lake. "Short- and Long-Range Effects of a Team Development Effort," in *Social Intervention: A Behavioral Science Approach,* Harvey A. Hornstein, Barbara B. Bunker, W. Warner Burke, Marion Gindes, and Roy J. Lewicki, eds. New York: The Free Press, 1971.

Bennis, Warren G. *Changing Organizations: Essays on the Development and Evolution of Human Organizations.* New York: McGraw-Hill, 1966.

Bennis, Warren G., and Herbert A. Shepard. "A Theory of Group Development." *Human Relations* 9 (4) (November 1956), 415–437.

Bennis, Warren G., Kenneth D. Benne, and Robert Chin. *The Planning of Change*. New York: Holt, Rinehart and Winston, 1961.

Blake, Robert R., and Jane S. Moulton. *The Managerial Grid: Key Orientations for Achieving Production through People*. Houston: Gulf Publishing Co., 1964.

Blake, Robert R. *Consultation: A Handbook for Individual and Organization Development*. Reading: Addison-Wesley, 1983.

Blanksten, George I. "Transference of Social and Political Loyalties," in *Industrialization and Society*, Bert F. Hoselitz and Wilbert E. Moore, eds. The Hague: UNESCO-Mouton, 1963.

Brace, Richard M. "Evolutionary Theory in Intellectual History and Its Meaning in Algeria," in *Social Change in Developing Areas: A Reinterpretation of Evolutionary Theory*, Herbert R. Barringer, George I. Blanksten, and Raymond W. Mack, eds. Cambridge: Schenkman Publishing Company, 1965.

Brintnall, Douglas E. *Revolt Against the Dead: The Modernization of a Mayan Community in the Highlands of Guatemala*. New York: Gordon and Breach, 1979.

Brinton, Crane. *The Anatomy of Revolution*. Revised edition. New York: Prentice-Hall, 1958.

Burns, James MacGregor. *Leadership*. New York: Harper and Row, 1978.

Carrasquilla, Tomás. "Reconquista." *El Correo Liberal obras completas* 27:2031–2035. Medellín, 1913.

Chomsky, Noam. *Aspects of the Theory of Syntax*. Cambridge: MIT Press, 1965.

Clark, James V. "Motivation in Work Groups: A Tentative View." *Human Organization* 19 (4) (Winter 1960).

Cottrell, W. Fred. "Technological Progress and Evolutionary Theory," in *Social Change in Developing Areas*, Herbert R. Barringer, George I. Blanksten, and Raymond W. Mack, eds. Cambridge: Schenkman Publishing Company, 1965.

Darwin, Charles. *The Essential Darwin*, Robert Jastrow, ed. Boston: Little, Brown and Co., 1984.

Davis, Louis E., and Albert B. Cherns and Associates. *The Quality of Working Life*. 2 vols. New York: The Free Press, 1975.

Dickens, Charles. *Oliver Twist*. Kathleen Tillotson, ed. Oxford: Clarendon Press, 1966.

Doughty, Paul L. "The Interrelationship of Power, Respect, Affection and Rectitude in Vicos," *The American Behavioral Scientist* 8 (7) (March 1965), 13–17.

Durkheim, Emile. *The Rules of Sociological Method.* Eighth edition. Sarah A. Solovay and John H. Mueller, translators; George E. G. Catlin, ed. Glencoe, Ill.: The Free Press, 1965.

Durkheim, Emile. *Suicide: A Study in Sociology.* John A. Spaulding and George Simpson, translators; George Simpson, ed. Glencoe, Ill.: The Free Press, 1951.

Eldredge, Niles, and Stephen J. Gould. "Punctuated Equilibria: An Alternative to Phyletic Gradualism," in *Models in Paleobiology,* Thomas J. M. Schopf, ed. San Francisco: Freeman, Cooper and Co., 1972.

Erikson, Erik H. *Childhood and Society.* New York: W. W. Norton and Co., 1950.

Erikson, Erik H. *Young Man Luther: A Study in Psychoanalysis and History.* New York: W. W. Norton and Co., 1958.

Erikson, Erik H. *Insight and Responsibility: Lectures on the Ethical Implications of Psychoanalytic Insight.* New York: W. W. Norton and Co., 1964.

Feldman, Arnold S. "Evolutionary Theory and Social Change," in *Social Change in Developing Areas: A Reinterpretation of Evolutionary Theory,* Herbert R. Barringer, George I. Blanksten, and Raymond W. Mack, eds. Cambridge: Schenkman Publishing Co., 1965.

Fluharty, Vernon L. *Dance of the Millions.* Pittsburgh: University of Pittsburgh Press, 1957.

Gabarro, John J. "The Development of Trust, Influence, and Expectations," in *Interpersonal Behavior: Communication and Understanding in Relationships,* Athos, Anthony C., and John J. Gabarro with the assistance of Jane L. Holtz. Englewood Cliffs: Prentice-Hall, Inc., 1978.

Gabarro, John J. "The Development of Working Relationships," in *Handbook of Organizational Behavior,* Lorsch, Jay W., ed. Englewood Cliffs: Prentice-Hall, Inc. (to be published).

Gordon, Thomas. *Group-Centered Leadership: A Way of Releasing the Creative Power of Groups.* Boston: Houghton Mifflin Co., 1955.

Gould, Stephen Jay. *Hen's Teeth and Horse's Toes.* New York: W. W. Norton and Co., 1983.

Graves, Nancy B., and Theodore D. Graves. "The Impact of Modernization on the Personality of a Polynesian People." *Human Organization* 37 (2) (Summer 1978), 115–135.

Hagen, Everett E. *On the Theory of Social Change: How Economic Growth Begins.* Homewood: The Dorsey Press, 1962.

Hagen, Everett E. "Wealth and the Economy," in *Comparative Theories of Social Change,* Hollis W. Peter, ed. Ann Arbor: Foundation for Research on Human Behavior, 1966.

Hagen, Everett E. *The Economics of Development.* Homewood: Richard D. Irwin Inc., 1980.

Henderson, L. J. *On the Social System.* Bernard Barber, ed. Chicago: University of Chicago Press, 1970.

Herbst, P. G. *Autonomous Group Functioning*. London: Tavistock Publications, 1962.

Hirschman, Albert O. *Journeys toward Progress: Studies of Economic Policy Making in Latin America*. New York: The Twentieth Century Fund, 1963.

Hirschman, Albert O. *A Bias for Hope*. New Haven: Yale University Press, 1971.

Hobsbawm, E. J. "Ideology and Social Change in Colombia," in *Ideology and Social Change in Latin America*, June Nash, Juan Corradi, and Hobart Spalding, Jr., eds. New York: Gordon and Breach, 1977.

Holmberg, Allan R. "The Changing Values and Institutions of Vicos in the Context of National Development," *The American Behavioral Scientist* 8 (7) (March 1965), 3–8.

Homans, George C. *The Human Group*. New York: Harcourt, Brace and Co., 1950.

Homans, George C., and David M. Schneider. *Marriage, Authority and Final Causes*. New York: The Free Press, 1955.

Hornstein, Harvey A., Barbara B. Bunker, W. Warner Burke, Marion Gindes, and Roy J. Lewicki, eds. *Social Intervention: A Behavioral Science Approach*. New York: The Free Press, 1971.

Hoselitz, Bert F. *Sociological Aspects of Economic Growth*. Glencoe: The Free Press, 1960.

Hoselitz, Bert F. "Main Concepts in the Analysis of the Social Implications of Technical Change," in *Industrialization and Society*, Bert F. Hoselitz and Wilbert E. Moore, eds. The Hague: UNESCO-Mouton, 1963.

Hoselitz, Bert F., and Wilbert E. Moore, eds. *Industrialization and Society*. The Hague: UNESCO-Mouton, 1963.

Inkeles, Alex, and David H. Smith. *Becoming Modern*. Cambridge: Harvard University Press, 1974.

Junkerman, John. "Leadership: The Search for the 'Heroic Man.' " *Harvard Business School Bulletin*. June 1984, 66–77.

Kahl, Joseph A. *The Measurement of Modernism: A Study of Values in Brazil and Mexico*. Austin: University of Texas Press, 1968.

Kerr, Clark, John T. Dunlop, Frederick H. Harbison, and Charles A. Myers. *Industrialism and Industrial Man*. Cambridge: Harvard University Press, 1960.

Kimberley, John R., Robert H. Miles, and associates, eds. *The Organizational Life Cycle: Issues in Creation, Transformation and Decline of Organizations*. San Francisco: Jossey-Bass Publishers, 1980.

Klein, Janice A. "Why Supervisors Resist Employee Involvement." *Harvard Business Review*. no. 5, 1984, 87–95.

Kuhn, Thomas S. *The Structure of Scientific Revolutions*. Chicago: University of Chicago Press, 1962.

Lawrence, Paul R., and Davis Dyer. *Renewing American Industry*. New York: The Free Press, 1983.

Lévi-Strauss, Claude. *The Scope of Anthropology*. Sherry O. Paul and Robert A. Paul, translators. London: Jonathan Cape, 1967.

Levinson, Daniel J., with Charlotte N. Darrow, Edward B. Klein, Maria H. Levinson, and Bruxton McKee. *The Seasons of a Man's Life*. New York: Ballantine Books, 1978.

Levy, Kurt L. *Vidas y obras de Tomás Carrasquilla*. C. Lopez Narvaez, translator. Medellín: Editorial Bedout, 1958.

Lewin, Kurt. "Frontiers in Group Dynamics: Concept, Method, and Reality in Social Science; Social Equilibrium and Social Change." *Human Relations* 1 (1) (1947), 5–41.

Lippitt, Ronald, Jeanne Watson, and Bruce Westley. *The Dynamics of Planned Change*. New York: Harcourt, Brace and Co., 1958.

López de Mesa, Luis. *Escrutinio sociológico de la historia Colombiana*. Bogotá, Colombia: Academia Colombiana de Historia, 1956.

Lorsch, Jay W., ed. *Handbook of Organizational Behavior*. Englewood Cliffs: Prentice-Hall, Inc. (to be published).

Maccoby, Michael. *The Leader*. New York: Ballantine Books, 1981.

Malinowski, Bronislaw. *Argonauts of the Western Pacific*. New York: E. P. Dutton and Co., 1932.

Manuel, Antonio. *Historia elemental del departmento de Antioquia*. Medellín: Editorial Bedout, 1952.

March, James G., ed. *Handbook of Organization*. Chicago: Rand McNally and Co., 1965.

Maslow, Abraham H. *Motivation and Personality*. New York: Harper and Brothers, 1954.

Mauss, Marcel. "Essai sur la don: Forme et raison de l'echange dans les societés archaiques," in *Sociologie et Anthropologie*. Paris: 1950.

Mayo, G. Elton. *The Human Problems of an Industrial Civilization*. New York: Macmillan, 1933.

Mayo, G. Elton. *The Social Problems of an Industrial Civilization*. Boston: Harvard University, Graduate School of Business Administration, 1945.

Mayo, G. Elton. *Some Notes on the Psychology of Pierre Janet*. Cambridge: Harvard University Press, 1948.

McCall, Morgan W., Jr., and Michael M. Lombardo, eds. *Leadership: Where Else Can We Go?* Durham: Duke University Press, 1978.

McGregor, Douglas. *The Human Side of Enterprise*. New York: McGraw-Hill, 1960.

McPhee, John. *In Suspect Terrain*. New York: Farrar, Straus, and Giroux, 1983.

Mead, Margaret. *New Lives for Old: Cultural Transformation—Manus 1928–1953*. New York: William Morrow and Co., Inc., 1956.

Migdal, Joel S. *Peasants, Politics and Revolution: Pressure Toward Political and Social Change in the Third World*. Princeton: Princeton University Press, 1974.

Monahan, Cynthia. "Bogotá's Gamins—They Defy Adult Society." *Christian Science Monitor*, August 15, 1974.

Nash, June. *The Mines Eat Us and We Eat the Mines: Dependency and Exploitation in Bolivian Tin Mines*. New York: Columbia University Press, 1979.

Nash, June, Juan Corradi, and Hobart Spalding, Jr., eds. *Ideology and Social Change in Latin America*. New York: Gordon and Breach, 1977.

Nash, June, Jorge Dandler, Nicholas S. Hopkins, eds. *Popular Participation in Social Change: Cooperatives, Collectives, and Nationalized Industry*. The Hague: Mouton Publishers, 1976.

Nash, Manning. *Machine Age Maya*. Glencoe: The Free Press, 1958.

Ortega y Gasset, José. *The Revolt of the Masses*. New York: W. W. Norton and Co., 1932.

Ouchi, William. *Theory Z: How American Business Can Meet the Japanese Challenge*. Reading, Mass.: Addison-Wesley, 1981.

Parsons, Talcott. *The Social System*. Glencoe: The Free Press, 1951.

Pascale, Richard T., and Anthony G. Athos. *The Art of Japanese Management: Applications for American Executives*. New York: Simon and Schuster, 1981.

Paz, Octavio. *The Labyrinth of Solitude: Life and Thought in Mexico*. Lysander Kemp, translator. New York: Grove, 1961.

Pfeffer, Jeffrey. "The Ambiguity of Leadership," in *Leadership: Where Else Can We Go?* Morgan W. McCall, Jr., and Michael M. Lombardo, eds. Durham: Duke University Press, 1978.

Piaget, Jean. *The Child's Conception of the World*. New York: Harcourt, Brace and Co., 1929.

Platt, John. "Hierarchical Growth." *Bulletin of the Atomic Scientists* 26 (9) (November 1970), 2–4, 46–48.

Poza, Ernesto J., and M. Lynne Markus. "Success Story: The Team Approach to Work Restructuring." *Organizational Dynamics* (Winter 1980), 3–25.

Radcliffe-Brown, A. R. *A Natural Science of Society*. Glencoe: The Free Press, 1957.

Reck, Gregory G. *In the Shadow of Tlaloc*. New York: Penguin Books, 1978.

Rice, A. K. *Productivity and Social Organization: The Ahmedabad Experiment*. London: Tavistock Publications, 1958.

Rice, A. K. *The Enterprise and Its Environment: A System Theory of Management Organization*. London: Tavistock Publications, 1963.

Roethlisberger, F. J. "Understanding: A Prerequisite of Leadership," in *Management and Morale*. Cambridge: Harvard University Press, 1941, chap. 3.

Roethlisberger, F. J. *Man-In-Organization*. Cambridge: Harvard University Press, 1968.

Roethlisberger, F. J. *The Elusive Phenomenon*. George F. F. Lombard, ed. Boston: Harvard University, Graduate School of Business Administration, 1977.

Roethlisberger, F. J., and W. J. Dickson. *Management and the Worker*. Cambridge: Harvard University Press, 1939.

Rohlen, Thomas P. *For Harmony and Strength*. Berkeley: University of California Press, 1974.

Rojas, Alfonso, and Charles H. Savage, Jr. *Social Organization in an Urban Factory in Colombia*. Alfred P. Sloan School of Management, Working Paper 201-66. Cambridge: Massachusetts Institute of Technology, 1966.

Ronken, Harriet O., and Paul R. Lawrence. *Administering Changes: A Case Study of Human Relations in a Factory*. Boston: Harvard University, Graduate School of Business Administration, 1952.

Rostow, Walt W. *The Process of Economic Growth*. New York: W. W. Norton and Co., 1952.

Rostow, Walt W. *The Stages of Economic Growth*. Cambridge: Cambridge University Press, 1960.

Savage, Charles H. *Management Behavior in a Developing Economy*. Cambridge: Inter-American Program in Civil Engineering, School of Engineering, Massachusetts Institute of Technology, 1962.

Savage, Charles H. *Social Reorganization in a Factory in the Andes*. SAA Monograph 7. Ithaca: Society for Applied Anthropology, 1964.

Savage, Charles H. *Village Ways and Factory Ways: A Study of the Interplay between Technology and Social Structure in a Traditional Andean Village*. Alfred P. Sloan School of Management, Working Paper 147-65. Cambridge: Massachusetts Institute of Technology, 1965.

Savage, Charles H. *The Particulars of Early Change*. Alfred P. Sloan School of Management, Working Paper 236-67. Cambridge: Massachusetts Institute of Technology, 1967.

Sayles, Leonard R. *Leadership: What Effective Managers Really Do . . . And How They Do It*. New York: McGraw-Hill Book Co., 1979.

Schlesinger, Leonard A., and Barry Oshry. "Quality of Work Life and the Manager: Muddle in the Middle." *Organizational Dynamics*. Summer 1984, 5–19.

Schopf, Thomas J. M. *Models in Paleobiology*. San Francisco: Freeman, Cooper and Co., 1972.

Selznick, Philip. *Leadership in Administration: A Sociological Interpretation*. New York: Harper and Row, 1957.

Sherif, Muzafer, ed. *Intergroup Relations and Leadership: Approaches and Research in Industrial, Ethnic, Cultural, and Political Areas.* New York: John Wiley and Sons, Inc., 1962.

Simmons, John, and William Mares. *Working Together.* New York: Alfred A. Knopf, 1983.

Soler, E. *The World of the Industrial Worker: Peru.* Alfred P. Sloan School of Management, Working Paper 185-66. Cambridge: Massachusetts Institute of Technology, 1966.

Soler, E., and Charles H. Savage, Jr. *Technological Impact on a Community in Transition—Peru.* Alfred P. Sloan School of Management, Working Paper 202-66. Cambridge: Massachusetts Institute of Technology, 1966.

Stinchcombe, Arthur L. "Social Structure and Organization," in *Handbook of Organization,* James G. March, ed. Chicago: Rand McNally and Co., 1965.

Stogdill, Ralph M. "Intragroup-Intergroup Theory and Research," in *Intergroup Relations and Leadership: Approaches and Research in Industrial, Ethnic, Cultural, and Political Areas,* Muzafer Sherif, ed. New York: John Wiley and Sons, Inc., 1962.

Tagiuri, Renato, and George H. Litwin, eds. *Organizational Climate: Exploration of a Concept.* Boston: Harvard University, Graduage School of Business Administration, 1968.

Taylor, Frederick W. *The Principles of Scientific Management.* New York: Harper and Brothers, 1911.

Toffler, Alvin. *Future Shock.* New York: Random House, 1970.

Trist, E. L., G. W. Higgin, H. Murray, and A. B. Pollock. *Organizational Choice: Capabilities of Groups at the Coal Face Under Changing Conditions.* London: Tavistock Publications, 1963.

Vidich, Arthur J., Joseph Bensman, and Maurice R. Stein. *Reflections on Community Studies.* New York: John Wiley and Sons, 1964.

Walton, Richard E. "From Control to Commitment in the Workplace." *Harvard Business Review* 2, March–April 1985, 77–84.

Weber, Max. *The Protestant Ethic and the Spirit of Capitalism.* Talcott Parsons, translator. New York: Charles Scribner's Sons, 1958.

Whyte, William F. *Street Corner Society: The Social Structure of an Italian Slum.* Third edition. Chicago: University of Chicago Press, 1981.

Whyte, William F. *Leadership and Group Participation.* New York State School of Industrial and Labor Relations Bulletin 24. Ithaca: Cornell University, 1953.

Winn, Peter. "Workers into Managers: Worker Participation in the Chilean Textile Industry," in *Popular Participation in Social Change: Cooperatives, Collectives, and Nationalized Industry.* June Nash, Jorge Dandler, and Nicholas S. Hopkins, eds. The Hague: Mouton Publishers, 1976.

Wolff, Kurt A. "Surrender and Community Study: The Study of Land," in *Reflections on Community Studies,* Arthur J. Vidich, Joseph Bensman, and Maurice R. Stein, eds. New York: John Wiley and Sons, 1964.

Zager, Robert, and Michael P. Rosow, eds. *The Innovative Organization: Productivity Programs in Action.* New York: Pergamon Press Inc., 1982.

Zaleznik, Abraham. *The Human Dilemmas of Leadership* New York: Harper and Row, 1966.

Zaleznik, Abraham. "Managers and Leaders: Are They Different?" *Harvard Business Review* 55 (3) (May 1977), 67–78.

Zaleznik, Abraham, C. Roland Christensen, and F. J. Roethlisberger. *The Motivation, Productivity and Satisfaction of Workers: A Prediction Study.* Boston: Harvard University, Graduate School of Business Administration, 1958.

Glossary of Latin American Terms

Abrazo	Hug, embrace
Aburrido	Bored. In Colombia this word connotes "tired of" or "fed up with."
Actividades	Activities
Aguardiente	Corn mash liquor
Aislado	Isolate
Animo	Spirit, motivation, courage
	Corn griddle cake
Barrio	Ward, quarter, precinct, neighborhood
Berraco	Male hog; board. In Colombia it carries connotations of daring, bravery.
Blanquero	Citizen of La Blanca
Bravo; bravito	Courageous, brave, fierce
Cachaco	A term used historically to describe dandies newly arrived from Spain or the sons of these Spanish immigrants.
Camahan	Young punk; zoot-suiter (colloq.)
Campesino	Peasant; country man
Candidato	Candidate
Cantina	Canteen, lunchroom
Casa	House, home
Cerámica	Ceramic
Chulu	Small tailor shop, open to the street
Compañerismo	Good fellowship, camaraderie
Completo	Complete, well-rounded
Conquistadores	Sixteenth-century Spanish conquerors in the Americas
Despedida	Leave-taking, farewell
Destino	Destiny, fate
Desviadores	Deviant members (of a work group)
Doctor	Honorary title used for a professional or educated person.
Don	Spanish title used before masculine Christian names; formerly given only to noblemen, now used widely.

Doña	Used before feminine Christian names; see don.
Duende	Goblin, ghost; male witch
Encomienda	Originally land or estates in America, including the inhabitants, granted to Spanish colonists; hence, any large agricultural estate worked by Indian or peasant labor.
Fiesta	Feast, holy day
Finca	Farm, ranch
Fogón	Fire box, cooking stove; gathering of soldiers and civilians around a fire.
Futbol	Football (i.e., the game called soccer in the United States).
Futbolista	Football player
Genio	Disposition
Hacienda	Farmstead; country property
Hombre	Man
Incompleto	Incomplete
Inquieto	Restless, anxious
Interacciones	Interactions
Junta	Meeting, council, committee
Loco	Crazy, mad, insane
Machismo	The ethic of machismo associated with maleness, i.e., strong, tough, self-sufficient.
Madre	Mother, motherly; affectionate
Maestro	Master
Maluco	Sickish, ill
Mayordomo	Overseer
Mensos	Silly, foolish, stupid, slow
Miembro regular	Regular member (of a work group)
Molleja	Gizzard, sweetbread
Montaña	Mountain
Montañeros	Mountain people
Mucha	Much, many
Muy	Very, very much
Nucleado	Nucleus; central; regular (member of a work group)
Nuevo	New
Padre de familia	Family head (male)
Pájaro	Bird; crafty fellow
Pantalero	A tailor who makes trousers
Pasta	Dough, pie crust, paste
Patrón	Boss; often sponsor, protector, owner, master
Peón	Unskilled laborer
Peso	Unit of money; paper money
Plata	Money
Policía	Police
Polilla	Moth

Primavera	Springtime
Pueblo	Small town, village
Puesto fijo	Fixed station or position
Querido	Dear, lover; also used as an adjective meaning "nice."
Quieto	Quiet, still, calm
Referencia	Report, account, narration; work-order
Ruana	Woven poncho typically worn by peasants in cool climates.
Sastre completo	Master tailor
Sentimiento	Sentiment; feeling
Simpático	Likeable, congenial, agreeable
Tienda	Store
Unido	United
Vaca	Cow
Viejo	Old, ancient. Often used affectionately, as in "viejito" or "viejita" (little old one).
Vigilante	Vigilant, watchful

Index